Norms and Necessity

Norms and Necessity

AMIE L. THOMASSON

OXFORD
UNIVERSITY PRESS

OXFORD
UNIVERSITY PRESS

Oxford University Press is a department of the University of Oxford. It furthers
the University's objective of excellence in research, scholarship, and education
by publishing worldwide. Oxford is a registered trade mark of Oxford University
Press in the UK and certain other countries.

Published in the United States of America by Oxford University Press
198 Madison Avenue, New York, NY 10016, United States of America.

Library of Congress Cataloging-in-Publication Data
Names: Thomasson, Amie L. (Amie Lynn), 1968– author.
Title: Norms and necessity / Amie L. Thomasson.
Description: New York, NY, United States of America : Oxford University Press, 2020. |
Includes bibliographical references and index.
Identifiers: LCCN 2019053766 (print) | LCCN 2019053767 (ebook) |
ISBN 9780190098193 (hb) | ISBN 9780197747162 (pb) |
ISBN 9780190098216 (epub) | ISBN 9780190098223 (online)
Subjects: LCSH: Normativity (Ethics)
Classification: LCC BJ1458.3 .T45 2020 (print) |
LCC BJ1458.3 (ebook) | DDC 111—dc23
LC record available at https://lccn.loc.gov/2019053766
LC ebook record available at https://lccn.loc.gov/2019053767

Paperback printed by Marquis Book Printing, Canada

For May, my favorite modal.

Contents

Acknowledgments

This work has been a long time coming, and I have so many people to thank for the numerous conversations, questions, and comments over the years that I am afraid I won't be able to name them all. But to everyone who took the time to talk with me about this, raise difficult questions, or give comments, I am extremely grateful. I am also very grateful to audiences at a number of universities and conferences where I was able to present parts of this work over the last decade—including Australian National University, Brown, University of Colorado, Georgetown University, University of Georgia, University of Memphis, University of Pittsburgh, University of Stockholm, and my own prior institution, University of Miami, and current institution, Dartmouth College. Wherever it may stand now, the generous feedback and in-depth conversations from so many fine philosophers certainly brought the final project miles beyond where it began.

For generously commenting on the (penultimate version of the) whole manuscript, I am especially grateful to Huw Price, Michaela McSweeney, and two anonymous referees from Oxford University Press. Special thanks also go to Mark Warren and Ted Locke, not only for numerous extended discussions about these issues over the years, but also for their insight into how to take the approach and run with it—in Mark's case, to addressing problems in meta-ethics, and in Ted's case, to problems of counterpossibles and other hyperintensional phenomena. Thank you for helping me make the view stronger, and giving me the inspiration to finally see this book into print. For very helpful comments on (parts or all of) earlier versions of the manuscript, and/or particularly helpful discussions, I would like to thank Karen Bennett, Simon Blackburn, Samuel Boardman, Robert Brandom, Eli Chudnoff, Jamie Dreier, Mark Lance, Jessica Leech, Italo Lins Lemos, Sam Levey, Takaaki Matsui, Irene Olivero, David Plunkett, Greg Restall, Sam Rickless, David Ripley, Ted Sider, Nick Stang, Tim Sundell, Christie Thomas, and Jack Woods. I would also like to thank my research assistant, Ira Richardson, for invaluable help with the final stages of research and final preparation of the manuscript, bibliography and index. Finally, I want to express my sincere thanks to my wonderful editor, Peter Ohlin, for his interest and confidence in the project from the beginning, through to his patience waiting for the final manuscript at the end.

I would also like to again express my gratitude to the National Endowment for the Humanities, for a grant in academic year 2013–2014 to support a project I then called "The Descent of Metaphysics," which eventually split into two and became *Ontology Made Easy* (2015) and the present volume.

Some of the material has previously appeared in print (though it has all been revised, sometimes to the point of unrecognizability, for the current volume). I would like to thank the following publishers for permission to use (revised) versions of (parts or all of) the following previously published articles. Early versions of the view were presented in "Modal Normativism and the Methods of Metaphysics" (*Philosophical Topics* 35, nos. 1 & 2 [2007]: 135–60) and in "The 2012 Nancy D. Simco Lecture: Norms and Necessity" (*Southern Journal of Philosophy* 51, no. 2 [June 2013]: 143–60). Revised versions of material from those articles are used here with permission of (respectively) the University of Arkansas Press and Wiley Blackwell. A version of Chapter 1 was previously published as "Non-Descriptivism about Modality: A Brief History and Revival," in *Baltic International Yearbook of Cognition, Logic and Communication*, Volume 4: *200 Years of Analytical Philosophy* (2009): 1–26, and is reprinted with permission of the New Prairie Press. Portions of Chapter 8 draw on "Experimental Philosophy and the Methods of Ontology," *Monist* 95, no. 2 (April 2012): 175–99, used here with permission of Oxford University Press. And a prior version of Chapter 7 was published as, "How Can We Come to Know Metaphysical Modal Truths?" in *Synthese* (June 2018; https://doi.org/10.1007/s11229-018-1841-5), and appears here with kind permission of Springer Science and Business Media B.V.

My greatest thanks go to my family. I want to express my love and gratitude to Peter Lewis for helping me in all of the necessary preconditions for this book, and for life—from home logistics to emergency philosophical discussions to moral support. And finally, enormous love and thanks go to my dear daughters Natalie and May, for their patience when I had to hide and work, for providing the happiest relief from philosophical difficulties when I wasn't working, and for their endless sweet loving support, which means the world to me. May: This one's for you.

Norms and Necessity

Introduction

Debates in metaphysics often revolve around questions about what
could, must, or *could not* be the case. When we discuss the persistence
conditions for things of a certain sort, we ask questions about whether
a person, say, *could* or *could not* survive a brain transplant or teleportation. When we ask about the identity conditions for works of art, we
ask what conditions *must be met* for entities A and B to be identical—
and so whether a whether a translated poem *could be* identical to the
original, or a post-restoration painting *could be* the same work of art as
a pre-restoration work with a very different surface appearance. These
are all *modal* questions. Debates about material constitution, similarly, often revolve around the question of whether or not the statue
and the lump of clay have different *modal properties*—as one apparently can, and the other cannot, survive being squashed—and whether
this entails that the statue and the lump are not identical. Modal issues are often involved in other central metaphysical debates as well.
Questions about supervenience, for example, are traditionally framed
in modal terms: in asking whether moral properties supervene on
nonmoral properties, we are asking whether there *could be* a difference
in moral properties without a difference in nonmoral properties. On
one prominent understanding, the relation of truthmaking is understood as necessitation: a truthmaker is characterized as something that
necessitates something being true (Armstrong 2004, 6–7). Modal issues clearly do not exhaust metaphysics—the existence questions that
concern ontologists, for example, are not modal in any obvious way.[1]

---

[1] Of course the two may come together. For modal concerns are often at issue in
addressing existence questions as well, as one attempts to uncover the *existence conditions*
for things of a certain kind (for example, what it would take for a work of literature to
come into existence), or to answer questions about whether or not there is anything with
the relevant *modal profile* of a statue, and so on. For extended discussion of existence
questions similar in spirit to the treatment of modality here, see Thomasson (2015).

Norms and Necessity. Amie L. Thomasson, Oxford University Press (2020). © Oxford University Press.
DOI: 10.1093/oso/9780190098193.001.0001

Nonetheless, modal questions are central to metaphysics and permeate a wide range of metaphysical debates.

After decades of focus on modal issues (especially following Kripke and Lewis), however, recent work in metaphysics has seen something of a turn to interest in grounding, essence, and other so-called post-modal notions instead. For modal notions alone (it is often said) are not fine-grained enough to capture the distinction between, say, when an entity A exists only in possible worlds where B exists, and cases in which A exists *in virtue of* B's existing, or A's existence is *grounded in* B's.[2] But while this turn to interest in grounding, essence, and the like has raised a number of important philosophical issues, it does not relieve us of the need to understand modality or render that project obsolete.

First of all, as most parties accept, claims about essence, grounding, and ontological dependence have central modal *consequences*, even if they are not equivalent to modal notions. For example, it is common to accept that if A is the full grounds of B, then A necessitates B.[3] Similarly, many accept that if a property P is essential to x, then x couldn't exist without being P; and that if A ontologically depends on B, then necessarily, if A exists, then B exists.[4] Second, if we can make progress on understanding our modal thought and talk, this may also aid us in understanding claims about grounding and essence.[5] So even those who care most about grounding or essence have reason to try to make sense of our talk about what could be, may be, or must be the case.

Moreover, modal claims themselves also play a central role in a wide range of issues in other areas of philosophy. Central issues in

---

[2] For influential arguments against the modal-existential account of ontological dependence, see Fine (1994b). Fine famously argues that if we define ontological dependence as: A ontologically depends on B if and only if, necessarily, if A exists then B exists, that entails that *everything* depends on a *necessary existent*. Yet it seems crazy to think, for example, that Socrates depends on the number two.

[3] See Bliss and Trogdon (2016, section 5) for the claim that this is the "default view among proponents of grounding that full grounding carries metaphysical necessity," along with further discussion of who accepts and who rejects the claim.

[4] Along these lines, Karen Bennett (2017, 47–57) argues that all of those relations she calls "building relations" are such that, if x builds y, then necessarily, if x then y.

[5] While this won't be my focus here, I return to this idea briefly in Section 6.3, and refer interested readers to Locke (2018) and (in progress) for further development.

the philosophy of language, for example, hinge on whether the name "Gödel" *would still apply to the same man* if it turned out that Schmidt were (unbeknownst to us) the true discoverer of the incompleteness of arithmetic.[6] Arguments in epistemology rely on claims about whether you *could* (say) come to know that there is a real barn in that field by seeing it, if (unbeknownst to you) most barns in that bit of country-side are facades.[7] Philosophers of mind address questions about, say, whether Swampman (a man-like creature spontaneously generated by lightning in a swamp) *could* think of or refer to objects;[8] about whether zombies (creatures just like humans except that they lack all conscious experience) are possible;[9] and about whether phenomenal qualities *must* have a physical realization. The list could be extended indefinitely. In short, questions about what *could, must,* or *could not* be permeate a wide range of philosophical debates in metaphysics and elsewhere. As a result, it would be a mistake to turn our backs on addressing questions about modality. We have as much reason as ever to be concerned with how to understand modal thought and talk, and with how to resolve debates about modal questions.

There are, at least on the surface, various sorts of modal claim: we commonly distinguish claims about distinctively metaphysical necessity from claims about the necessity of pure logical or mathematical truths. We also commonly distinguish—and in my view, it is impor-tant to distinguish—claims of metaphysical necessity and possibility from claims of *nomological* necessity (that is, what is necessary, given the laws of nature—e.g., that it is nomologically necessary that gases expand when heated) and empirically grounded counterfactuals (e.g., that if I were to drop this glass onto the tile floor, it would break). All of these are distinguished again from the modal expressions involved in discussing and issuing permissions and obligations on the one hand (concerning what we may or must do) and also from epistemic modal

---

[6] See Kripke (1980) for the original discussion.

[7] Goldman (1976) introduces the case to philosophical discussion, crediting Carl Ginet with the idea.

[8] For the original thought experiment, see Davidson (1987), who characterized Swampman as a Davidson-duplicate, generated just as Davidson himself is killed by lightning.

[9] See Chalmers (1996) for development of the zombie thought experiment.

expressions (e.g., about what might turn out to be the case) on the other hand. The possibilities and necessities discussed in metaphysics—as well as those at issue in the other philosophical debates mentioned—are generally thought of as specifically *metaphysical* necessities rather than as strictly *logical* necessities, or as *nomological* necessities.[10] This book is focused squarely on modal claims and questions of this distinctively metaphysical sort—the sort that metaphysics, rather than the natural sciences, is generally thought to be in the best position to study. I will speak about other sorts of modality, such as logical or nomological necessities, only in passing.

The target here is to understand metaphysical modal "claims," "statements," or "truths." By a modal claim I shall mean not a mere modal sentence, but rather what is said (on a given occasion, in a given language) in uttering a modal sentence.[11] For context-sensitive sentences containing modal terms may be true in some contexts, false in others (e.g., "My favorite number is necessarily even"). What we are interested in is the truth or falsehood of what is said in uttering that modal sentence on a given occasion (e.g., that four is necessarily even). That is what I shall call the modal claim.[12] By "modal term" I shall mean terms like the metaphysician's "necessary" and "possible" (as

---

[10] Though it is sometimes a matter for debate whether, say, the necessities involved in debates in the philosophy of mind are physical or metaphysical.

[11] Kirk Ludwig similarly understands a "statement" as "a fully meaningful declarative sentence, if it is context-insensitive, or an utterance of one, if it is context-sensitive" (in progress, 1)—provided, of course, that the utterance itself is understood as fully meaningful, not as a mere sequence of noises.

[12] Some may be tempted to suggest that what *explains* the truth of a modal claim is that it expresses a certain modal *proposition* that is true—and thus that the proper starting point is in analyzing modal *propositions* rather than modal terms or claims. But, given the deflationary approach to ontology I have defended elsewhere (Thomasson 2015), this viewpoint is not only not obligatory, it is misguided. On the minimalist approach outlined above—and defended for the case of propositions in greater detail by Stephen Schiffer (2003) and Michael McCracken (2009)—we can allow that there are propositions, yet deny that propositions are entities that can do deep explanatory work to show why our sentences are true. Instead, on this view, talk of propositions is derived by hypostatization from more basic sentences. We may indeed be able to infer that a given statement (or meaningful sentence) is true if and only if the proposition it expresses is true, but that equivalence does not show that there is an asymmetric *explanation* of the truth of the sentence in terms of that of the proposition. Thanks to Eli Chudnoff and Matti Eklund for making this worry apparent to me. Another virtue of starting with modal terms and claims is that this makes it more natural to raise questions about their function and use—questions that figure prominently in this work.

they are currently used, keeping their meaning fixed), though it is of course not merely the English terms that are in question here, but any that express the same concept in a different language (e.g., the German metaphysician's *notwendig* and *möglich*). Dealing first and foremost with modal claims does lead to certain limitations: it doesn't enable us to discuss modal *beliefs*, if we think that these may sometimes be non-linguistic. While I think it is clearest to begin with cases of modal claims and the modal terms used in them—since it is much easier to express them and examine them than it is for (allegedly) non-linguistic modal beliefs—the approach to be developed here may be extended to cover non-linguistic modal beliefs as well, as long as beliefs are thought to involve concepts that are themselves rule-governed in ways analogous to the corresponding terms. In any case, however, my primary target is to understand modal claims made in debates in metaphysics, and these of course are made using language. For that purpose, starting simply by understanding the status of these modal terms and claims (made using language) is entirely appropriate.

Modality presents a range of familiar and first-rate philosophical problems. The ontological problems are well known: Should we accept that there are modal facts or properties or essences? If so, what are they, how are they related to the non-modal, and how is it that they can vary even when the non-modal properties (say of a statue and the lump that constitutes it) do not? Should we accept that there are other possible worlds? If so, what are they? The epistemological problem of how we can know modal facts is even more notorious, and has been familiar at least since Hume—for it seems that modal facts can't simply be perceived or otherwise empirically detected.[13]

But the real quarry here concerns the methods of metaphysics. For although metaphysical debates so often revolve around modal questions, there has been a great diversity of opinion about all prominent metaphysical modal questions. Competing theories have continued to proliferate about what the conditions are for persons to be identical, whether works of art are essentially tied to their artist or

---

[13] Scott Shalkowski (1994, 669) similarly describes the two fundamental questions for modal metaphysics as accounting for the "ontological ground" of modality on the one hand, and our epistemic access to modal truths on the other.

historical context, what sorts of change a statue could survive, and so on. One aim here is to step back from these first-order debates to address the meta-level and methodological questions: What is going on in these modal debates? How are we to understand modal questions like these, and how can we go about resolving them? How can we determine who is right and who is wrong where different judgments are made about what is metaphysically possible or necessary?

I will argue that modal questions do not require a special form of philosophical insight or intuition into features of reality for their resolution. For properly understood, modal terms do not function to describe or track special modal features of reality that we must discover to render our verdict. Instead, they serve as perspicuous ways of mandating or enforcing, reasoning with, and renegotiating rules. Speakers who master the relevant terms or concepts are in a position to acquire modal knowledge, given their conceptual and reasoning abilities and (in some cases) knowledge of empirical facts. We require no form of special philosophical insight to undertake modal metaphysics, and we can see the work of the metaphysician as primarily on the conceptual side—not as discerning what the "essential" or "modal" features of reality are, but rather as expressing semantic or conceptual rules and their consequences in the object language, under conditions of semantic descent—or implicitly advocating for changes in the rules.

This work forms part of a larger project, aiming to clarify the epistemology and methods of metaphysics. The overall goal is to argue that metaphysics requires no distinctive and mysterious epistemology; that instead, the questions of metaphysics (or at least those that are well-formed and legitimate, answerable questions)[14] can be answered by conceptual and/or empirical work, leaving nothing that is (in Theodore Sider's terms [2011, 187]) "epistemically metaphysical." I undertook this work for existence questions in *Ontology Made Easy* (2015), arguing that existence questions can be answered by straightforward conceptual and/or empirical methods. If I can expand this approach here to those metaphysical questions that

---

[14] For discussion of some questions that are not well-formed and answerable, see Thomasson (2009).

are explicitly or tacitly modal, we will have come a long way toward demystifying the epistemology of metaphysics, and clarifying how debates are best resolved. Of course this may not yet address all metaphysical questions. If some, say, grounding questions, questions about the nature of time, questions about truthmaking or about consciousness, are not properly understood as either metaphysical modal questions or existence questions, they would have to be handled separately. I will leave examination of such questions for elsewhere. Nonetheless, the aim of this volume is to take us another big step along the way, while also making progress directly on the venerable historical problems of modality.

1. Problems for the Descriptivist Assumption

The assumption I wish to call into question in this book is the assumption that metaphysical modal statements are *descriptive* or *representational* in character.[15] It is an assumption that mostly goes unnoticed. It is certainly not an articulated theory, but rather a way of looking at things that finds various expressions, and that influences the kinds of questions thought to be legitimate and pressing.

In one sense it might seem just obvious that metaphysical modal statements are descriptive—if I say "Mary is necessarily human" this sounds similar in form to saying "Mary is unusually tall"; both are indicative in form and are naturally thought of as "describing" (or "representing") Mary in certain ways. I certainly do not wish to deny these obvious truths.[16] It is a familiar point in the pragmatics literature in philosophy of language, however, that "the force of a speech act . . . is not to be read off its mood, whether imperative, indicative, or interrogative" (Langton 2015, 6).[17] Nor, I will suggest, is its function.

---

[15] Huw Price (2011) uses the terminology "representational" and puts the point in terms of denying that all discourse is "e-representational." See Price (2011) for the original formulation and criticisms of the representationalist/descriptivist assumption.

[16] Huw Price similarly notes that those he calls "non-factualists" (our non-descriptivists) may accept that moral claims, for example, are "statements in some minimal sense" (2011, 56).

[17] So familiar that Langton says she will simply take this point "for granted" (2015, 6).

The philosophical assumption of descriptivism goes beyond accepting the above truisms: it involves an assumption about function. Many of the basic terms in our language seem to serve the function of tracking certain features of our environment, with which they are meant to co-vary, enabling us to get around better. So, for example, it is plausible that terms such as "wolf" and "river" serve a descriptive tracking function. To assume that a term is descriptive in our sense is to assume that it serves that function. Huw Price (2011) calls terms that serve this function "e-representations," those whose job "is to co-vary with something else—typically, some *external* factor, or environmental condition" (2011, 20). Where terms serve this kind of function, it is natural to think of them as aiming to correctly represent what there is (and is not) in the world—and as answerable to the world in the sense that we look to the world to determine whether what we say using those terms is true or false. As it is often put, when discourse is descriptive in this way, we look to the world to find "truthmakers" for our claims about wolves or rivers, features of the world that "explain how sentences about the real world are made true or false" (Mulligan, Simons, and Smith 1984, 288). Adhering to the descriptivist assumption thus often leads to questions about what things in the world could serve as truthmakers for our discourse.

The descriptive assumption has somewhat invisibly dominated work on modality over the past half-century or more. As a result, it is widely assumed that "the problem of modality is a problem about truthmakers for modal propositions" (Roy 2000, 56). Since the obvious truthmakers to posit are modal facts or properties, the descriptivist assumption has led to an increasing tendency to accept what we may call a form of "heavyweight modal realism," according to which there are distinctively modal properties or facts that *explain* what it is that *makes* some modal statements true.[18] So, when a philosopher says: "A person can survive a transplant of her brain into another body," or "A

---

[18] As will become clear below, I call this view "heavyweight realism" rather than simply "realism," since I think there are realist options available that are not committed to the explanatory claim. I will argue below for a form of non-explanatory "simple" realism as falling out of the normativist approach to modal discourse. The heavyweight realist view, as I shall present it, is roughly the same as what Simon Blackburn (1993) has called "hyperrealism."

painting cannot survive a process that involves replacing forty percent of the original surface paint (that would not be a matter of restoring but destroying the original painting),"[19] it is tempting to think of their statements as simply describing what modal properties people or paintings have (the modal property of [not] possibly-surviving-this-change), just as we describe the person or painting as having other properties (weight, color, etc.). Alternatively, we might think of modal statements as attempts to describe modal *facts* in the world, and as holding true if those modal facts indeed obtain.

But heavyweight modal realism faces serious ontological problems, as it sits uncomfortably with the otherwise dominant trends in metaphysics toward naturalism and physicalism. Frank Jackson called problems like this—of "locating" some sort of interesting entity "within the scientific account" of the world—"location problems" (1998, 3), and argued that "serious metaphysics by its very nature raises the location problem" (1998, 1).[20] Huw Price (2011, 186) speaks analogously of various "placement problems."

Defenders of heavyweight modal realism clearly face a "location" or "placement" problem. For how are these modal facts or properties supposed to fit into the natural world? They do not seem to be physical properties or facts like those investigated by the empirical sciences—so what are these modal facts or properties supposed to be, and why should we think there are such things? How are they related to the non-modal facts or properties studied by the natural sciences? More generally, how can any philosopher of a vaguely empiricist or naturalist persuasion find suitable truthmakers for modal claims in the (actual) physical or natural world?

[19] Mark Sagoff (1978) defends a view about art along these lines.

[20] Jackson argued that "the location problem can only be solved by embracing what I call the 'entry by entailment' thesis" (1998, 1)—that is, that a "putative feature of the world" has a place in some metaphysical account if and only if "the feature is entailed by the account told in the terms favoured by the metaphysics in question" (1998, 5). Price goes on to propose an alternative approach to handling such "placement problems" by way of a "subject naturalist" account that takes seriously also what science tells us *about human linguistic behavior*—which may include rejecting the idea that linguistic items "represent" something non-linguistic, which must be "located" in a scientific description of the world. See Price (2011, 188–90). See also Price's comparison of his approach with Jackson's in Price (2011, 77–79).

If we begin by assuming that modal statements serve a descriptive function and go on to ask what features of reality they describe, or what their truthmakers are, we face even more formidable epistemological problems. If we think of modal statements as aiming to describe modal facts or properties that should make them true, then the natural story to give about how we acquire modal knowledge is that we do so by discovering what modal properties an object has, or what modal facts obtain. But how are we to do that? As Hume observed long ago, there seems no prospect of giving an empirical account of our knowledge of modality—so what sort of account can we give? Even if one thinks, with Barbara Vetter, that one can acquire knowledge of dispositions or potentialities empirically (having observed many glasses shattering, we infer that glasses are *disposed* to break on sharp impact; 2015, 11–13), the same methods cannot ground knowledge of distinctively *metaphysical* modality. For the same observations of the statue/lump of clay lead to different modal conclusions: that the statue would not survive a squashing while the lump would. The well-known grounding problem arises precisely because no non-modal/non-sortal properties that could be empirically known seem capable of grounding the difference in the *metaphysical* modal properties (identity and persistence conditions) attributed to the statue and the lump.[21] If we have no idea how we are to gain this specifically *metaphysical* modal knowledge or to determine what counts as reasonable grounds for accepting metaphysical modal claims or for revising them, it is small wonder that we have such difficulty coming to agreement on the modal issues that permeate metaphysics.

One prominent alternative to heavyweight modal realism is David Lewis's (1986) possible worlds realism. On this view, we need not accept that there are any distinctively *modal* features of this world. Instead, we accept that there are many other concrete worlds causally and spatiotemporally disconnected from our own—call these the (merely) possible worlds (our actual world is also a possible world). This approach promises to not only make sense of our straightforward

---

[21] For discussion of the grounding problem, see Zimmerman (1995), Bennett (2004), Burke (1992), and Thomasson (2007, Chapter 4).

modal talk, but also to vindicate our talk of possible worlds—talk that has proven extremely useful in adding expressive power that enables us to articulate metaphysical positions that cannot be expressed without quantification over possible worlds (Lewis 1986, 16).[22] Lewis's possible worlds approach gives us truthmakers for both simple talk about what is possible and necessary, and for possible worlds talk, within the compass of a reductive view of modality. For, as Lewis emphasizes, we needn't posit distinctively *modal* properties or facts. Instead, the idea is that the operators "possibly" and "necessarily" in modal statements can be simply replaced with quantifiers over possible worlds, where it is the (non-modal) facts of those worlds that determine whether the modal statement is true or false. Thus, to use Lewis's own example, "It is possible that there be a talking donkey" is true just in case there is some world in which there is a donkey that talks. So Lewisian possible worlds realism still enables us to understand modal statements as descriptions, but they are seen as attempted descriptions not of *modal* features of *our* world, but of *non-modal* facts in one or more of the possible worlds (including our actual world).

Those who seek truthmakers for modal propositions thus have the option of rejecting heavyweight modal realism and adopting possible worlds realism, treating the facts of these possible worlds as truthmakers for our modal propositions.[23] This hardly seems a more palatable ontological view, however—indeed, few have been genuinely willing to countenance the idea that there are such other worlds, or that they could adequately serve as non-modal truthmakers for our modal propositions (Divers and Melia 2002; Jubien 2007).

Lewis's work on possible worlds contributed to an explosion of philosophical work on modality, generating several new sub-industries. One sub-industry involved debates about whether we should accept that there are merely possible entities at all, or instead insist on

---

[22] For example, formulating global supervenience theses that enable us to capture claims such as that no two worlds could differ in their moral properties without differing in their nonmoral properties requires quantification over possible worlds.

[23] I do not mean to suggest that Lewis himself thought of his possible worlds as truthmakers for modal propositions, only that possible worlds realism along Lewis's lines is capable of supplying the truthmakers that the truthmaker theorist needs.

some form of "actualism."[24] Another sub-industry arose in attempts to develop alternative ways of understanding possible worlds as actually existing abstract entities such as maximally consistent sets of propositions (Adams 1974, 225), or as maximal possible states of affairs (Plantinga 1974).[25] A third sub-industry focused on questions about whether objects may be identical across possible worlds, and if so whether we need to offer criteria of transworld identity (and how we could do so).[26]

This massive expansion of philosophical work on modality, however, generally ignored, or led us astray from, the original philosophical puzzlements about modality: questions about what the truthmakers could be for modal discourse, or, more basically still, of how to understand modal discourse—what its function would be, and whether it would need truthmakers. Since it is those questions that I primarily aim to address in this book, I will have little to say here about these post-Lewisian swaths of philosophical work on modality.[27]

In any case, even if we are content to allow that there are Lewisian possible worlds, a massive problem of *relevance* remains—a problem that was raised in various forms in prominent reviews of *The Plurality of Worlds* by Nathan Salmon (1988), Graeme Forbes (1988), William Lycan (1988), and Allen Stairs (1988). The problem is that our modal statements just don't seem to be *about* what goes on in other worlds, even if there are such worlds (Stairs 1988, 344); these don't seem like *relevant* truthmakers; nor do the goings-on in other possible worlds seem relevant to assessing the truth of, or the ways we care about,

---

[24] See Bennett (2005) and Menzel (2018) for a good overview of debates about actualism, and further references to related work. Debates about actualism themselves seem to presuppose a form of descriptivism about modal discourse. As Menzel characterizes the problem: "What makes actualism so philosophically interesting, is that there is no obviously correct way to account for the truth of claims like 'It is possible that there are Aliens' without appealing to possible but nonactual objects" (2018, introduction).

[25] For critical discussion of a range of "ersatzist" views, see Lewis (1986, Chapter 3).

[26] For a good overview of the literature on transworld identity, see Mackie and Jago (2017).

[27] Though I will have a bit to say about how to understand possible worlds talk in Chapter 6. Thanks to an anonymous referee for suggesting that I should make clear why I am not engaging (much) with those areas of literature.

counterfactuals.[28] In the words of Simon Blackburn, this "sounds like a change of subject" (1993, 73). Graeme Forbes puts the point as follows: "If one asks 'What makes it necessary that there are no married bachelors?', Lewis's answer, 'Because in no world is there a married bachelor,' is rather unilluminating. Surely the correct answer would refer to the definition of 'bachelor'?" (1988, 227). Such observations suggest that even if we accept the ontology of possible worlds, its *relevance* to the modal question remains in doubt. And that, in turn, might suggest that it's a mistake to think that modal claims aim to *describe* facts about other worlds.

Lewis's possible worlds realism also faces daunting epistemological problems parallel to those that trouble the heavyweight realist. For given the causal isolation of the other possible worlds from our own, it remains unclear how we could know anything about them, or about what claims they make true. Lewis argues that causal acquaintance cannot be necessary for knowledge, as we have mathematical knowledge without being causally acquainted with numbers. Indeed, he argues that causal acquaintance is only needed for knowledge of what is *contingent* (1986, 109–12). But to suggest that one (in any case) needs *some* account of how we can have knowledge without causal connections is not yet to *give* any such account, nor does it give us any positive idea of how modal knowledge may be acquired. Lewis is quite upfront that he provides no general analysis of modal knowledge, adding only that this "is a problem for everyone (certain skeptics and conventionalists excepted)" (1986, 113). (In Chapter 7 I will go on to suggest that non-descriptivist heirs to the conventionalist approach can indeed avoid the problems of modal knowledge better than other views—and that this is an important advantage for the approaches to modal discourse defended here.) Instead, Lewis (1986, 104–15) simply suggests that we commonly come to have the modal *beliefs* we do (regardless of whether or why they count as *knowledge*) by way of engaging in imaginative experiments guided by a principle of recombination (1986, 113–14).[29]

---

[28] In the latter form this is the famous "Humphrey" objection Kripke (1980, 45 n.3) raises against Lewis. Michael Jubien (2007, 104) makes a similar point.

[29] For further critical discussion of Lewis's reply to the knowledge problem, see Bueno and Shalkowski (2004).

Both heavyweight modal realism and possible worlds realism thus leave us with a crisis in modal epistemology. This crisis in modal epistemology also leads to a crisis in understanding the methods of metaphysics. For if a great portion of metaphysical debates are about either explicitly or tacitly modal issues, to the extent that we are without a good story about how we can acquire modal knowledge, we're also left without an understanding of how we can acquire knowledge in metaphysics. It certainly doesn't seem that we can come to know what modal properties or facts there are, or what's going on in merely possible worlds, by anything like the standard sorts of empirical enquiry used in the natural sciences. So by what methods are we to investigate the modal questions in metaphysics? How are we to adjudicate among competing modal claims that play a central role in metaphysics and other areas of philosophy? Without a clear answer, the methodology is left completely mysterious. Small wonder, then, that there has been so little agreement about the answers to these questions.

These diverse problems—ontological problems of saying what the modal facts or properties are and how they fit into a physicalistic ontology (or, alternatively, of defending the idea that there are many concrete possible worlds); epistemological problems of explaining how to acquire knowledge of the relevant modal facts, modal properties, or possible worlds; and allied methodological problems about how to go about answering metaphysical modal questions and adjudicate debates about their answers—all arise from a common source. All arise from treating modal statements *descriptively*, taking a modal claim to be an attempt to describe certain properties or features in this or another possible world that are capable of explaining what makes the modal claim true. This is a formidable array of problems. If we think of the problem of modality as the problem of finding truthmakers for modal propositions, then it is, to say the least, a very tough nut to crack. Reminding ourselves of these familiar problems should motivate us to look for an alternative approach, in hopes of finding one able to bypass the problems that have arisen from the tacit descriptivist assumption.

2. The Attractions of the Normativist Approach

If we examine the history of treatments of modality over the past century, it becomes clear that there is an alternative. In the early days of analytic philosophy, a more deflationary approach to modality held sway: one that denied that modal statements serve a descriptive function. The approach was suggested by early conventionalists like Schlick[30] (1918), and developed in a new way by Wittgenstein in the *Tractatus* (1922/1933), which in turn influenced the later modal conventionalism of the logical positivists.[31] The approach reappeared in a more sophisticated expressivist (or, more broadly, non-descriptivist) vein in the work of the later Wittgenstein, Ryle (1950/1971), and Sellars (1958), and more recently in work by Blackburn (1987/1993) and Robert Brandom (2008).

The view defended here is developed in that tradition. I call the view "modal normativism" since, on this view, basic metaphysical modal claims do not have the function of tracking or describing special modal features of this world—or other possible worlds. Instead, on this view, modal language serves the function of mandating, conveying, or renegotiating rules or norms in particularly advantageous ways. For metaphysical modal discourse, I will argue, the rules in question are semantic rules.[32] Modal normativism does not aim to reduce the modal to the non-modal, still less to eliminate it. The hope is instead to provide a way of understanding *metaphysical* modality in terms of *deontic* modality (modal claims concerning permissions and obligations). More specifically, the hope is to make sense of claims about metaphysical necessity by way of understanding semantic rules and the ways we communicate, enforce, and renegotiate them.

If we could make a view along these lines work, it would be very attractive indeed. One virtue of the view is that it gives us hope of a more

---

[30] Schlick, in turn, was developing ideas originating in Hilbert's *Foundations of Geometry* and attempting to generalize them to the cases of logic and mathematics. See Baker (1988, 187ff).

[31] A neo-conventionalist view has also been developed by Alan Sidelle (1989).

[32] This may also include using metaphysical modal claims as ways *advocating for* certain semantic rules, rather than merely conveying the actual rules. I return to this idea in Section 8.6.

unified account of modal terms—whether they are used in ethics, metaphysics, or science. For on the normativist view championed here, we can see metaphysical modal expressions, like deontic modal expressions, as serving a normative function. Indeed, there is some hope for getting a more unified view of modal terms as implicitly mandating and conveying norms: of behavior (unconditionally: morals), or behavior (in certain social circumstances: conventions, laws, game rules, instruction by authority); of use of terms (metaphysical); of reasoning (logical); or of empirical inference to future occurrences based on evidence (causal). If we took our metaphysical modal expressions to be describing special features of the world, while our deontic ones express permissions and obligations, we would have a deeply divided account of modality. For even those who are willing to treat moral deontic modal terms as describing special moral features of reality—what is permissible or obligatory—tend to become uneasy at the prospect of applying this across the board to all deontic modals including nonmoral ones such as those governing conventions (you must eat your rice with your fork) or authority (you may play after you've finished your dinner). And there is reason for thinking that a unified account of modal terms is desirable, for the same class of expressions tends to be used across the languages of the world regardless of whether the modality in question is alethic, deontic, or epistemic.[33] It would be bizarre if this were so although the terms were completely ambiguous. Moreover, uses of modal terms to express obligation, necessity, and possibility are acquired together at around age three (Wells 1985, 159–60 and 253)—giving additional evidence that there is some connection among these concepts.

More importantly for our purposes, a view like this, if we can make it plausible, would be extremely attractive from a philosophical standpoint. One advantage is the ontological advantage that comes from not thinking of modal properties or possible worlds as things our modal claims aim to describe or track, and that are capable of explaining what

---

[33] More precisely, there is apparently little evidence of the "logician's" distinctive sense of alethic modality in natural language—native speakers make no clear distinction between this use and the epistemic use (Palmer 1990, 6–7). But the deontic and epistemic meanings "tend to be expressed by a single class of modal expression in the languages of the world" (Papafragou 1998, 371).

makes them true. As I will argue in Chapter 6, the normativist may allow that we become entitled to accept that there are modal facts and properties—and even other possible worlds—but not in the sense of "positing" them to "explain" the truth of our modal claims (hence the difference from heavyweight/explanatory realism). The ontological entitlement to say that there are such things is explanatorily "downstream" from such truths, rather than explaining what makes them true. The most important advantage of a normativist approach is the epistemological advantage of avoiding the notorious difficulties heavyweight realist views and possible worlds realist views face in explaining our knowledge of modal facts. If we think of ourselves as trying to truly describe the modal facts or possible worlds (the presence of which could make the claims true), it is very difficult to see how we could have any (quasi-)perceptual or intellectual access to these modal facts or properties or worlds. The normativist demystifies modal knowledge by considering the move from *using* language to knowing *basic* modal facts to be a matter of moving from *mastering* the rules for properly applying and refusing expressions (as a competent speaker) to being able to explicitly *convey* these rules and their consequences in the object language and indicative mood.

A third, related, advantage of the normativist view is its helpfulness in clarifying the methodology of metaphysics and justifying the use of intuition in modal debates. If we think of metaphysicians as trying to "detect" modal properties of objects, the hopes of adjudicating debates about the modal features of persons or works of art seem slim. For no one, it seems, has any useful answer to the question of how they are supposed to be detected. Moreover, although it is common to rely on intuitions to support metaphysical views, it's not clear how to justify *why* intuition should be thought to be a reliable guide to the modal features of the world, when it certainly fails to be a reliable guide about most other features (see Sosa 2008, 233). But on the normativist view we have good reason for thinking that intuitions of competent speakers may play a useful role in revealing and making explicit the *actual* semantic rules, and thereby in discerning specifically *modal* facts that correspond to the semantic rules. Nonetheless, as I will argue in Chapter 8, some uses of metaphysical modal claims may be fruitfully seen as engaged in what David Plunkett and Tim Sundell (2013) have called "metalinguistic negotiation": as ways of *advocating for* changes the rules—whether to precisify them or alter them in other ways, in order to serve various purposes.[34] Where such moves are at stake, we do well to bring to the surface the pragmatic element in addressing these debates. Given the notorious difficulties facing heavyweight realism about modality, these methodological, epistemological, and pragmatic benefits of being a modal normativist are very attractive indeed.

3. The Plan of This Book

I begin in Chapter 1 by undertaking some philosophical archeology. I will first trace the roots of this alternative non-descriptive approach to modality in the work of Schlick, Ayer, Wittgenstein, Ryle, and Sellars. But despite this august list of defenders, the view has largely been abandoned and forgotten. Here I will examine the reasons why it was (sometimes wrongly) dismissed, and why the view was largely left abandoned in the wake of other emerging challenges.[35]

In Chapter 2 I begin to develop modal normativism as a contemporary non-descriptive view by showing what alternative account it gives of the function of modal discourse. In Chapter 3 I aim to show how the view manages to avoid the difficulties that kept historical forms of modal non-descriptivism off the table for decades—in particular by giving an account of the meaning of metaphysical modal terms that is connected with the earlier view of their function, and yet gives an account of meaning that remains stable even in embedded contexts, enabling us to avoid the notorious Frege-Geach problem. In Chapter 4 I aim to show that the form of modal non-descriptivism advocated here also is able to meet later challenges, accounting for the sorts of *de re* and a posteriori necessities identified by Kripke. Chapter 5

---

[34] See Plunkett (2015) and Thomasson (2017a) for developments of the idea that certain metaphysical debates may be seen as engaged in metalinguistic negotiation.

[35] Though a few brave souls—including Blackburn (1993) and Brandom (2008)—have recently made efforts to revive it, as have I (Thomasson 2007b, 2009, 2013a, 2018). Others, including Hacker (1996), Baker (1988), and Wright (1980), have made efforts at gaining a better understanding of the later position of Wittgenstein and its plausibility.

deals with a range of other apparent counterexamples, along with worries about whether the reliance on rules involves us in circularity. Chapters 6 through 8 give the core of the positive case for the view. For in these chapters I discuss the considerable attractions of the modal normativist position, showing how it enables us to mitigate ontological worries (Chapter 6), avoid the epistemological difficulties of more heavyweight positions (Chapter 7), and clarify the methodology of the (explicitly or tacitly) modal parts of metaphysics (Chapter 8)—making clear why traditional approaches involving intuitions or thought experiments are relevant, while at the same time allowing that the work of metaphysics can be deep and worldly. Such promising features are sufficient motivation for developing a detailed contemporary non-descriptivist view of modal discourse and showing how it measures up against competing theories of modality. In the concluding chapter, I return to the big picture, showing the ways in which a neo-pragmatist appreciation of the different functions language may serve, along with a deflationary easy approach to ontology, have come together to help solve the problems of modality. Combining these approaches is not only promising for handling the problems of modality but also develops a strategy that may prove useful in addressing a range of other venerable philosophical problems.

1

The Rise and Fall of Early
Non-Descriptive Approaches

Recent work on modality has been dominated by the assumption that modal statements serve the function of describing some special features of our world, or features of other possible worlds—an assumption that leads to a variety of ontological, epistemological, and methodological problems for metaphysics.

The problems of understanding modal discourse are certainly not new, however. If we look back to early twentieth-century analytic philosophy we can find the roots of an entirely different, non-descriptivist approach to modality. In this chapter I aim to unearth the history of this approach. I will argue that not only is such an approach available, it has generally been dismissed and buried for the wrong reasons. This work should clear the way for reviving an approach along these lines and provide some suggestions for how to develop a non-descriptivist view.

Analytic philosophy generally traces its roots back to British empiricism, and more immediately to the empiricism of the logical positivists. Understanding how claims about possibility and necessity could be true and how we could come to know them was a central problem for thinkers in both traditions. Their focus was not so much on the modal claims made in metaphysics (though these also were discussed) as on understanding what it could mean to say that the truths of logic and mathematics are not just true but *necessarily* true, and how we could know that they are necessarily true. Nonetheless, looking at earlier work on these modal claims will provide useful background for examining the metaphysical modal claims that are the focus of attention in this book.

Norms and Necessity. Amie L. Thomasson, Oxford University Press (2020). © Oxford University Press.
DOI: 10.1093/oso/9780190098193.001.0001

1.1 The Pre-History: Challenges for Empiricism

Empiricists face challenges in accounting for modal truths precisely because *modal* features of the world do not seem to be empirically detectable. As David Hume argued, we cannot be thought to know *necessary* matters of fact (or rather: to know that any matter of fact holds necessarily) on the basis of experience of the world. For however well a statement may be confirmed through experience, that only shows that it *does* (so far) hold, not that it *must* hold (1777/1977, 39–53; cf. Ayer 1936/1952, 72).

This, of course, leaves a significant problem in understanding our knowledge of the truths of mathematics and logic. Empiricists cannot think of them as truths about empirically undetectable abstract objects, so a natural alternative is to think of them as empirical generalizations (rather than as necessary truths), and to see them as grounded in experience. John Stuart Mill famously treated the axioms of logic and mathematics as merely well-confirmed observational hypotheses:

> And so, in all cases, the general propositions, whether called definitions, axioms or laws of nature, which we lay down at the beginning of our reasonings, are merely abridged statements, in a kind of shorthand, of the particular facts, which, as occasion arises, we either think we may proceed on as proved, or intend to assume.
>
> (1843/1875, 220; cf. Baker 1988, 173)

Even the principle of non-contradiction Mill considers "to be, like other axioms, one of the first and most familiar *generalizations from experience*" (1843/1875, 321; italics mine). Logic, on Mill's view, "rests on completely universal empirical truths" (Skorupski 1998, 48).

But major problems notoriously arise for this account, since the validity of the statements of logic and mathematics is not determined in the same way as that of empirical generalizations. As A. J. Ayer argues, we don't take purported counterexamples to provide evidence, for example, that two plus two really is *not* four, or that the angles of a Euclidean triangle really *don't* add up to 180 degrees: "Whatever instance we care to take, we shall always find that the situations in which a logical or mathematical principle might appear to be confuted are accounted for in such a way as to leave the principle unassailed" (Ayer 1936/1952, 77). The fact that the principles of logic and mathematics cannot be confuted by experience, Ayer holds, gives reason for doubting that they are empirical generalizations.

Of course the empiricist needn't treat principles of logic and math as generalizations from "external" experience of the world; one may take them to be psychological principles derived from experience of our minds and reasoning processes. Although Mill is often considered a founder of psychologism (e.g., by Husserl 1901/1970, 90–97), this is contested. For although Mill held that logicians must draw on laws of psychology to achieve their aim of instilling clear thinking, he was clear that the laws of logic themselves are universal empirical generalizations about the world—not about our judgments (Skorupski 1998, 47–50). In any case, psychologism was another option open for the empiricist to take about logical and mathematical truth, and was prevalent in nineteenth-century German philosophy (e.g., of Jakob Friedrich Fries and Friedrich Beneke).

But psychologism was subjected to devastating critiques at the hands of Frege and Husserl (following Bolzano and Lotze's earlier criticisms). According to Frege and Husserl, psychologism confuses the *act* or process of thinking with the *content* of the thought and the *object* thought about. As Frege wrote:

> Never take a description of the origin of an idea for a definition, or an account of the mental and physical conditions through which we become conscious of a proposition for a proof of it. A proposition may be thought, and again it may be true; never confuse these two things. We must remind ourselves, it seems, that a proposition no more ceases to be true when I cease to think of it than the sun ceases to exist when I shut my eyes.
>
> (1884, VIe)

That is, whether we are talking about trees, mathematics, or logic, the *object* considered (number, proposition, etc.) is different in principle from (and can't be reduced to) the *act* of thinking about it, or the (repeatable) *way* in which one thinks of it. Husserl also argues extensively against psychologism in the *Logical Investigations*, arguing (among other reasons) that logical laws cannot be based on psychological laws, as the former are apodictically certain, whereas the latter are merely probable (1901/1970, 98–102). Moreover, if they were based on psychological laws, the truth of the laws of logic would entail the existence of psychological occurrences, though it does no such thing (1901/1970, 104–8). On Husserl's view, the very *meaning* of discourse about logic and math is misconstrued if we take it to be "about" acts of consciousness.

The alternative Frege and Husserl favored—to take the statements of logic and mathematics as being *about* abstract entities and their interrelations—appeared not to be one that the empiricist could embrace. Thus, in light of the problems generated by previous attempts, by the early twentieth-century empiricists were in the market for a new approach to understanding the truths of logic and mathematics.

Ayer would later summarize the options for the empiricist as follows:

> [I]f empiricism is correct no proposition which has a factual content can be necessary or certain. Accordingly, the empiricist must deal with the truths of logic and mathematics in one of the two following ways: he must say either [following Mill] that they are not necessary truths, in which case he must account for the universal conviction that they are; or he must say that they have no factual content, and then he must explain how a proposition which is empty of all factual content can be true and useful and surprising . . . if we can show either that the truths in question are not necessary or that they are not "truths about the world," we shall be taking away the support on which rationalism rests. We shall be making good the empiricist contention that there are no "truths of reason" which refer to matters of fact.
>
> (1936/1952, 72–73)

The second option for the empiricist is to deny that the necessary truths of logic or mathematics are factual claims at all—that is, in effect, to take a non-descriptivist approach to modal discourse suggesting that, although they are expressed in the indicative mood, modal statements do not aim to describe features of the world—neither of psychological nor non-psychological entities in the world. It is this non-descriptivist approach that newly emerged in early analytic philosophy, and that is of interest here.

1.2 Conventionalism and Its Motives

The basic statement of the positivist view of necessity, and often the only one passed down to us, is that "the truths of logic and mathematics are analytic propositions or tautologies" (Ayer 1936/1952, 77)—statements that thus say nothing about the world.[1] It also formed the core of the view that came to be known, perhaps unfortunately, as "modal conventionalism."

Although he never used the term "conventionalism," the view that came to be known as modal conventionalism arose in the work of Moritz Schlick (1918). Generalizing Hilbert's approach to geometry, Schlick argued that the necessary statements of mathematics and logic are not *descriptive* statements saying something about the world, precisely because they *say nothing* at all. On Schlick's view, necessary truths are instead implicit definitions of concepts. Since definitions are conventional, they then might also be said to be "conventions of symbolism," which say nothing about the world (Baker 1988, 199), although they enable us to use these symbols to say things about the world.

Two central problems arose for Schlick's initial formulation of conventionalism (Baker 1988, 215). First, it seems to involve treating the truths of logic as based on arbitrary conventions, when they seem not to be arbitrary. Second, it faces a regress problem most famously raised by Quine in "Truth by Convention" (1935/1976), where it is put forward primarily as a problem for Carnap's conventionalism about logical truth. As Quine argues, if we think of logical truths as including those expressed in basic axioms (taken as implicit definitions) *and any truths that follow from those*, we apparently need logic "for inferring

---

[1] For important recent revivals of the conventionalist idea that necessity should be understood in terms of analyticity, see Sidelle (1989) and Ludwig (in progress).

logic from the conventions" (1935/1976, 104), and so cannot take conventionalism to provide a complete account of logical truth.

Although Schlick introduced the approach, the idea that necessary propositions—at least of logic and mathematics—say nothing, and thus cannot be thought of as *descriptions* at all—was popularized by Ludwig Wittgenstein's work in the *Tractatus* (1922/1933), which even later members of the Vienna Circle routinely acknowledged as the greatest influence on their view (Baker 1988, 208). Rather than thinking of logical and mathematical propositions as implicit definitions (or following from these), Wittgenstein held that they are one and all empty *tautologies*:

6.1 The propositions of logic are tautologies.

6.11 The propositions of logic therefore say nothing. (They are the analytical propositions.)

(1922/1933; cf. Hacker 1996, 32)

Tautologies thus understood do not *describe* anything (not even relations among logical objects)—they combine meaningful signs in such a way that all content "cancels out" (Baker 1988, 214). They say nothing either about the world or about language or logical "objects" themselves.

The Tractarian formulation enables us to avoid both of the problems faced by Schlick's view. First, it needn't involve treating logical truths as arbitrary. Instead, these truths (the tautologies) are true given only their *logical structure* (rather than their status as implicit stipulations or definitions). Second, we avoid the regress problem. On Wittgenstein's view, all logical truths are equally tautologies, as can be shown from truth-table notation, and so we avoid the need to presuppose logic in order to infer derivative logical truths from the definitional axioms (cf. Baker 1988, 215). So, although critical remarks like those mentioned have been influential in keeping any views resembling conventionalism at bay, they do not apply to views like the Tractarian or later Wittgensteinian one.[2]

---

[2] Of course other forms of conventionalism may need to face (again) these lines of objection. For other replies to the regress problem, see Dummett (1991, 202), Boghossian (1997, 374), and Thomasson (2007, 32–37).

But although the propositions of logic do not *say* anything, according to the Wittgenstein of the *Tractatus*, their importance lies in what they *show*—or, more precisely, in what is shown by the fact that the propositions of logic are tautologies:

> The fact that the propositions of logic are tautologies *shows* the formal—logical—properties of language, of the world.
> That its constituent parts connected together *in this way* give a tautology characterizes the logic of its constituent parts.
>
> (1922/1933, 6.12)

For example, if two propositions "p" and "q" form a tautology when they are combined as "p→q," that *shows* (but does not say) that q follows from p (1922/1933, 6.1221). Moreover, "Every tautology itself shows that it is a tautology" (1922/1933, 6.127). Thus in the *Tractatus* we can see not only the idea that logical propositions are not descriptions, but also that they serve some other function: showing, rather than saying.

Much influenced by the *Tractatus* (see Hacker 1996, 46), the positivists adopted the idea that the necessary propositions of logic and mathematics are tautologies or analytic claims, marrying it with the following understanding of analyticity: "a proposition is analytic when its validity depends solely on the definitions of the symbols it contains" (Ayer 1936/1952, 78). The positivists' view is often summarized as the view that necessary/analytic propositions are those whose truth depends on our linguistic conventions (which define the terms used), and labeled as a form of "modal conventionalism."[3]

But how should we understand the idea that the truth of necessary/analytic propositions "depends on our linguistic conventions"? If one takes modal claims to be attempted descriptions, and assumes that the problem of modality is the problem of saying what it is that explains why certain modal claims are true, then it is natural to read the positivists as providing the answer that linguistic conventions serve as the truthmakers for modal statements. This also provides a

---

[3] A modern conventionalist view is developed by Sidelle (1989), in a way that enables conventionalists to account for *de re* and a posteriori necessities. See Chapter 4 for discussion.

straightforward way of understanding the idea that the truth of these propositions "depends on our linguistic conventions," and indeed a way of understanding it that is consistent with empiricism. Some positivists wrote in ways that invite this (mis)interpretation; for example, Carnap treats a sentence as L-true (necessarily/analytically true) "if and only if it is true *in virtue of* the semantical rules alone, independently of any extra-linguistic facts" (1947, 174, italics mine). Alan Sidelle's recent defense of conventionalism more directly invites this reading:

> Conventionalists, of course, are free to believe that there are true statements of the sort described [true statements beginning with "necessarily"]. Where they differ from realists is over the grounds of this necessity, or, to borrow Armstrong's phrase, over the "truth-makers" for modal statements.
>
> (1989, 6)

Sider, one of the most recent vocal critics of conventionalism, explicitly interprets the view in that way. He takes the view to be that "By adopting certain rules governing the use of logical words like 'all,' language users somehow make 'all horses are horses' true" (2011, 98), and goes on to dismiss the "notion of truth by convention" as "thoroughly confused" (268), since the convention "plays no role in explaining why [an analytic sentence] is true, or necessary" (268–69); the conventionalist may be right that analytic claims are necessary, but that does not "secure a truth-making role for the convention" (101).

Taking conventionalism to be the view that conventions serve as the truthmakers for modal statements, however, is historically inaccurate and philosophically catastrophic.

1.3 Criticisms of Conventionalism

The thought that conventionalism was committed to the view that linguistic conventions serve as truthmakers for modal statements provoked a barrage of criticism that led to decades of neglect of similar approaches to modality, and even to the dominance of heavyweight realist views of modality as reactions against the apparent failings of conventionalism. Indeed, modal conventionalism is still regularly invoked and dismissed on the basis of objections that arise when we understand modal conventionalism on this model (e.g., Boghossian 1997; Sider 2003 and 2011).[4] As Sider puts it, "The old 'linguistic' or 'conventionalist' theory of necessity has few contemporary adherents, for the most part with good reason" (2003, 199). As a result, even those who now defend versions of non-descriptivism tend to avoid association with, or even much discussion of, their conventionalist predecessors.

A first standard objection is that conventionalism makes "the truth of what is expressed *contingent*, whereas most of the statements at stake in the present discussion [logical, mathematical, and conceptual truths] are clearly necessary" (Boghossian 1997, 336). For if analytic statements were "actually about language use" (Sider 2003, 199)—if, for instance, "All bachelors are men" meant "It is a linguistic convention that 'bachelor' is to be applied only where 'man' is applied"—then it would clearly be contingent, since we might have adopted other linguistic conventions to govern these symbols. This not only seems wrong (it certainly *seems* necessary that all bachelors are men) but also would block the attempt to explain necessity in terms of analyticity, and analyticity in terms of linguistic conventions (since analytic statements would no longer be seen as necessarily true). Sider expresses a similar worry as follows: if "necessarily P" says that P "is true by convention," then "necessarily P" itself "would apparently turn out contingent, since statements about what conventions we adopt are not themselves true by convention" (2011, 268). But then we would have to give up

---

[4] Boghossian attributes the "metaphysical" form of conventionalism—which he characterizes as the idea that "a statement is analytic provided that, in some appropriate sense, it *owes its truth value completely to its meaning, and not at all to 'the facts'*" (1997, 334)—to the positivists, and calls it a "discredited idea" of "dubious explanatory value and possibly also of dubious coherence" (1996, 364). He does, however, show greater sympathy for what he calls the "epistemological" version of the idea of "truth by virtue of meaning," characterized as the position that a statement is true by virtue of its meaning "provided that grasp of its meaning alone suffices for justified belief in its truth." He attributes the latter view to Carnap and the middle Wittgenstein, and defends it against certain Quinean criticisms.

the axiom (of modal system S4) that if P is necessary, it is necessarily necessary.[5]

The second, related, criticism is that the very idea of truth by convention is untenable, since it (allegedly) requires that we can *make* certain statements (the analytic or basic modal ones) true "by pronouncement," but (as Boghossian puts it) "how can we make sense of the idea that something is made true by our meaning something by a sentence?" (1997, 336). Sider develops the argument further as follows:

> I cannot make it the case that it rains simply by pronouncing, nor can I make it the case that it does not rain simply by pronouncing. . . . Therefore, I cannot make it the case that either it rains or it doesn't rain, simply by pronouncement.
>
> (2003, 201; see also his 2011, 104)

But while these are the most influential and frequently cited reasons for dismissing modal conventionalism, they are historically inaccurate, as they miss the point of the original view. To take all those who are labeled as "conventionalists" to be defending the view that the necessary truths of logic and mathematics are descriptive claims *made true by* our adopting certain linguistic conventions ignores the really interesting and promising aspect of their proposal, and of the Wittgensteinian view that inspired it—namely, that the propositions of mathematics and logic should not be thought of as *descriptive* claims in need of truthmakers at all. It is that (mis)interpretation of the view, not the view itself, that is thoroughly confused.

Ayer, for example, is much more careful than the critics of conventionalism would have us believe, in not suggesting that necessary truths are descriptions *made true by* the adoption of linguistic conventions; instead they are "entirely devoid of factual content," and thus describe neither the (language-independent) world, nor our linguistic conventions. He suggests that analytic statements serve some other function than describing—they "*illustrate* the rules which

---

[5] Sidelle responds to this line of criticism in his reading (1989, 7).

govern our usage" of the terms or logical particles (1936/1952, 80), "*record* our determination" to speak in certain ways, "*[call] attention to the implications* of a certain linguistic usage," or "*indicate* the convention which governs our usage of the words" (1936/1952, 79; italics in each case are mine). Note that in all this talk of what analytic statements do—*they illustrate, call attention to*, or *indicate* our rules, usages, or linguistic conventions—there is no talk of them *describing* these things (or anything else). And this careful choice of words is not accidental, for Ayer well understood that the crucial insight of Wittgenstein's view (and the crucial insight needed to make the view workable) was denying that necessary propositions are descriptive at all (cf. Ayer 1985, 60–67).

Not only does Ayer avoid the mistake of taking analytic statements to be *about* our linguistic conventions (they are, as he often—following Wittgenstein—insists, about nothing), he also shows awareness of the problems that would arise with that view, responding directly to the first standard objection as follows:

> [J]ust as the validity of an analytic proposition is independent of the nature of the external world, so is it independent of the nature of our minds. It is perfectly conceivable that we should have employed different linguistic conventions from those which we actually do employ. But whatever these conventions might be, the tautologies in which we recorded them would always be necessary.
>
> (1936/1952, 84)

In short, it seems unjust to reject views like Ayer's and the early views of Wittgenstein for the reasons customarily given for dismissing "modal conventionalism." Indeed, Sider admits that his arguments are directed against the notion of truth by convention understood as the view that "We can *legislate-true* the truths of logic" (2011, 103). But if this is, as I have argued, a misunderstanding of the view, the criticisms leave the basic approach untouched. To the extent that (in the contemporary context) the name "modal conventionalism" suggests the view that modal claims are made true by our (adopting) conventions, it is simply a misleading name. The crucial insight of these views instead lies in the idea that modal statements *do not even aim to describe* features of the world.[6]

Thus, in what follows, I will turn to examine developments of what I will call "modal non-descriptivism." As I develop my own non-descriptivist approach to metaphysical necessity, I will return in section 3.4 to show in detail how it is able to avoid the classic criticisms of conventionalism.

1.4 Later Non-Descriptivism and the Normative Function of Modal Discourse

Despite the many changes in Wittgenstein's views over time, a crucial point that remains constant is the idea that necessary truths should be understood not as *descriptions* but rather as tautologies that say nothing.[7] (But, importantly, Wittgenstein's understanding of what a tautology is evolves, so that in the later work a tautology is considered to be any proposition that can be ascertained to be true exclusively by appeal to rules of grammar [Baker 1988, 39].)

---

[6] As an anonymous referee pointed out, some might have doubts that Ayer's version of the view entirely avoids the worries about conventionalism. One might, for example, still maintain that it is a contingent matter whether a certain string of symbols "illustrates" a linguistic convention. As the referee helpfully suggested, there may be responses available here, for example by insisting that the relevant conventions should be understood not as governing mere *strings of letters* (where the connection might seem contingent), but rather as governing meaningful *terms* (or even: *whatever plays a certain role* in our language). In any case, the central points for the present are (1) that the standard criticisms of conventionalism involve misinterpreting the view as a view about the *truthmakers* of modal claims, leaving it an open question whether criticisms in the vicinity could be resurrected to apply to the actual view, and (2) that the real point of these views was to reject the functional assumption behind the truthmaker approach—leaving a route open to explore.

[7] Nonetheless, there are many crucial changes and differences, as detailed in Baker (1988, 116ff.). First, Wittgenstein's later work is anti-metaphysical: he doesn't see his results as grounded in the essence of propositions, but rather in the way the term "proposition" is used: p v ~p and ~(p& ~p) are rules, rules that tell us what a proposition is. If a logic is made up in which the law of the excluded middle does not hold, there is no reason for calling the substituted expressions propositions (Wittgenstein 1932-5/1979, 140). Second, he abandons the assumption that atomic statements are independent—they are organized instead into *Satzsysteme*. Third, he no longer makes a distinction between the tautologies of logic and analytic claims: any implication between two atomic propositions is now called a tautology (even, e.g., nothing can be red and green all over) because it cannot be false (Baker 1988, 136).

In the *Tractatus*, Wittgenstein is mainly concerned to emphasize the fact that the necessary truths of logic (which he then held to be the only necessary truths) lack descriptive content. He retains this view in his later work, insisting that the propositions of logic do not fulfill a descriptive function. The universality of a claim like 'p v ~p' is not like that of 'all apples are sweet'; it's not describing something that holds of all propositions (1932–35/1979, 139–40). But in his later work he also broadens his focus to include analytic statements more generally, along with some claims of metaphysical necessity, and raises the crucial question: If these propositions do not serve to describe the world, what is their function? "Why, if they are tautologies, do we ever write them down? What is their use?" (Wittgenstein 1932–35/1979, 137). Clearly we don't inform by means of them: if, for example, you ask me how many people will be present, and I tell you that "if there are fifteen, there will be fifteen," I have told you nothing, given you no information (Wittgenstein 1939/1976, 280). But we still need a positive view of what the function or use of these forms of language *is*, if it is not descriptive.

The answer Wittgenstein suggests is that (reputed) necessary propositions have a *normative* or *prescriptive* function—much the same as rules do. While this is the general insight, the precise relation to rules must be specified carefully, and may vary for different kinds of (reputedly) necessary claims. Arithmetical equations are understood as rules for transforming empirical propositions (about quantities)—which of course is not to say that they give us predictions about what the results will be if anyone calculates:

> Are the propositions of mathematics anthropological propositions saying how we men infer and calculate?—Is a statute book a work of anthropology telling how the people of this nation deal with a thief etc.? . . .
>
> The prophecy does *not* run, that a man will get *this* result when he follows this rule in making a transformation—but that he will get this result, when we *say* that he is following the rule.
>
> (1956/1978, §65–66; cf. Ayer 1985, 63)

Propositions of logic are said to "reflect" rules for reasoning in the sense that "P ergo Q" is a rule of inference if and only if "P→Q" is a tautology (Baker 1988, 135)—though the tautology itself states nothing (not even a rule of reasoning or "grammatical rule").
As Hacker describes Wittgenstein's later view of analyticity:

> Analytic propositions such as "Bachelors are unmarried" . . . are, despite the fact that we talk of them as being true, rules in the misleading guise of statements (as, indeed, we say that it is true that the chess king moves only one square at a time). "Bachelors are unmarried" is the expression of a rule which licenses the inference from "A is a bachelor" to "A is unmarried."
>
> (1996, 49)

What, then, of purported metaphysical *necessities*? As Wittgenstein succinctly put it, "Essence is expressed by grammar" (1958, §371). The later Wittgenstein

> rejected the common assumption that what are conceived of as metaphysical truths are descriptions of anything, that the "necessary truths" of metaphysics are descriptions of objective necessities in nature—that the "truths" of metaphysics are truths about objects in reality at all. Rather, what we conceive of as true metaphysical propositions are *norms of representation, rules for the use of expressions in the misleading guise of descriptions of objects and relations.*
>
> (Hacker 1996, 102; italics mine)

Thus, even the reputed necessary truths of metaphysics are said to "disguise" or "hide" grammatical rules:

> [W]hen we meet the word "can" in a metaphysical proposition [e.g., "A and B can't have seen the same chair, for A was in London and B in Cambridge; they saw two chairs exactly alike"] . . . [w]e show that this proposition hides a grammatical rule. That is to say, we destroy the outward similarity between a metaphysical proposition and

an experiential one, and we try to find the form of expression which fulfils a certain craving of the metaphysician which our ordinary language does not fulfill and which, as long as it isn't fulfilled, produces the metaphysical puzzlement.[8]

(Wittgenstein 1958, 55)

The idea that modal statements serve an implicitly normative (rather than descriptive) function surfaces again in the work of Gilbert Ryle and Wilfrid Sellars, though they expand the issue further, discussing modal expressions as they appear in what Ryle calls "hypotheticals" (what we would now call conditionals of the form: "If P, then Q") and in statements of scientific laws. Frank Ramsey had developed an idea along these lines two decades earlier, arguing that universal generalizations (which he called "variable hypotheticals") "are not judgments but rules for judging. 'If I meet a φ, I shall regard it as a ψ'" (1929, 137). Assertions of causal laws, Ramsey argued, are just a special case of variable hypothetical, and as such "express an inference we are at any time prepared to make" (1929, 134).[9]

Echoing and developing Ramsey's point, Ryle argues that hypotheticals of the form "If P, then Q" should not be thought of as asserting (truth-conditional) relations between statements, propositions, or facts. Instead, delivering a hypothetical statement is a way of giving instruction in how to wield or follow arguments. Saying "If P, then Q" is not making an assertion, but licensing one: "[T]he author of a hypothetical statement is neither using nor mentioning any premiss statements or conclusion statements. He is showing, empty-handed, how to use them" (Ryle 1950/1971, 248). In other words, such an author is licensing us, if we have P, to infer Q. But this is emphatically not to say that hypothetical statements are *about inferences:* "It

---

[8] Compare Ayer's similar treatment of the apparent metaphysical proposition that a material thing cannot be in two places at once (1936/1952, 58).

[9] Thanks to Huw Price for pointing out the connection to Ramsey. For further discussion of Ramsey's position and its relation to later pragmatist work, see Price (2017). Marion (2012) interestingly traces Ramsey's position that universally quantified claims are "rules for the formation of judgments" to a 1921 paper by Hermann Weyl. He also argues that Ramsey's work on variable hypotheticals was an influence on the shift of Wittgenstein's views from the Tractarian approach to meaning, to the pragmatist approach characteristic of Wittgenstein's subsequent work.

must be realized that asserting '*if p, then q*' is not making a report of any inference or a comment on any inference" (240). Such hypothetical statements are not to be taken as *descriptions* at all. The questions "'What exactly do hypothetical statements assert to characterise what?' . . . or, more generally, 'What do such statements describe?' or 'What matters of fact do they report?'" are thus misguided, and positing "Necessary Connections between Facts, or Internal Relations between Universals, and the like" to answer those questions is unnecessary (243). For hypotheticals do not aim to describe but rather serve the different function of explicitly instructing in and licensing the inference from P to Q. This point, as Ryle himself argues, is directly relevant to understanding modality, since "the differences between modal and hypothetical statements are in fact purely stylistic," as the only way to negate a hypothetical statement (If you walk under a ladder you come to grief before the day is out) is to insert a modal verb (No: you *may* walk under a ladder and not come to grief) (244). (I shall return to this important point in Chapter 2.)

Ryle develops a parallel understanding of statements of scientific laws in *The Concept of Mind*, insisting again that these are not factual statements describing any features of the world, but instead fulfill a different function:

> A law is used as, so to speak, an inference-ticket (a season ticket) which licenses its possessors to move from asserting factual statements to asserting other factual statements. It also licenses them to provide explanations of given facts and to bring about desired states of affairs by manipulating what is found existing or happening.
>
> (1949, 121)

Sellars (1958) develops a similar treatment of statements of scientific laws, which he treats as having the function of *justifying* or *endorsing* inferences from something's being an A to its being a B (cf. Brandom 2008, Chapter 4). To say "'Being A physically entails being B' . . . contextually implies [without asserting] that the speaker feels himself entitled to infer that something is B, given that it is A" (Sellars 1958, 281). To make first-hand use of modal expressions is to be involved in *explaining* a state of affairs or *justifying* an assertion. "The primary use of 'p entails q' is not to state that something is the case, but to explain why q, or to justify the assertion that q" (283). Like other modal non-descriptivists, Sellars also shows awareness of the potential pitfalls of modal conventionalism:

> It is sometimes thought that modal statements do not describe states of affairs in the world, because they are really metalinguistic. This won't do at all if it is meant that instead of describing states of affairs in the world, they describe linguistic habits. It is more plausible if it is meant that statements involving modal terms have the force of *prescriptive* statements about the use of certain expressions in the object language.
>
> (283)

Taking basic statements of necessity not to be descriptive, but, in some sense, prescriptive or normative, is the key move that unites Wittgenstein's later treatment of logical, mathematical, and metaphysical necessities, Ryle's handling of hypotheticals, and Sellars's treatment of physical necessities. All of the views canvassed so far have in common the crucial feature that they deny that modal discourse should be taken as descriptive at all—whether of other possible worlds, modal features of the actual world, or platonic essences. Making this move explicitly enables us to avoid the standard criticisms of conventionalism, for the key move for the non-descriptivist is to emphasize that the expressions in question do not even attempt to describe features of the world, and so have no need for truthmakers (not that they have as truthmakers our making certain legislations or adopting certain conventions).

1.5 Why the Non-Descriptivist Approach Was Lost

So why were views like these abandoned, to the extent that they are not even on the table in contemporary discussions of modality—where, as I mentioned at the outset, the question is usually posed as that of finding the truthmakers for our modal claims, simply *presupposing* that these claims are to be understood descriptively?

One problem seems to be the frequent failure to understand the view. In some quarters, at least, the functional monist assumption—that all discourse has the function of tracking/describing some portion of reality—seems to have made such views practically impossible to see. A prime case in point is in the introduction to Armstrong's *Truth and Truthmakers*, where he insists on the need for truthmakers for counterfactuals, and criticizes Ryle for appealing to dispositions without saying what the truthmakers are for dispositional statements:

> I think [Ryle] was quite right to claim an essential role for dispositionality in the elucidation of our notion of the mental . . . But we need then to go on to consider the question of the truthmaker for these dispositional truths. What is there in the world in virtue of which these truths are true? Ryle had no answer.
>
> (2004, 3)

He goes on to excoriate Ryle for letting dispositions "hang on air," calling this "the ultimate sin in metaphysics" (2004, 3).[10] But this criticism rests on a spectacular failure to understand Ryle's point about disposition-talk: "Dispositional statements are neither reports of observed or observable states of affairs, nor yet reports of unobserved or unobservable states of affairs. They narrate no incidents" (Ryle 1949, 125). Instead, as Ryle emphasizes, dispositional talk serves a different function: licensing inferences.

But there is also a more legitimate reason non-descriptivist views of modality fell out of view. Non-descriptivist or expressivist views in general were thought to fall prey to the "Frege-Geach" or "embedding" problem raised by both Peter Geach (1965) and John Searle (1969). While the problem has become most notorious in meta-ethics, it applies across the board to a range of non-descriptive views about various sorts of subject matter. In fact, Geach himself discusses not only views about moral discourse but also about truth, negation, and existence, among others.

---

[10] This is an idea that has been more recently voiced in Sider's view that the truthmaker principle is useful as a way to "rule out dubious ontologies" and "catch cheaters" who would accept truths without saying what "robust ontology" makes them true (2001, 40–41).

In each case, the non-descriptivist insists that the expressions in question are used not to describe but to do something else (such as commend an action or license an inference). Searle's basic admonition is this: don't confuse what speech act an expression is commonly *used* to perform with what the word *means* (1969, 137–38). For suppose we take some form of expression, and argue that it is not used as a description (requiring truthmakers) but rather is used to do something else. Moral expressivists, for example, are tempted to say that to call an action "good" is to commend it. But commending is a certain type of speech act, and while it may be true that the most basic or typical uses of "good" are in speech acts of commendation, the word "good" may also be used in many other sorts of complex expression, in which it often does not involve performing the speech act of commending at all:

> Calling something good is characteristically praising or commending or recommending it, etc. But it is a fallacy to infer from this that the meaning of "good" is explained by saying it is used to perform the act of commendation. And we demonstrate that it is a fallacy by showing that there are an indefinite number of counter-examples of sentences where "good" has a literal occurrence yet where the literal utterances of the sentences are not performances of the speech act of commendation; nor are the utterances explicable in terms of the way the rest of the sentence relates the utterance to the performance of the speech act of commendation.
>
> (Searle 1969, 139)

So, for example, "If this is good, we should buy it" contains the term "good," but in that context (since the term is embedded in a hypothetical construction) it is clearly used without commending anything.[11] Similarly, "Either this is good or this is bad" contains the term "good" without using it to commend. So it seems that either the original account did not give us the *meaning* of the term "good" (but only an

---

[11] Geach (1960, 223) makes a similar point, expressed as the need to distinguish between "calling a thing 'P' " (which involves the speech act of assertion) and "predicating 'P' of a thing" (which may be done in embedded contexts without asserting that it is P).

account of its typical use), or that "good" must have a different meaning in an embedded context.

The latter move is problematic, however, for if we hold that the term changes meaning in embedded contexts, we are left unable to account for our ability to reason validly like this:

1. If protecting the lives of others is good, then so is protecting your own life.
2. Protecting the lives of others is good.
3. Protecting your own life is good.

The argument seems clearly valid, yet if "good" means something different in the unembedded context (2) than where it is embedded in a conditional (1), then the argument is invalid on grounds of equivocation. The moral of the story has been thought to be that expressivists need to say not just how basic moral claims are typically *used* (for performing what sorts of speech act), but also of what they *mean*—with contents that may be the same across speech acts with varying force.[12] Searle applies his criticism not only to expressivist views in ethics, but also to what he calls "speech act" analyses of "true," "know," and one modal term: "probably," criticizing the view that the word "probably" is used to qualify commitments.[13]

Geach also explicitly criticizes Ryle's (1950/1971) view of "hypotheticals" as *licensing* inferences rather than as *describing* relations among propositions. What Geach says directly about Ryle's view is sketchy and uncharitable at best. He first criticizes what he takes to be Ryle's argument that "If P then Q" can't be taken to be describing a relation between statements. He takes Ryle's argument to be based on the view that the antecedent and consequent are not asserted and so cannot be *statements*. But Ryle's view that a hypothetical does not assert a relation between *statements* is based primarily on the ability to convert hypotheticals such as "If today is Monday, then tomorrow is Tuesday"

---

[12] Allan Gibbard is often thought to have met this challenge on the moral side by giving an account of the contents of moral propositions in terms of pairs consisting of a world and a system of norms (Gibbard 1990, 2003; see also discussion in Dreier 1996, 44–45).

[13] A view he attributes to Toulmin (1950).

to modal statements of the form: "It cannot be Monday today and not be Tuesday tomorrow," where the clauses no longer even appear in propositional form at all (for "be Monday today" is not a proposition). Thus this argument does not hinge on the terminology "statement" but would apply equally well if we used Geach's own preferred terminology of propositions (as Ryle himself notes [1950/1971, 245]).

Geach (1965, 451–52) also argues against what he takes to be Ryle's view that "If P then Q" does not form a premise in the argument from P to Q. But this seems to be a misreading that misses the deep point Ryle is making: Ryle does not deny that hypothetical statements may serve as premises in explicit *modus ponens* arguments. Rather, he denies that inference rules should be identified with premises: for even if we have both premises, we should still need an inference rule to license us to make the relevant move (from "P" and "If P then Q" to "Q"). And what we are *doing* in asserting a hypothetical statement (he suggests) should be understood as making explicit a rule of inference. Moreover, Ryle is making the radical and insightful move of suggesting that our practices of making inferences, and accepting or rejecting inferences, are prior to those of explicitly stating arguments with hypothetical premises. Thus, he urges, we should see the hypothetical (If P then Q) as a way of explicitly instructing and licensing others to make (particular) inferences from P to Q, rather than seeing the inference from P to Q as eliding the full argument with the hypothetical premise suppressed. This is an approach that would be developed much later by Robert Brandom (1994, 100–101). Brandom, following Ryle, takes logical vocabulary as a later, more sophisticated development than the practice of making, endorsing, accepting, and rejecting inferences. Making explicit hypothetical statements, on this view, has the function of enabling us to express our implicit inferential commitments in an explicit way: as contents of potential propositional commitments.[14]

---

[14] Ryle's central claim, as we have seen, is that a hypothetical statement itself should not be thought of as describing anything at all but rather serves a different function, of licensing those who have P in hand to infer Q. Against this, Geach writes: "Particular readings of 'p' and 'q' may make 'p, therefore q' into a logically valid argument; but it is not in general logically valid, and if not, then no power in heaven or earth can issue me a 'license' that makes it logically valid" (1965, 452). But this seems to misconstrue the position along the lines of the common misunderstandings of conventionalism, taking it to be the view that our acts of legislation *make* certain statements true—rather than as the view that the statements in question have a different function than describing.

In any case, despite the shortcomings of Geach's particular comments about Ryle, it does seem that the general point Geach makes later in that article (and that Searle makes in his chapter) could also be wielded against Ryle's analysis of hypotheticals. For even hypothetical statements can be further embedded, say as "*It's not true that* (if you break a mirror then you will get bad luck)"—but in that context the if-then statement can't be seen as licensing an inference from breaking a mirror to the onset of bad luck. Thus, even if we accept Ryle's view that hypotheticals do not function to describe a relation (between statements, propositions, or anything else), but rather most basically serve to license inferences, we cannot use that as an account of the meaning of hypotheticals.

The general lesson of the Frege-Geach problem is that anyone who offers a non-descriptive reading of the function of some area of discourse should shy away from saying that they are giving the *meaning* of the expression: to give the function is not to give an account of the meaning. For non-descriptive approaches to be plausible, this lesson must be taken on board, and some other account of the meaning must be given. Yet, to retain the ontological and epistemological advantages the non-descriptivist sought, that meaning cannot be given by appealing to certain objects or properties the terms refer to. Another account of meaning is required (one that also preserves the validity of standard inferences made using sentences containing those terms). I will return in Chapter 3 to discuss how a contemporary non-descriptivist about metaphysical modality might discharge that debt.

The historical story thus far has made it clear that the non-descriptivist about modal discourse has difficult waters to navigate. Treat the discourse as *made true by* our linguistic conventions or stipulations and you run into the classic problems of conventionalism. Deny that it is descriptive talk that needs truthmakers at all, and hold that it serves a different function, and you risk running aground on the Frege-Geach problem, since the same function is not served in embedded contexts. Given the difficulties that arise on both sides, perhaps it is not such a wonder that many concluded that these waters could not be successfully navigated at all, leaving the approach abandoned and nearly forgotten for decades.

There may also be other reasons why non-descriptive approaches were left behind—reasons more sociological than philosophical. As

I have argued above, one reason seems to have been failure to really understand the position—a failure that may arise from the ubiquity of the functional monist assumption that all indicative sentences serve the same, describing, function. Wittgenstein's earlier Tractarian view was typically (if wrongly) assimilated to the conventionalism of the logical positivists, which (as mentioned in Section 1.3) in turn was widely believed to have been deeply problematic. But as I have argued in Sections 1.2–1.4, the standard criticisms of "conventionalism" miss the real point of the view, and it is clearly misguided to reject all forms of modal non-descriptivism by association with the view that necessary truths are made true by our adopting certain conventions. To the extent that non-descriptivist views were (or are) rejected for these reasons, the rejection clearly rested (or rests) on a simple failure to understand the position—a mistake bred in the tendency to cleave to the descriptivist assumption.

Another reason that Wittgenstein's later views have had little influence may be historical, owing to the scattered and late-breaking nature of his remarks on modality. (And even once they appeared, Wittgenstein's later views were often dismissed by faulty association with conventionalism.[15]) Wittgenstein's mature view is not made

---

[15] Indeed, according to Hacker (1996, 255), one of the key factors in this was a review of Wittgenstein's *Remarks on the Foundations of Mathematics*, in which Dummett accuses him of an extreme and untenable form of conventionalism, writing, "Wittgenstein goes in for a full-blooded conventionalism; for him the logical necessity of any statement is always the direct expression of a linguistic convention. That a given statement is necessary consists always in our having expressly decided to treat that very statement as unassailable" (Dummett 1959, 329).

But, as Hacker (1996, 255–64) and Baker (1988, 263) bring out in some detail, this rests on a serious misunderstanding of Wittgenstein's position. Dummett takes Wittgenstein to adopt the extreme conventionalist position that we must separately decide to treat each statement of logic as unassailable since Wittgenstein denies that propositions in logic follow from each other. But, as Baker argues, when Wittgenstein makes this denial, the point is that it is a category mistake to say that propositions of logic "follow from" each other, as inferences in empirical reasoning might: " 'Radical conventionalism' mistakes the observation that it is *nonsense* to say that an a priori proposition follows from something in the sense in which an empirical proposition follows from others for the claim that an a priori proposition is *independent* (i.e. does *not* follow) from all other propositions" (Baker 1988, 263). To think (as conventionalists did) that we can verify a logical proposition by showing that it follows from a more basic one is again to make the mistake of thinking that the question "What makes a proposition of logic true?" is an appropriate one—whereas on Wittgenstein's view this is a nonsensical question that arises from mistakenly treating a priori sentences on the model of empirical propositions.

explicit except in scattered passages of his later works (which, however insightful they may be, can hardly be said to be developed into a full-blown theory of modal discourse ready to be weighed up against that of competitors). And many of the later works in which the relevant remarks appeared were not published until after (some long after) his death in 1951,[16] by which point there had already been a major shift in philosophy from interest in ordinary language approaches to the dominance of a scientistic Quinean approach—and with it a great decline in interest in Wittgenstein's views, and a decline in awareness of the possibilities of functional pluralism.

Still another reason for the lack of influence of Wittgenstein's later approach may lie in his cryptic and cantankerous style, which alienated him from many analytic philosophers. Indeed, there has been a huge backlash against Wittgenstein, at least partly brought about by both his style and his embrace of conclusions many philosophers found intolerable—for example, that modal claims could not be true, that metaphysicians were simply led astray in talking of modal facts or properties, and (worst of all) that metaphysics in particular, but also philosophy more generally, was largely misleading nonsense, in need only of therapy. Although I will suggest below that modal non-descriptivism fits naturally with a certain sort of deflationary approach to metaphysics, I will also argue that the non-descriptivist approach is extricable from these unpopular theses, and so can be made far more palatable than Wittgenstein cared to make it. My aim here, as elsewhere, is not to eliminate metaphysics, but rather to press for a reinterpretation of what metaphysics (often) has been up to, and what it can legitimately be up to, and to do so in a way that avoids the epistemological mysteries that bring metaphysics into ill repute. I aim, in short, not at a slash-and-burn elimination of metaphysics, but at a reinterpretation and rehabilitation that may both demystify metaphysics and show what it has to offer.

---

[16] *Remarks on the Foundations of Mathematics* was published in 1956, *Cambridge Lectures 1932–35* in 1979, *Lectures on the Foundations of Mathematics* in 1976.

1.6 New Barriers to Modal Non-Descriptivism

I have said a little about why non-descriptivism was abandoned, but there are perhaps even more important, prominent reasons why no view along these lines has been revived. For even if the Frege-Geach problem could be overcome (on this, see Chapter 3), other major barriers to non-descriptive approaches have arisen from the work of Quine and Kripke. Quine's criticisms of analyticity, which were widely taken on board, made it seem unpromising to try to understand modality in terms of analyticity; and Kripke's apparent discoveries of a posteriori necessities gave new life to the idea that modal facts should be thought of as discoverable features of the world—not in any way tied to linguistic rules.

Quine's criticisms of the very notion of analyticity in "Two Dogmas of Empiricism" (1951) were directed primarily at Carnap, and (even assuming they are successful) would apply directly only to those who (with the positivists) seek to classify necessary statements as analytic statements, where the latter are in turn understood as logical truths and those reducible to logical truths by substituting synonyms for synonyms. But if instead we work with a broader understanding of necessary truths as something like rules for the use of terms "in the misleading guise of descriptions" (Hacker 1996, 102) we may avoid those particular problems, since (as Wittgenstein often emphasized) grammatical rules may take a wide variety of forms and needn't always be rules that simply license the substitution of synonyms.

Such a view does, however, still rely on making a distinction between expressions that serve as object-language expressions of semantic rules for using the terms, and those that simply *employ* terms in accord with those rules (cf. Boghossian 1997, 382–83)—roughly, a distinction between *regulative* and *descriptive* claims. It seems that Quine would have rejected this distinction as well. For he expressed doubts that a behavioral criterion could be given to distinguish cases in which we *establish* conventions from cases in which we simply follow or violate rules (unless the introduction of a convention is made quite explicit in stipulated definitions):

> On the other hand it is not clear wherein an adoption of the conventions, antecedently to their formulation, consists; such

behavior is difficult to distinguish from that in which conventions are disregarded. . . . In dropping the attributes of deliberateness and explicitness from the notion of linguistic convention we risk depriving the latter of any explanatory force and reducing it to an idle label.

(1935/1976, 105–6)

It seems that Quine would have similar doubts about whether we can distinguish behaviorally between utterances that are object-language expressions of semantic rules, and those that are descriptive uses of terms in accord with (or in violation of) those rules. But even if Quine would have rejected the distinction, the question is: would he have been justified in doing so?[17] If his reason for rejecting this distinction is that it is inconsistent with his behaviorism, those not committed to behaviorism needn't follow him there.[18] Those who are willing to accept that there may be differences between regulative utterances (used as a way of conveying meaning-constituting rules, enforcing or pressing for changes in them) from descriptive utterances (made simply using rule-governed terms) thus have no reason to reject a non-descriptivist approach to modality on the basis of Quine's arguments against analyticity.[19]

The second reason given in "Two Dogmas" for rejecting an analytic/synthetic distinction comes from adopting a holistic account of confirmation. But as I (2007, 37) and others (e.g., Glock 1996) have argued elsewhere, Quine's holism also gives us no reason to deny a distinction between utterances that are implicitly regulative, and those that are descriptive. We may still accept that, as science develops, any statement of a theory is revisable—even those that are implicitly regulative. The

---

[17] Hans-Johann Glock has argued convincingly and in some detail that Quine's attacks on the idea of "truth by virtue of meaning" give us no reason to abandon a Wittgensteinian account of necessity (1996, 204–24).

[18] Richard Creath (2004, 49) argues that the bottom line of Quine's reasons for rejecting the analytic/synthetic distinction as formulated by the Vienna Circle was its failure to be based on a behaviorally observable difference—a point Quine himself acknowledges later, writing: "Repudiation of the first dogma, analyticity, is insistence on empirical criteria for semantic concepts: for synonymy, meaning" (1991, 272). So it should come as no surprise that his objections to accepting a distinction between (prescriptive) acts of rule-constitution and simply following/violating rules come down to the same bedrock.

[19] I give further responses to Quine's attacks on analyticity in Thomasson (2007, 29–37).

point is only that some revisions involve not denying the descriptive truth of a claim, but rather renegotiating the "rules" of the language we use to make the claims (just as we may choose to revise the rules of college basketball to make the games more efficient, less dangerous to players, etc.). I will return to this topic when I come to the idea of metalinguistic negotiation in Chapter 8.

In any case, Quine's influence seems to be an important part of the historical story of why non-descriptivist approaches to modality remained off the table. Around the time of Quine's "Two Dogmas" came his rise to prominence, especially in American philosophy, and with it interest in his scientistic approach, conceiving of philosophy as no different in kind than natural science. This involved obliterating the distinctions among uses of language and assimilating them all to a single, scientific-explanatory use. Quine's rejection of the analytic/synthetic distinction also led many to abandon altogether the ordinary language approach to philosophy—and with it the methodology of trying to dissolve problems like that of modal discourse by seeking to understand the function of that discourse.

Later criticisms of the notion of analyticity, such as those raised by Timothy Williamson (2007), do not rely on behavioristic concerns or views about confirmation. These have laid further challenges to those who would seek to understand necessity in terms of analyticity. In any case, suspicions about analyticity have no doubt played a significant role in keeping off the table views that tie necessity to analyticity, and any non-descriptivist who wishes to take that route owes a defense of the notion of analyticity. While I do not make use of the notion of analyticity here, I defend the idea that there are semantic rules governing our expressions against Quinean objections and Williamson's later objections elsewhere (2007 and 2015, respectively).

Another important factor in accounting for why non-descriptivist views of modality remain off the table and tend to be met with suspicion is Kripke's rise. Although Kripke's (1980) arguments appeared after non-descriptivist approaches to modality had already faded from philosophical consciousness, his "discovery" of a posteriori necessary truths (such as "Necessarily, water is H_2O") seemed to put the last nail in the coffin of the idea that necessary truths may be identified with truths that are analytic, and to give reason for thinking that we should accept genuine *de re* modal facts in the world—that is (roughly), modal facts tied to objects, not to our ways of thinking or talking about things. Indeed, his work was taken to suggest that modal features must be real, discoverable parts of the world, which seemed to rule out the idea that apparently necessary truths could be known merely by reflection on the rules governing our use of terms. Any fully developed non-descriptivist account of modality thus must have something to say about how we can make sense of Kripkean a posteriori and *de re* necessities (or give a compelling argument that there are no such things that we need to account for). Sidelle (1989), Kirk Ludwig (in progress), and Jakob Schieder (2016) have each recently tried to show how one may retain something like the conventionalist's idea that necessity can be accounted for in terms of analyticity (or, more broadly, meaning or reference-determination) while still accommodating *de re* and a posteriori necessities. I will return in Chapter 4 to show how the normativist view developed here can meet those challenges.

It now seems we have a reasonably comprehensive understanding of what happened to modal non-descriptivism: early conventionalist approaches were dismissed based on widely accepted criticisms, which were largely based on serious misinterpretations of the view—taking it to be the view that modal truths are made true by our conventions. Later non-descriptivist approaches (e.g., by the later Wittgenstein, Ryle, and Sellars) made it clear that modal statements should not be taken as having a descriptive function at all, but they, too, were often misunderstood given assumptions of functional monism and the popularity of the truthmaker principle. More worryingly, such views faced the Frege-Geach problem, which seemed to show that they could not identify the meanings of modal statements with what they are characteristically *used* to do. Later work by Quine and Kripke seemed to raise further barriers to the idea that necessity could be understood in terms of analyticity, and Kripke's a posteriori necessities provoked a renaissance of the idea that modal features are discoverable features of the world. These, combined with the ascendancy of a truthmaker approach to metaphysics (particularly owing to David Armstrong, following C. B. Martin), have kept non-descriptivist approaches to modality largely off the table, and have contributed to the popularity of heavyweight modal realisms, even among those who have qualms about what modal properties or facts could be, how they could fit into the natural world, and how we could come to know about them.

1.7 A Non-Descriptivist Revival

It would be inaccurate, however, to suggest that non-descriptivist approaches to modality have been *completely* off the table. The idea has appeared in a paper by Simon Blackburn (1987/1993) and has recently been given a compelling development by Brandom (2008). In "Morals and Modals" (1987/1993), Blackburn provides the first, brief revival of the non-descriptivist approach to modality. There, he applies his general quasi-realist approach to the problems of modality, and argues that it is misguided to think of the problem of modality as the problem of finding the truthmakers for our modal claims. As he writes:

> We allow possibilities, rule out impossibilities, and insist upon necessities. This is not describing anything ... It is more like adopting a norm, or a policy or a rule that a thesis be put "in the archives," above the hurly-burly of empirical determination. The decision dictates how we shall treat recalcitrant evidence.
>
> (60)

Instead, he suggests, we can make sense of our "modalizing talk"—for example, of saying that something is necessary, as an expression of the fact that we find its denial inconceivable: we can make nothing of denials of it, or of what would count as a recalcitrant experience, we can't see how we could have gone wrong in thinking it true (70).

Brandom (2008) provides the most developed contemporary version of a non-descriptivist approach to modality. He begins from what he calls the Kant-Sellars thesis about modality: that "the ability to use ordinary empirical descriptive terms such as 'green,' 'rigid,' and 'mass' already presupposes grasp of the kinds of properties and relations made explicit by modal vocabulary" (97). Thus you can't (with Hume and Quine) claim to understand non-modal vocabulary (and to have mastered its use), but claim to just not understand modal vocabulary. For in mastering non-modal vocabulary, you must already engage in the practices that our modal vocabulary makes explicit, and so at least have some *implicit* grasp of modality.

The idea is that modal vocabulary just enables us to state explicitly the conceptual commitments that are implicit in what one is *doing* in using ordinary empirical vocabulary, reasoning with it, making, accepting, or rejecting inferences, and so on. On this view, modal vocabulary has a very different role than first-order, descriptive vocabulary, and it would be a category mistake to treat modal claims on the same model as descriptive claims, and think of them as describing a range of modal facts or properties. The primary role of alethic modal vocabulary is not to describe modal facts or properties; instead, "the expressive role characteristic of alethic modal vocabulary is to make explicit semantic or conceptual connections and commitments that are already implicit in the use of ordinary (apparently) non-modal empirical vocabulary" (99).

On Brandom's view, in order to use (apparently) non-modal concepts (like cup, lion, etc.) at all, you must be prepared to accept and reject certain counterfactual inferences involving the concept. As Brandom puts it, "One has not grasped the concept cat unless one knows that it would still be possible for the cat to be on the mat if the lighting had been slightly different, but not if all life on earth had been extinguished by an asteroid-strike" (97). Moreover, to make assertions using a concept, one must be prepared to treat these counterfactual inferences involving the concept as having a "certain *range of counterfactual robustness*, that is, as remaining good under various merely hypothetical circumstances" (104–5). So, for example, to use the concept of *lioness* in asserting that the lioness is hungry, one must be prepared to accept some counterfactual inferences (e.g., that if there were prey nearby it would be in danger), and treat these as remaining acceptable if we strengthen the antecedent in certain ways (e.g., if there were prey nearby *and it were sleeping*, the prey would be in danger), but as unacceptable if we strengthen it in other ways (e.g., if there were prey nearby *and the lioness were trapped in a cave*, the prey would be in danger). But then in being a competent speaker, you've already mastered all you need to grasp modal vocabulary. For modal vocabulary just provides a way to make explicit those commitments to the ranges of robustness of these different material inferences. So, if we endorse the conditional "if p then q" (e.g., "if there is visible prey, the lioness will take interest in it"), we can state this instead in explicitly modal terms, by saying (at least subject to the relevant conditions) "it's not possible that (p and not-q)"—for example, it's not possible that there be visible prey and the lioness not take interest in it (104).

Brandom's approach has much in common with the treatment of modality I shall recommend—most especially in treating modal vocabulary not as descriptive but rather as serving to make explicit certain norms of use mastered by competent speakers. But I focus squarely on claims of *metaphysical* necessity, whereas Brandom is concerned more directly with the sorts of modal talk involved in expressing physical necessities, counterfactuals, and hypotheticals.[20] He draws no firm distinction between what we normally think of as metaphysical necessities (e.g., "Necessarily, all donkeys are animals"), and nomological necessities (e.g., "Necessarily, donkeys exposed to fire die"); both are, on his view, ways of restating certain counterfactual inferences ("If my first pet had been a donkey, it would have been an animal" or "If you put a donkey in a fire it will die") (122). By contrast, I think that there is a difference in principle between those (nomological) modal claims that license inferences based on empirical evidence, and those (metaphysical) modal claims that do so based on conceptual competence; there is a difference in our mode of knowledge of each sort of modal (more on this in Chapter 7), in the appropriate ways of confirming or disconfirming each sort of claim. (But to say that there is a difference in principle is not to say that it is always totally clear which is which, nor is it to say that metaphysical modal claims are *unrevisable*—see Chapter 8.) It is the latter sort of modal claim that is especially at issue in metaphysics, and in which I am especially interested here.

Our goals are also different, for Brandom's main quarry in *Between Saying and Doing* is to better understand certain features of language: particularly, gaining a new picture of the relations between meaning and use, especially by specifying the different sorts of pragmatic and semantic relations that can hold between different sorts of vocabulary (such as ordinary empirical and modal vocabulary). By contrast, my aim is to show that this approach to metaphysical modality can deal with the ontological and epistemological problems of modality better than the dominant heavyweight realist competitors, and to examine its impact for understanding the methods of

---

[20] Later, in Chapter 5, Brandom also provides a way of introducing logical and modal vocabularies in terms of relations among our commitments and entitlements—especially relations of incompatibility and "commitive consequence."

metaphysics. To that end, I aim to show how (and in what sense) the normativist view developed enables us to provide an account of modal truth without the need for truthmakers (Chapter 3) and gives a promising answer to the vexed question of how we can acquire modal metaphysical knowledge (see Chapter 7). I also aim to show that it has the resources needed to respond to the most important criticisms of non-descriptivism (Chapters 3, 4, and 5). So although our views begin from a similar insight, given their different goals and contexts, the work done in this volume should not seem redundant even for those who already know and embrace Brandom's work on the subject.

1.8 Where Do We Go from Here?

I've tried above to outline the main historical story of why non-descriptivist views of modality arose and why they fell out of favor. Looking back at the story makes it clear that a non-descriptivist view has to be stated very carefully to be plausible and to avoid the problems of certain forms of conventionalism. It must be made clear that the point is that basic modal claims don't have the function of describing at all, and so do not need truthmakers. But at the same time, as has become clear, to avoid the Frege-Geach problem non-descriptivists must not identify the meaning of a modal claim with its function or force, and must show how modal claims remain meaningful even in force-stripping contexts, and may be used in reasoning (Chapter 3). The historical overview has also brought to light further challenges that await the non-descriptivist, including showing how to account for *de re* and a posteriori necessities (both of which I undertake in Chapter 4). But it is well worth facing up to these challenges. For the mainstream views of modality on the table, from heavyweight modal realisms to possible worlds realism, have such serious ontological problems, and leave modal epistemology at bottom so mysterious, that we might have better hope of working the kinks out in a non-descriptivist view than of fitting the former views into our overall philosophical program.

2

The Function of Modal Discourse

I suggested in the Introduction that a great many of the problems about metaphysical modality, which lead to problems about the methods of metaphysics, arise from the "descriptivist assumption": that is, the assumption that modal discourse serves the function of *describing* either some features of our world, or features of other (possible) worlds. Most often, this is just one instance of a functional monist assumption: the assumption that *all* discourse serves a descriptive function. Given the ubiquity of this assumption, the question "what function does modal discourse serve?" has seldom been asked in discussions of metaphysical modality. Instead, most authors simply assume that the function of modal discourse is to track and describe some portion of reality—the only problems being to say what portion of reality that is, and how we could come to know it.

The problems that arise from the descriptivist assumption, however, are sufficient to motivate looking again at the nearly forgotten non-descriptivist alternative. In this chapter I aim to clarify and develop one such non-descriptivist approach in clear contemporary terms. The approach I will consider here (as heir to the non-descriptivist tradition of Wittgenstein, Carnap, Ayer, Sellars, and Ryle) is one that denies that metaphysical modal terms function to *describe* features of the world (or to describe other worlds) that serve as the truthmakers for modal sentences.

But it is important to be clear about what it is to deny that the function of metaphysical modal terminology is descriptive. As mentioned in the introduction, it is certainly not to deny that modal claims are expressed in the indicative. Nor is it to deny that there is a clear sense in which, when we say "Margaret Mead necessarily comes from the genetic origin she actually has" there is a sense in which we are describing Margaret Mead and saying something true about her. Instead, the

Norms and Necessity. Amie L. Thomasson, Oxford University Press (2020). © Oxford University Press.
DOI: 10.1093/oso/9780190098193.001.0001

fundamental point is about what the *function* of modal terminology is. As Ryle puts it:

> [T]he truth that sentences containing words like "might," "could" and "would . . . if" do not report limbo facts does not entail that such sentences have not got proper jobs of their own to perform. The job of reporting matters of fact is only one of a wide range of sentence-jobs.
>
> (1949, 120)

So what is the basic "sentence-job" of metaphysical modal claims, if not to report some sort of (ordinary or strange) facts?

There are two importantly different ways to interpret this question. The first is: What is the use of having terms such as the metaphysical "necessarily" and "possibly" in our language? What function does such terminology serve in our overall linguistic apparatus? The second is: What is the point of our *uttering*, on a given occasion (or: in typical instances), a sentence that makes a metaphysical modal claim?[1] I will call the first the "functional" question, and the second the "use" question, and address the functional question first. The use question will become relevant again in Chapter 8, and I return to it there.

The answers to the functional question and the use question may come apart. For example, a deflationist about truth may see the linguistic *function* of having a truth predicate as serving as a device of generalization. But on a given occasion of use, if Sally says, "That politician is a crook" and I say, "That is so true," the point of my utterance may well be to *endorse* Sally's claim (as P. F. Strawson [1949] observed that "true" is commonly used to *endorse* or *confirm* a previously made statement, rather than to metalinguistically *describe* a sentence as possessing the property of truth).

What do I mean by "function" here? I certainly do not intend to offer a full theory of function—that would be a book of its own. But it may be useful to say a little about what I do and do not mean. I do not mean

---

[1] These correspond roughly to what Michael Williams (2015) identifies as the "practical significance" clause versus the "expressive/performative (speech act) function" clause of a functional analysis, that serves as part of his Explanations of Meaning in terms of Use (EMUs). I return to discuss Williams's account in Chapter 3.

to identify the function of a piece of vocabulary with how it is used on a given occasion, nor with its intended function (since most pieces of language are not intentionally designed at all). Nor do I aim, as Herman Cappelen does, to merely attribute a disquotational notion of function, such that the function of "salmon" is to denote salmon (2018, 187). If that is the only notion of function we admit, we are committed to a functional monist assumption, and foreclose the option of a non-descriptive approach.

There have been two large trends in understanding the notion of function in post-Darwinian biology: in terms of evolutionary/selection history (a historical story about what the ancestors of such things did that accounts for their reproduction and survival) ("proper function"), and in terms of a thing's current capacities/dispositions, with particular attention paid to the role such things play in the overall system in which it is embedded (what Beth Preston calls "system function" [Preston 1998, 221]). In neither case do we need to identify function with what anyone intends the function to be.

The notion of proper function has been most famously developed by Ruth Millikan, who is not concerned merely with biological functions, but rather explicitly aims to identify functions of "language devices" that are "not found either by averaging over idiolects or by examining speaker intentions" (1984, 4). On Millikan's view (roughly), a member of a "reproductively established family" has as its proper function whatever its ancestors did that contributed to the reproductive success of the family, which contributes to explaining the existence of that member (1984, 28). Millikan explicitly applies the view to cultural products, including language, as much as to biological entities such as hearts and lungs. Meaningful linguistic devices, on her view, are also members of "first-order reproductively established families" (1984, 29), and Millikan argues that "language devices must have direct proper functions at some level or levels. It must be because they correlate with functions that they proliferate" (1984, 31). This is clearly a view on which the (direct) proper function of a concept or term need not be identified with anyone's intentions or beliefs about what the function is, nor with the actual dispositions of speakers to use the term in certain ways, or an average over the relevant ways in which, or purposes for which, it is used.

The other dominant approach to function is to adopt a "system function" view like that defended by Robert Cummins (1975). On this model, the function of an item is whatever it *does* within the system as a whole—whatever its current capacities contribute to the capacities of the whole. As Preston describes it, such accounts of function enable us to give a compositional analysis "of the capacities of containing systems in terms of their component parts" (Preston 1998, 225). As Preston argues, these two notions of function—as proper function and as system function—must not be conflated, but we also need not consider them rivals. Instead, we may need to recognize them as "equally important for a viable general theory of function"—whether we are concerned with the functions of biological entities or of artifacts (1998, 226). Typically new proper functions begin life as *system* functions: it is because these entities can do something for the system that they (and their later copies) tend to be kept around; that is why identifying what a range of vocabulary *can* do (its system function) can be a useful tool in determining its *proper* function.

It is plausible that many of our terms (including many of those that come early in language-learning) serve the function of describing our world in the sense that they aim to track certain features of our world, to co-vary with environmental conditions.[2] Terms such as "wolf," "river," and "copper" plausibly come into language with this function, and the typical *use* of uttering simple assertions involving these terms (like "there is a wolf") is again plausibly to report on and track important features of our environment.

But the functional story need not always take that form. As Ryle (1949) noted, we have reason to look for a non-descriptive story particularly in cases where the descriptivist assumption leads us to puzzles, problems, or paradoxes[3]—for example, where ontological

---

[2] These are what Huw Price has called "e-representations" (2011, 20–21).

[3] Thanks to Christie Thomas for pressing this question. Of course, saying that one has particular reason to look for an alternative functional story in such cases is not to say that one must take a straight descriptivist tack for other areas of discourse. There is, as Price has long pointed out (2011), the option of being a global expressivist, though even there we do best to respect a distinction between those terms that serve an "e-representational" function of tracking features of the world, and those terms that serve other sorts of function. It is the motivations for looking for the "other," non–e-representational functions that I am discussing in this paragraph. For more on the prospects for a global pragmatism, see also Thomasson (2019).

placement problems arise in figuring out what the "entities" described could be, or how they could relate to physical objects; where epistemological puzzles arise because we do not seem to have the same way of "detecting" the relevant facts as we do for straightforward empirical truths; where "motivational" puzzles arise about how such properties or objects could do the job they are supposed to do (say, of motivating action, norming our belief, guiding our credences, or guiding our theorizing).[4] Some areas of discourse for which one or more of these problems have classically arisen—and for which alternative, nondescriptive views have been developed—include morality, truth, mathematics, probability, meaning, and modality. Deflationists about truth, for example, treat the function of the truth predicate not as describing a property possessed by some propositions, but rather as serving as a device of generalization: enabling us to express generalizations ("Everything Sally said is true") that would otherwise require knowledge (of what various things Sally said) we might lack, and repetition we might rather do without (Sally said P and P, Sally said Q and Q, and so on) (Horwich 1999, 104–5). Stephen Yablo similarly gives an analysis of the function of nominalized number talk as enabling us to express infinitely many facts in a finite form—certain scientific laws, for example, could only be expressed in uncountably many sentences of infinite length if we were unable to quantify over numbers (2005, 94). Alejandro Perez Carballo (2016) goes further to argue that the point of mathematical practice isn't to descriptively gather "mathematical information," but rather to structure logical space in an epistemically useful way—one that structures the space of possibilities in a way that is conducive to discovering and understanding what the world is like (2016, 461). Mark Lance and John O'Leary Hawthorne (1997) develop the view that discourse about meaning has a normative function. Moral expressivists treat the function of ethical discourse as expressing

---

[4] A classic argument that moral properties would have trouble being action-guiding traces to Hume, who writes, "Reason is wholly inactive, and can never be the source of so active a principle as conscience, or a sense of morals" (in section 3.1.1 of *Treatise of Human Nature*). More recently, such arguments were made prominent by Mackie (1977). For more on the puzzles of why chances, even if there are any, should be credence-guiding, see Lewis (1994). For the puzzle of why "naturalness" should guide our theorizing, see Dasgupta (2018).

attitudes or coordinating plans rather than as tracking moral facts or properties (Blackburn 1993, Gibbard 2003). The goal here is to give a similar non-descriptivist story for modal discourse that shows it as earning its keep by serving a function other than describing.

So what is the function of having modal terminology in our language?[5] Deontic modal discourse, about what one must or may or ought to do (full stop, in the case of moral discourse, or in order to meet some local standards or achieve some contingent goal), wears its normative function on its sleeve—such discourse is quite naturally seen as serving a normative function of influencing, coordinating, or guiding actions.[6] And as detailed in Chapter 1, despite the dominance of the descriptive assumption, the functional question has occasionally been raised for certain forms of modal discourse. Wittgenstein held that *logical* truths "reflect" rules of reasoning, and that *metaphysical* claims are norms of representation; "disguised" grammatical rules. Ryle (1949) took statements of nomological necessities to serve as inference tickets, entitling us to make inferences, while Sellars (1958) similarly took statements of scientific laws to serve the function of justifying or endorsing inferences.[7] Despite their differences, these suggestions share a common theme: the idea that the function of modal discourse is, broadly speaking, normative—whether it has to do with conveying rules of reasoning, or speaking, of making empirical inferences, or adjusting our expectations and explanations. Take

---

[5] It is worth noting that this is separate from the question of the function of having possible worlds talk—an issue addressed by David Lewis (1986). I will turn to address the issue of the function of possible worlds talk and our ability to preserve it (on a modal normativist view) in Chapter 6. Here I am concerned only with the function of more basic talk of what is necessary or possible.

[6] Though even normative discourse is often read as serving to describe some transcendent normative facts or naturalistic facts about patterns of behavior. See Lance and O'Leary-Hawthorne (1997, Chapter 3) for discussion, and insistence that normative judgments serve instead to endorse or propose a standard.

[7] There have also been recent suggestions about the function of counterfactual reasoning, from those who do not hold non-descriptive views. Timothy Williamson (2007) has argued that the function of *counterfactual* reasoning ("if the bush were not there, the rock would have rolled into the lake") is to facilitate learning from experience, improve future performance, and give clues to causal connections (2007, 140–41). Boris Kment similarly suggests that the function of counterfactuals is to enable us to better evaluate explanatory claims, to predict, to intervene, and even to regulate our evaluative judgments and emotions—by comparing what happened to what could have easily happened (2014, 13).

this thought—that modal discourse serves a normative function—as a suggestive idea. The main goal of this book is to develop and defend a specific version of this idea in far more detail for metaphysical modal claims, and to demonstrate the advantages of doing so.

But why should we want specifically *modal* terms to help us with such normative functions? After all, there are other ways of expressing and conveying norms, such as with commands, or with a stick. I will turn first (in section 2.1) to the question of why modal language is a particularly useful way of expressing and conveying norms. To make it clear and precise, I will focus on the role modal terms serve in enabling us to convey the rules of games.

And what normative function specifically is served by *metaphysical* modal vocabulary? I will turn to this in section 2.3. The basic view I will defend here is that the function of having metaphysical modal vocabulary is that it enables speakers to convey semantic rules (or their consequences)[8] in particularly useful ways, while remaining in the object language. If something along these lines is the right way of understanding metaphysical modal discourse, then the whole way the problem of modality is usually set up in metaphysics—as the problem of finding truthmakers for our modal claims—gets off on the wrong foot, setting up an unnecessary pseudo-problem that calls for dissolution rather than solution.[9]

---

[8] In some cases, speakers convey the rules they think there *are*. In other cases, they *advocate* for the rules they think there *ought to be*. I return to this idea in Chapter 8.

[9] Micheala McSweeney raised an interesting question for me at this point: Even if I am right that this is how our metaphysical modal discourse *does* function, why couldn't the serious metaphysician introduce a set of "schmodal" terms that function *descriptively*? I can only gesture at a response here, though the question is in some ways parallel to the question of why, even if my analyses about the actual English quantifier (given in *Ontology Made Easy*) are apt, serious metaphysicians could not retreat to Sider's "plan B" and introduce a new quantifier stipulated to carve at the ontological joints (a point I address in Thomasson 2015, Chapter 10). An initial response is to ask for more information: What would these "schmodal" terms be, how would they function, what rules would they follow? If I am right that our actual modal terms serve a *normative* function, it is hard to see how any descriptively functioning terms could be closely related enough to them to count as "modal" at all. Suppose someone said, "OK, I see how our salutation terms function. But now I want to introduce *schmal*utation terms, which are like those, but function descriptively—to talk about the *schmal*utational features of reality." I think we would have no idea what these could be, or by what rights we would come to think there was any relation (other than phonetic) between the introduced terms and our familiar salutational terms.

Since the view is an heir to work in the conventionalist and expressivist traditions, one important task is showing how it can avoid or overcome the problems thought to plague these prior views. In Chapter 3 I will show how a modern non-descriptivist can face up to the challenge presented by the Frege-Geach problem, and show why it doesn't fall prey to the problems commonly raised for conventionalism, thereby overcoming the two main historical challenges to views along these lines.

Of course other challenges await the normativist. In Chapter 4 I will address the later Quinean and Kripkean barriers that arose to resurrecting views along these lines, showing how the modal normativist may account for Kripkean *de re* and a posteriori necessary truths. In Chapter 5 I discuss other putative counterexamples, along with concerns about whether the account is subject to charges of circularity.

2.1 Games, Necessities, and the Advantages of Modal Terminology

What function does it serve to have terms like "possible" or "necessary" in our language?[10] Looking at the role modal terms can serve in giving the rules of games can help us understand the way modal terms enter the language and why they serve useful functions that could not be served by expressions of the rules in the form of imperatives (or methods of more brute force).

---

[10] Notice that the focus is squarely on the function of modal *language* or its use. One might separately raise questions about why we need modal *concepts*. And there we might take very seriously views of the form found in Kant, Husserl, and Brandom to the effect that even our ordinary descriptive, perceptual concepts are implicitly modal—governed by rules regarding (say) what it would take for a given experience to (continue to) count as a perception of a plate. The present discussion does not address these deep issues, but only the question of why we would want explicitly modal terms in our language. (One might similarly distinguish questions about why it's useful to be able to count from why it's useful to have nominative terms for numbers in our language; or why it's useful to be able to distinguish the true from the false from why it's useful to have a truth predicate in our language).

Games have rules that must be in force, and to which players must subject themselves if they are to play the game.[11] In one standard and familiar form, rules are issued in imperatives; for example, the second rule of Scrabble is: "2. Complete your turn by counting and announcing the score for that turn." But rules need not be stated in the imperative form, for—provided the context is clear, as it is, for example, on the box top of a board game—the rules may also be stated in the indicative mood, either in universal indicative form (e.g., "Each player completes his/her turn by counting and announcing the score for that turn"), or in superficially singular form (e.g., "A player completes a turn by counting and announcing the score for that turn"[12]).

There are various advantages to stating rules in the indicative form, rather than in the imperative form. At least where contextual cues are lacking, utterances in the initial command form might be mistaken for *advice* (e.g., about how to improve one's game, ensure that no misunderstandings arise) rather than for mandates of rules that must be in force if the game is to be played.[13] That problem is avoided by using the indicative mood. More importantly, shifting to the indicative mood enables us to express conditionals that we can use in making explicit our ways of reasoning with rules. We could not make all of these ways of reasoning explicit in the imperative form, since imperatives cannot be embedded in the antecedents of conditionals. So, for example, in the indicative form we can make explicit our ways of reasoning among rules (e.g., as "If black always moves first, then white never moves first"), but no parallel expression is available in the imperative form ("If black: move first, then" isn't even grammatical). Similarly, in the indicative we can express what follows from rules combined with empirical facts; for example, "If black moves first, and Christina is the black player, then Christina moves first." If we are limited to the imperative formulation, we can indeed make the parallel

---

[11] Notice that this is not the same as saying that players must invariably *follow* the rules, only that they must be subjected to them in the sense that they are open to criticism if they violate them, etc. Nor is it to say that these rules are *unrevisable*. I will return in Section 2.4 to discuss whether games are to be individuated in terms of constitutive rules (see Lance and O'Leary-Hawthorne 1997, Chapter 3).

[12] Scrabble Game Rules, Parker Brothers, 1999.

[13] At least: in force at a time. I return in Section 2.4 to issues about the identity of games over time. Thanks to Crispin Wright for suggesting the useful term "mandate" here.

move and say: "Black: move first," and, noting that Christina is the black player, go on to say: "Christina: move first," but we cannot express the relation between these commands.

But while we may engage in simple reasoning with indicative expressions of rules, there are limits to what we can do, and it is fraught with dangers. For a simple indicative statement of a rule may be mistaken for a description of what happens to occur in such games (in the universal case) or in a particular game (in the singular case). Call statements of rules (and their consequences) statements with "regulative" status. Without an explicit marker for what does and does not have regulative status, it is not clear how to reason with the claims in question, or what the status of the conclusions is when we do reason with them. For from "The black player moves first," as regulative, we may conclude "White doesn't move first," as regulative. But from "The black player moves her leftmost piece," as descriptive, we may not conclude "The black player does not move her rightmost piece" and take this as regulative. Without an explicit modal term, we have no mark of whether an indicative statement is to have a regulative or descriptive status, and so we have no way to guard against this kind of mistake.

Moreover (as Ryle pointed out [1950/1971]), when using simple indicatives, we have no way of expressing permissions, or reasoning from rules to permissions. So, while we may express the rule "Black moves first" in a simple indicative, we cannot express the permission: "Kings *may* move both forward and backward" without inserting a modal verb.

Adding a modal verb ("Black *must* move first") thus brings several advantages to stating rules.[14] It makes it explicit that the expression has a regulative rather than descriptive status, and so is not easily mistaken for a descriptive report of what happens to occur in these games.[15] It thereby enables us to avoid mistakes: once we have added a modal verb, it no longer looks valid to reason from "The black player moves her leftmost piece" to "The black player *must* not move her rightmost

---

[14] Other modal verbs may also be used; for instance, the rules of baseball are stated in terms of what players "shall" do—where again this should not be mistaken for a prediction.

[15] However, modal formulations still (like the imperative formulation) might be mistaken for advice out of context (as a tennis coach might say: you *must* use your upper body to put more power in your serve). Thanks to Elizabeth Barnes for pointing this out.

piece." It also enables us to express conditionals that make explicit our ways of reasoning with rules (among rules, from rules to facts, and between rules and permissions). Finally, neither the imperative form nor the non-modal indicative on its own enables us to express *permissions* as well as requirements. We can say: "Do x" or "Do not do x," but when the option is left open, we must resort to introducing a modal (or deontic) term, saying "You *may* do x" or "x is permitted." Similarly, as Ryle pointed out (1950/1971, 244), questions about the rules may be asked without modal terms (e.g., "Does each player take a turn every round?") and positive answers may be given in non-modal indicative form: "Yes, each player takes a turn every round." But a negative answer can only be given by inserting a modal verb (e.g., "No, a player *may* choose to skip a turn"). Thus, the modal indicative formulation has the crucial advantage over the alternative methods of expressing the rules, that it enables us to express permissions as well as requirements.[16]

But despite their differences in structure and mood, the various ways of expressing the same rules of a game (in the form of a command, universal indicative, singular indicative, or modal indicative) are often used interchangeably and all serve the function of stating the rules of games.[17] It is important to note, however, that the view is not that these modal statements are descriptive *reports that* a particular command was given (the truthmaker for which would be the utterance of the command), or reports that a particular rule is in force. None of the earlier statements of rules are the same as *reports about rules* such as "The box top states that each player must complete his/her turn by counting and announcing the score for that turn." The latter may be made true by utterances of commands; the former are not, for they are *statements of* rules (and of what follows from them), not *statements about* rules.

These observations provide the basis for an interesting hypothesis about the function of modal discourse: that modal talk enters

[16] Thanks to Robert Brandom for this point.
[17] For example, the Scrabble rules (Parker Brothers, 1999) continue from a singular description of a rule "1. The first player combines two or more of his or her letters to form a word," to the explicit command form in the next rule: "2. Complete your turn by counting and announcing the score for that turn." Othello rules (Pressman Toy Corporation, 1990) use the universal indicative: "Black always moves first."

into language as a way of expressing rules or norms in the indicative (rather than imperative) mood. On this view, the most basic function of modal terms is to enable the expression of rules and their logical consequences, while making the regulative status of what is said more explicit than it is in the other forms of expression, enabling us to express conditionals connecting them to other rules, and to make explicit our ways of reasoning with them, and enabling permissions as well as requirements to be expressed.

If this is along the lines of the right story about the role of modal terms in a language, then it is no accident that grammatically modal terms include not only "possible" and "necessary," but also the "can," "may," "must," and "shall" characteristic of deontic modalities and uttered in stating commands and rules in an impersonal indicative form. The rules or norms expressed in various cases may vary across different sorts of modal expression, while the role of modal terminology in expressing these rules or norms in particularly useful ways remains constant. We thus have hope of gaining a unified understanding of modal terms: all are involved in enabling us to explicitly express and reason with rules and permissions. The ability to provide a unified account gives an important advantage, since it enables us to explain why these terms (for alethic, deontic, and epistemic modalities) tend to come together across a wide range of languages (Papafragou 1998, 371), and why children tend to learn to use modal terms for obligation, necessity, and possibility at around the same age (Wells 1985, 159–60 and 253). These commonalities would be masked by descriptive approaches to metaphysical modal statements, which would take claims of metaphysical necessity and possibility to be descriptions of features of the world, while "may," "must," and "shall" are more naturally taken as issuing permissions or obligations.

2.2 The Function of Metaphysical Modal Terminology

Where modal terms appear in stating rules of games, we are not so tempted to see them as attempting to describe features of the world (our true obligations when playing checkers?). There, it's easy to see their role as particularly advantageous ways of giving rules and permissions. But when modal terms are introduced in making claims about what's metaphysically necessary, many metaphysicians are tempted to see them as attempting to describe essences, modal properties, or features of all possible worlds.

The thesis of this book, however, is that that is a mistake: in metaphysical modal claims, no less than on the box tops of games, we should see modal terms as having the function of enabling us to convey and reason with rules and permissions in particularly advantageous ways.

But what norms or rules are at issue in metaphysical modal claims? Roughly, taking a normativist approach to specifically metaphysical modalities is a matter of seeing the role of *metaphysical* modal terminology as enabling us to make explicit, endorse, or renegotiate the rules of use of our terms (and what follows from them) in particularly useful ways (cf. Brandom 2008, 99). By "terms" I mean certain meaningful pieces of language, not a mere series of typographical marks or sounds (after all, we allow that there are homonyms: cases in which two different terms may have the same sound, often as well as the same spelling). I do not mean to take a stand on the identity conditions for words or terms here—that in itself is of course a metaphysical modal question, and so would be better addressed after achieving a clearer understanding of the methodology for resolving metaphysical modal questions.[18] I mean only to insist that, as I use the term "term" (or "word") I mean to refer not to the (mere) marks or sounds, but rather to a meaningful and working piece of language. Just as the rules of chess governing how the king may move should not be understood as rules regarding what may be done with a given piece of plastic, but rather rules that govern whatever is to play the relevant role in the game; so, similarly semantic rules, as I consider them, should be seen as applying not to merely physical strings of marks or sounds, but to whatever is to play the relevant role in the language.[19]

Many different sorts of rules may govern speaking a language, or, more narrowly, using a term, including syntactic rules, semantic rules,

---

[18] Though see Irmak (forthcoming) for a nicely developed ontology of words. See also Kaplan (1990).

[19] Thanks to an anonymous referee for suggesting this way of putting things.

and pragmatic rules. In addressing issues of metaphysical modality, my focus will be on *semantic* rules for use of noun terms, particularly rules regarding the conditions under which a term is to be applied or refused (rules I have elsewhere [2007a, 2015] called "application conditions"),[20] or other conditions under which it may be introduced; and rules regarding when a name or sortal term may be applied again to one and the same entity (these I have elsewhere [2007a] called "co-application conditions"). Semantic rules themselves may take many different forms. Call a rule an "intra-language," or "language-language," rule if it is a rule for using one term that may be stated in the metalanguage in terms of other terms (e.g., "apply term A only where you may apply term B"). But there may also be *world-language* rules: the sort of rules taught through ostensive definition. These will play a crucial role in accounting for Kripkean *de re* and a posteriori necessities (see Chapter 4).

In any case, to say that language has semantic rules is not to say that these rules may all be *stated* in a metalanguage, nor that competent speakers must be capable of reciting these rules—instead, they must simply be masters at *following* them. In fact, it seems reasonable to hold that our language must include some "semantically basic terms"[21]— that is, terms that cannot be learned just by way of learning definitions stated in other terms. And if that is so, then it can't be the case that the semantic rules of use for all of our terms can be (informatively) stated verbally. Nonetheless, since books must be written in words, it will make the structure of the view easier to see to focus on cases in which at least some of the rules can be verbally stated.

The rules relevant to claims of metaphysical necessity are *semantic* rules. However, metaphysical modal claims do *not state* the rules in the way that claims like "The black player must move first" do. Statements *of* semantic rules would have to be made in the metalanguage. And (like statements of rules of games) they might be expressed in various grammatical forms: a semantic rule for using the term "bachelor" may be stated in the imperative mood: "Apply 'bachelor' only where 'man'

---

[20] For more on how to understand application conditions, see Thomasson (2015, Chapter 2).

[21] To use a term of Philip Pettit's (Pettit 2002, 128).

applies." This command, like other rules, may also be stated in the indicative mood either as a universal claim (" 'Bachelor' is always applied only where 'man' applies") or a singular claim (" 'Bachelor' is applied only where 'man' applies"). While this is in the indicative mood, its status as a statement of a rule may be made explicit by adding a modal auxiliary (" 'Bachelor' *must* only be applied where 'man' applies").

These metalanguage statements of semantic rules are not the same as metaphysical modal statements: in the former, the key term "bachelor" is mentioned, not used—it states a rule for properly *using* the term *mentioned*. An alternative is to use semantic descent to *convey* semantic rules in the form of *object language* indicatives. So, for example, we can engage in semantic descent to move from " 'Bachelor' must only be applied where 'man' applies" to "Bachelors must be men," or (more clearly avoiding scope ambiguities) "Necessarily, whatever is a bachelor is a man." What is characteristic of basic claims of metaphysical necessity, then, is that they give object-language ways of *conveying* (without stating or describing) the semantic rules governing some of the very terms *used* in making the claim. While metaphysical modal claims do not *state* semantic rules, the modal verb nonetheless *makes explicit*, but does not report, that what follows is (presented as) an object-language formulation of a rule of use.

As in other cases, having modal verbs at our disposal brings various advantages: it enables us to make explicit that the expression has a regulative rather than descriptive status, and so helps us avoid mistakes in reasoning with rules. It also enables us to express conditionals that make explicit our ways of reasoning with rules, so we can say "if it is necessary that there be collective intentions for there to be money, then there can't be a world in which there is money but nothing else."

As mentioned in Section 2.1 for the case of games, another function of modal terminology is that it enables us to give permissions as well as imposing requirements, and this again carries over to the uses of metaphysical modal claims. How can we (while remaining in the object language) convey *permissible* ways of speaking? One way we can do this is by *demonstration,* simply *using* that term properly (in accord with the rules). So we can, for instance, begin to teach a child the proper use of the term "man" by simply applying the term in the course of making an assertion—say, "*That* is a man." But there are limits to how much we can convey by these methods. We might, for example, want to convey that, unlike "bachelor," "president" may (as far as its rules of use are concerned) be applied to a woman, but there is no woman to whom we may apply the term in asserting "*That* is the president." An important use of the term "possibly" in claims of the form "Possibly p" is to convey that "p" uses the terms involved properly (in accord with the rules), but without *asserting* p; we may convey this permission by saying, "It is possible that a woman be president." But nor does "Possibly p" *describe* the statement "p" as in accord with the linguistic rules: it remains in the object language, and doesn't *mention* p at all. Basic (unembedded) statements of the form "Possibly p" may be used to *endorse* a certain use of terms as in accord with the rules (or to disavow claims to the effect that "necessarily, not-p) without *reporting on* the rules of use for terms, and without *asserting* p.

The fact that these semantic rules are conveyed in the object-language, not the metalanguage, brings additional advantages—though it also brings with it additional risks that these metaphysical modal statements will be mistaken for descriptions of features of the world, rather than ways of conveying rules and their logical consequences. Why is it advantageous to convey *semantic* rules in the *object*-language, under conditions of semantic descent, rather than stating them in a metalanguage—particularly when this may mislead us into thinking that they aim to describe modal features of the world?

One advantage of using the object-language is simply that it is less cumbersome, and more familiar to most speakers who don't happen to be linguists or philosophers. But there is more to it than that: for semantic rules may take many forms. The rules reflected in standard analytic claims like "All bachelors are men" are *intralanguage* or *language-language* rules: rules governing when one expression is to be applied, stated in terms of when another expression is to be applied. But clearly not all rules of a language can be given simply by giving definitions in other terms of the language, or else the language would not be learnable at all—there would be no "way in," so to speak. There must be some "semantically basic" terms, the rules for which are introduced in other ways if language is to be learnable at all. Rules for introducing semantically basic terms may instead take the form of world-language rules. Such world-regarding rules are set up at least in part by (explicit or implicit) ostensive definitions (e.g., "*This person* is to be called 'Natalie'").[22] World-regarding rules cannot be fully stated in the metalanguage since we need an object-language term (e.g., a demonstrative) to perform the ostensive definition (and set up the rule). Nonetheless, rules like these may be conveyed in object-language modal statements involving demonstratives or names. Acknowledging the presence of semantic rules of many different forms, including world-language rules, is crucially important. For it enables us to handle the challenges raised by Kripkean cases of *de re* and a posteriori necessities, as I will argue in Chapter 4.

2.3 Uses of Metaphysical Modal Claims

The function question and the use question must be treated separately, but there are important connections between them. For given the *function* of modal terminology in enabling us to express rules and their consequences in useful ways, it should not be surprising if basic modal claims are often *used* to convey, enforce, or advocate for certain semantic rules. In everyday contexts (outside the metaphysics room), a common use of basic claims of necessity is to answer questions raised by those uncertain of how to use the terms. "Do bachelors have to be male?" might be raised by speakers of English as a foreign language, and a proper answer would be, "Yes, bachelors must be male." The fact that the claims so uttered are often used to guide others in the proper use of terms or to enforce proper usage is also made evident by the fact that responses in the metalanguage, which state the rules of use, such as "Yes, 'bachelor' means 'unmarried man'" would serve equally well as a response to the question. Utterances of the form "Necessarily p" thus are often used to make it clear that it would be improper to *deny* that p (or to say anything that would entail its denial)—and correlatively that it is obligatory to accept that p. Claims of the form "Necessarily p" may

---

[22] These parallel rules of make-believe games: we may have a *de dicto* rule that (whatever is a) stump is to count as a bear, or a *de re* rule that Natalie is (to count as) the queen. Similarly, social rules may be *de dicto* (whoever is a citizen must pay taxes) or *de re* (this river is to count as the state boundary). For differences in these forms of social rule, see "Foundations for a Social Ontology" (Thomasson 2003).

also be used to *correct* or *condemn* uses that involve denying p, but again without *reporting on* the linguistic rules or on the statement p. So, for example, "Necessarily, all bachelors are men" (or "Bachelors must be men, dear") may be used to correct a child who has said "Aunt Laura is always going to stay a bachelor, isn't she?" This is not the only way statements of metaphysical necessity can be used, however: another common use is not to convey (or [re-]enforce) the *actual* rules governing our terms, but rather to *advocate for* changing those rules to new ones—rules the speaker thinks there *should* be.[23] (I will return to this idea in Chapter 8.) Where metaphysical modal claims are used in these ways—to convey, enforce, or advocate for semantic rules—it is natural to see those who utter them as *doing* something other than describing.

Yet once we have separated out the functional question from the use question, a further question arises. Even if metaphysical modal terminology has a fundamentally non-descriptive function in the language, and metaphysical modal claims are *often* used in these non-descriptive ways, can't they also be used descriptively? Don't metaphysicians often aim to use a metaphysical modal claim descriptively when they say, for example, "a statue necessarily retains its shape"?[24]

Speakers may certainly think of themselves as using modal discourse to describe the world when they make metaphysical modal utterances. And if they do so in an everyday (not theoretically loaded) sense of "describing," they are not making a mistake. If one says, "a statue necessarily retains its shape," one may be making an assertion, the literal semantic content of which *is* world-oriented content about statues.[25] Moreover, if it does give object-language formulation of a

---

[23] That is, they may be used in engaging in what David Plunkett and Tim Sundell have called "metalinguistic negotiation." See their (2013) for a general exposition of the idea of metalinguistic negotiation, and Plunkett (2015) and Thomasson (2017a) for application of this idea to understanding certain philosophical disputes.

[24] There are interesting interpretive questions about whether a given philosopher, on a given occasion, uses a metaphysical modal claim descriptively—one can't assume they are always used that way, even in metaphysics. In Thomasson (2017a) I discuss certain historical cases in which it is not so obvious that metaphysical modal claims are used descriptively.

[25] Huw Price (2011, 56) makes the point that non-descriptivists (non-factualists, in his parlance) needn't deny that some utterances of the relevant kind are assertions—though it treats the category of assertions as relatively superficial, overlaying more crucial functional distinctions.

semantic rule, it may even say something true. So, a speaker makes no mistake if she thinks of her modal utterance as describing the way the world is, in the sense of expressing an indicative truth, the literal semantic content of which is about the world, and that entitles us to say, of statues, that they have the modal property of not surviving drastic changes in shape. The modal normativist accepts that modal claims are world-oriented in their literal semantic content, and insists that they are not *descriptions of* our language, concepts, or rules—though the pragmatic point of uttering them is often to call attention to those linguistic rules. One way to put the point, following Huw Price, is to allow that an utterance of a metaphysical modal claim may make a (minimal) *statement* understood as an utterance we can sensibly say is (minimally) true—that is, that it is an utterance that "provides a well-formed substitution into the context 'It is true that P' " (2011, 66).

But on the normativist view it *would* be a philosophical mistake to think of such utterances as serving to track modal features of the world, which they must mirror to be true, and which serve to assess and explain the truth of the modal claim. For if the functional analysis given here is correct, metaphysical modal terms are not in the business of tracking features of the environment in that way: their entry rules establish no such "link" between worldly features and the proper use of the term, and the success conditions for their use require no such link.

Nonetheless, if we allow that metaphysical modal discourse may be used descriptively, even in the deflationary sense, don't all the same philosophical problems for modality arise again? For if we allow that metaphysical modal discourse can "describe" modal facts and properties even in the everyday sense, can't we then go on to ask about the modal facts and properties that are described—what they are, how we know them, and by what methods we can resolve debates about them? And if so, what has been gained by insisting on the non-descriptive functional analysis of the vocabulary?

Actually, the classic problems don't arise in the same way—on the contrary, we can make major new progress on the old ontological, epistemological, and methodological problems of modality by giving up the descriptivist's functional assumption. Showing this in detail is the task of Chapters 6, 7, and 8. But before turning to explore these advantages of adopting the normativist view of the function of modal discourse, we must do more to show that the view is plausible and defensible. This requires showing how to give an account of the meaning of modal terms (motivated by this functional account) that can avoid the embedding problem that plagued earlier non-descriptive accounts, showing how we can account for a posteriori and *de re* necessities, and how we can overcome various other objections. I undertake that defensive work in Chapters 4 and 5, aiming to showing that the view is plausible, before coming back to show what ontological, epistemological, and methodological benefits may be gained by adopting the normativist's functional account. But first, before turning to that work, it may be worth saying a bit more about how I understand semantic rules, and confronting an objection that might arise to the analogies I draw on between semantic rules and rules of games.

2.4 How Should We Understand the Semantic Rules?

In laying out a view of the function and uses of metaphysical modal terms, I have relied on the idea that our terms are being governed by semantic rules, analogous to rules of games, where these rules are conveyed, endorsed, or renegotiated through claims of metaphysical necessity. The analogy with games, however, might raise worries—and confronting those worries here may help make clear what I do, and do not, (need to) presuppose about these semantic rules.[26]

Games such as organized sports and board games make their rules clear and explicit, and (in the case of organized sports at least) they have clear procedures for changing their rules, so that one can know reasonably precisely what the rules are and when they have been changed. But this sort of explicitness, obviousness, and precision is missing in the case of rules of use for natural-language terms.

The examples I use throughout the book of (what I take to be) plausible renderings of semantic rules for various terms are admittedly tentative and open to challenge and are the products of *interpreting* our practices and their norms—not just reading the box top of a board

---

[26] Thanks to Rebecca Kukla for pressing this point.

game, or a list of league rules. Working from the analogy of clear, explicit formal rules (rather than the tacit, collective, informal rules governing natural language) is nonetheless—or perhaps for that very reason—useful, since we can examine how rules work, what happens in cases of rule change, and the like more clearly while abstracting from the surrounding noise of whether we have ably interpreted the norms governing any particular ordinary expression.

Acknowledging these differences between the implicit and informal rules governing ordinary language and the explicit formal rules of (institutionalized) games, in the wider context, only helps my project. While it's important for the view to make use of the idea that semantic rules govern our expressions, as mentioned at the outset, I am not committed to the idea that competent speakers could articulate these rules or state them explicitly. (This certainly seems not to be the case for grammatical rules, which few competent speakers could articulate, though they are implicit in our practices—not only of speaking, but also of interpreting and correcting others, etc.) Nor am I committed to the view that the relevant rules are fully determinate, precise, or unchangeable. A more plausible view might be that these, like so many other norms, are implicit in our practices rather than explicitly accepted or even considered, and that they are typically open-textured and up for renegotiation.

Paying attention to the embedded, implicit nature of the relevant semantic rules gives room for the modal normativist to answer an objection, and to give a far more plausible and robust account of the work of metaphysics. For if we thought of the semantic rules as being as clear and obvious as the rules of institutionalized games, it might seem there is precious little work for metaphysicians to do, and little explanation of why they would ever disagree (we turn them into inexplicably squabbling readers of box tops). But if we acknowledge the implicit and embedded nature of these rules, there is far more work to do—work every bit as difficult as that of linguistics. This includes work in interpreting from our practices what the rules are, and, even more deeply, work in figuring out what the rules *ought to be*, or more broadly what language (with what rules) we ought to adopt. I will return to these methodological issues in Chapter 8.

Thinking of the semantic rules as analogous to rules of games might lead us to further objections, however. For games are typically thought to be governed by *constitutive rules*—rules that must be in force if that very game is to be played at all.[27] Analogously, the idea that our terms are governed by semantic rules might be thought to commit us to the idea that these are *constitutive* semantic rules—rules that must be in force if that very term is to be used at all.[28] This seems to commit us to the idea that when we change the semantic rules, we are no longer using the same term at all—and this might be thought to make it impossible for speakers to communicate, or to undermine possibilities of genuine disagreement. I have addressed the concern about barriers to communication elsewhere (2014), and the work of David Plunkett and Tim Sundell (2013) gives a fine basis for replying to worries that speakers who used terms with different meanings couldn't be thought to genuinely disagree. But while I do not think these are genuine problems for the constitutive rule view, I also do not mean to commit myself to the idea that the semantic rules are "constitutive" in the above sense.

Even in the case of games, it is controversial whether or not the rules should be thought of as constitutive. Mark Lance and John O'Leary-Hawthorne challenge the idea that games have constitutive rules. Citing the changes in the rules of the National Basketball Association that were introduced in response to the unexpected skills of Wilt Chamberlain, they write that if we held that there is a fixed set of rules definitive of a game, "then it would seem we must conclude that a different game was being played post-Wilt from the one played pre-Wilt" (1997, 191). Yet that would be an unreasonable conclusion, they suggest, which would require us to say "that every record book is mistaken since they all take statistics before and after Wilt to have been set in the same game" and that those who talk about basketball would be subject to an ambiguity of which they are unaware (1997, 191). In the case of chess, which underwent a phase in which the rules were changed every

---

[27] Talk of games having "constitutive rules" was popularized by Searle (1995), but the way of characterizing constitutive rules here is mine.

[28] I made use of this idea myself in some earlier work on the topic. But I have now dropped the term "constitutive" and changed my views on this, for reasons I aim to make clear here.

few days, they argue, "this would imply that new games were being invented each few days," when "In fact no such thing was happening" (1997, 192). And so they conclude "there is no aspect of any game that is *in principle* immune to revision without loss of identity" (1997, 194). There is no a priori rule "for deciding when a change in rules entails that we have a new game, an a priori line between the essential and the accidental feature of a game" (1997, 194).

So the question of whether or not games—or terms—have constitutive rules is tied to questions about the *identity conditions* for games (or terms). It is itself a metaphysical modal question.

From my current point of view, there is something right and something wrong about what Lance and O'Leary-Hawthorne say. What's right is that any apparent or even explicit rules of a game are constantly open to renegotiation. But I would not express this by saying that "In fact" no change of game was happening, that it was "*really*" the same game (nor would I say that it "*really wasn't*"). The point at issue here concerns identity conditions for games, and given the normativist point of view, these should themselves be object-language reflections of the rules of use for "game" (or more specific game terms such as "basketball" or "chess"). But the co-application conditions for "game" (reflected in object-language claims about identity conditions for games) are themselves every bit as open-ended and open to renegotiation as other semantic rules are. In different contexts, with different purposes, we may have different criteria for what should count as "the same game." The sense Lance and O'Leary-Hawthorne have in mind seems to be the *historical* sense, in which *continuity* of a historical practice plays a central role in game identity over time. For other purposes, in determining the legality of a move, the accuracy of refereeing, or even the impressiveness of statistics, we might want to individuate games more finely with reference to their current governing rules—or the most important among them.[29] I do not think

---

[29] Another sense in which we might speak of individuals (or communities) as "using the same term" despite certain differences in the constitutive rules is not merely historical, but also, following Joseph Rouse, if we can see there as having been "something . . . continuously at stake in the development of the practice in which they occur" (2014, 37). To the extent that there is not only a continuity in rules, but also in the broader function the term serves in the practices of a community, we may have an interest in counting it as "the

there is an independent matter of metaphysical fact to be discovered here about whether it is "really" "just the same game." But such metaphysical claims as we can legitimately make I think are reflections of the rules that govern (or perhaps: should govern) our term "game," or various more specific game terms.

Consider the game of football (using the term in its North American sense, not in the European sense applied to what North Americans would call "soccer"). American football and Canadian football developed from the same original sport (a form of rugby) and share most of the same rules. Are they playing "the same game"? Consistently with the normativist approach, I don't think there is a deep metaphysical discovery to be made here. They are playing the same game in a sense (historical continuity and similarity speak in favor). But in another sense they are not: the rules vary in ways that can lead to different optimal strategies, different outcomes, and so on.

Now let us come back to the case of semantic rules. The important point for our present purposes is not to make a metaphysical claim that *there really are* semantic rules without which *we would have a different term*. The point is that we should understand metaphysical necessities as object-language reflections of semantic rules (and what follows from them). With terms, as with games, there are various methods by which we might individuate them, according to our purposes: as with games, we might be interested in individuating them by their particular rules or inferential role, or by historical continuity, or by phonetics, spelling, or various other methods. The rules governing "same term as" themselves seem to be open-textured, and open to renegotiation. Here, as elsewhere, we must remember to engage in bootstrapping: these claims about what is necessary or possible while being "the same term"

same term" despite the variations of rules (though we can still diagnose certain disputes as pseudo-disputes when we can diagnose changes in the rules). This would work well, for example, if we wish to say that "marriage" hasn't changed meaning, despite changes (in many states and countries) in the constitutive rules for what counts as a marriage: as long as having the term (and corresponding institution) continues to fulfill largely the same social and legal functions, we have understandable reason to treat "marriage" in 1953 and "marriage" today as not mere homonyms. (For further discussion, see my forthcoming.) But we can still eliminate pseudo-disputes about what marriage "really is" or what the true meaning of "marriage" is, and focus more clear-headedly on genuine pragmatic disputes about how we should set the rules governing what counts as "marriage."

must be subjected to the same analysis as other claims of metaphysical necessity and possibility.

In short, in understanding our terms as having certain semantic rules, we are not prevented from acknowledging that these rules are often partial, indeterminate, and changeable, in ways that mean we often must engage not in conceptual analysis or explication, but rather turn to conceptual (re-)negotiation—implicitly addressing "external" questions about what terms we should use and how we should be using them. In Chapter 8 I will return to this idea, and its consequences for how normativists understand the work of metaphysics.[30]

---

[30] If I am right that metaphysical modal judgments have a normative function, then Lance and O'Leary-Hawthorne themselves should see them, like they see other normative judgments, as having a different point than describing. As they put it, normatives may amount to attempts to change something or to endorse the status quo, and "exist only within a context within which the *issue* of whether or not to change our practice is salient" (1997, 207).

3

The Meaning of Modal Discourse

In attempting to undermine the assumption that metaphysical modal terms serve a describing function, I have developed an alternative view, on which they serve a normative function. I have argued that modal discourse enters language not in an effort to describe modal features of the world, but rather as a perspicuous way of making rules (and their consequences) explicit. I have also tried to show why modal language, so introduced, is useful, as it enables rules to be formulated in the indicative (without risk of their being mistaken for descriptions), so that we can also reason from rules and among rules, and enabling permissions as well as requirements to be formulated. So understood, we can see the uses and attractions of introducing modal forms of speech without thinking that they are introduced (like the names of newly discovered antipodean marsupials) in an attempt to describe discovered features of the world.

I have then given reason for thinking that metaphysical modal claims typically serve the same sort of function: enabling us to convey rules (this time, semantic rules for the terms or concepts we use), in the useful form of object-language indicatives, while also enabling us to give permissions as well as imposing requirements. Typical uses of such basic claims of necessity, I have argued, are to convey these rules (or their consequences) to those who are unsteady with the terms, to correct or condemn misuses, or to enforce or advocate for certain rules—in each case, while *using* (rather than mentioning) the very terms in question.

As emphasized in Chapter 1, this view is in the same family as earlier non-descriptivist views, such as Ryle's view that talk of laws serves to license inferences. But to make any view of this sort plausible requires that we address the embedding or "Frege-Geach" problem, as well as showing that the view does not fall prey to the classic criticisms of conventionalism.

Norms and Necessity. Amie L. Thomasson, Oxford University Press (2020). © Oxford University Press.
DOI: 10.1093/oso/9780190098193.001.0001

The Frege-Geach problem, in its basic form, is that one cannot give an account of the meaning of a troublesome term by saying what it is *used to do* (say, treating the meaning of "good" as given by noting that the term is characteristically used to commend), since "good" may also appear embedded in the context of conditionals ("if this is good, we should buy it") or negations ("what he did was not good"). In such cases "good" is not used to commend at all. But we must assume it has the same meaning in these contexts in order to make sense of the validity of simple modus ponens arguments involving the term ("if this is good, we should buy it," "this is good," so "we should buy it").[1] The same problem of course would arise if we took the work in Chapter 2 to be giving the meaning of "(metaphysically) necessary" as conveying a semantic rule in the object-language. For expressions of the form "Necessarily p" may also occur in embedded contexts. If I say "If it is metaphysically necessary that persons A and B be spatio-temporally continuous to be identical, then teleporting a person is impossible," I am not aiming to convey any semantic rules (say, for the term "person"). I speculated in Chapter 1 that the threat of the Frege-Geach problem may have been a major factor in keeping non-descriptivist views of all sorts off the table. In the current context, for the normativist approach to have any hope of acceptance, we must show how to avoid that problem.

3.1 The Relation between Function and Use

In Chapter 2, I have not purported to give any analysis of the *meanings* of our modal terms—only of their *function*. Addressing the functional question, I have argued, requires addressing two separate (but related) questions. First, what is the function of modal terminology? Why is it useful to have such terminology in our language at all? Second, how are basic modal claims typically *used*—what are they used to do?[2]

---

[1] The problem is widely discussed in the meta-ethics literature, particularly among those in the broadly expressivist tradition. For responses see (among others) Blackburn (1998, 2006), Charlow (2013), Dreier (2006), Gibbard (1990, 1994, 2003).

[2] This parallels Michael Williams's distinction between the "practical significance" of a piece of vocabulary and its "expressive/performative (speech act) function" (2015).

Distinguishing these facets of the functional question not only adds clarity but also enables us to make a new approach to the Frege-Geach problem.[3] In its original formulation, the objection was raised against attempts to give the *meaning* of a term by appeal to its *use*. As Searle put it, many analyses go astray by giving an analysis of what speech act an expression is commonly *used* to perform (e.g., that "good" is used to commend or "true" to endorse a statement) with what the word *means* (1969, 136–41). Peter Geach similarly sums up the error as attempting "to account for the *use* of a term 'P' concerning a thing as being a *performance* of some other nature than describing the thing" (1960, 223; italics mine). For any given term may be used in a variety of ways, and yet we think the meaning remains constant.

The functional analysis given here, by contrast, takes off primarily from analyzing not how the terms are commonly *used* (what speech act they are used to perform), but rather from the *function* such terminology serves in a language (which then plays a role in explaining how the terminology may be used). That functional analysis does not itself vary even when there is variation in the uses to which the term is put, just as the function of a penny doesn't change when it is used to open a battery compartment.

Giving this functional analysis is also not a matter of giving the term's meaning. But it does provide the basis for giving a meaning analysis: we can give the meaning by giving the rules of use that enable the term to fulfill its function—rules that remain constant even in embedded contexts. Since we also believe modal claims and reason with them, whatever account we give should also enable us to make sense of how these beliefs and this reasoning are possible.

The best way to meet this challenge seems to me to combine the modal normativist account of the *function* of modal language with a deflationary inferentialist approach to its *meaning*. Michael Williams (2015) distinguishes two components of a pragmatist Explanation of Meaning in terms of Use (EMU), each of which is subdivided into two parts. The first is the functional component, which involves (1) a clause

---

[3] Mark Warren (2014, 2015) develops a form of moral inferentialism and a response to the Frege-Geach problem that runs along lines in some ways parallel to the approach I take for modal discourse here.

identifying what the term does for us and why it is useful to have a term like this in the language (this corresponds to the answer to the "function" question given in Chapter 2) and (2) a clause identifying "what we are doing in deploying the word in question (typically in a non-embedded declarative sentence)" (corresponding roughly to the answers to the "use" questions) (2015, 165).[4] The second is the content-determining component, which gives the *meaning*—determining what we are *saying* when we use the term.[5]

The two parts of the analysis are closely related. As Williams makes clear, the analysis is still *functionally* driven: the content-determining component articulates the *rules* that the term follows that enable it to serve the *functions* identified in the functional component (as well as enabling it to be *used* in these characteristic ways).[6] That enables us to make clear why we would want to have a term that followed these inferential rules. As Huw Price puts it, we can then see "functional pragmatics not as an addition tacked on to deal with problems of force and tone, but as a complement to the theory of sense whose task is to explain how there come to be uses of language with senses of a particular sort" (2011, 56). In that sense, the functional account still fulfills an explanatorily basic role, yet we can clearly avoid falling prey to the Frege-Geach problem.

So, for example, we can give a pragmatist account of the term "true" by first offering an account of the function of the truth-predicate, and then developing an account of the meaning of the term in terms of its inferential role—where that role in turn is what enables it to perform its typical function. On Horwich's version of truth deflationism, the function of the truth predicate is to serve as a device of generalization (2010,

---

[4] Williams labels these the "practical significance" clause and the "expressive/performative (speech act) function" clause respectively. For simplicity and coherence with the earlier terminology, I will refer to them simply as the "function" clause and the "use" clause.

[5] Williams further subdivides the content-determining component into a "material inferential" clause specifying the inferential role of the term, and an "epistemic character" clause, identifying whether those inferences licensed are a priori or open to empirical revision. Here, I will leave to the side the epistemic clause (coming back later to discuss modal epistemology), and will focus on the entry and exit rules for the terminology in giving the content-determining clause.

[6] Though there is no assumption that this set of rules is *uniquely* suited to fulfilling the relevant functions.

4), enabling us to replace endless statements of the form "Sally said that Copenhagen is in Denmark and Copenhagen is in Denmark; Sally said that the spark plugs were dead and the spark plugs were dead; Sally said that there were termites in the roof beams and there were termites in the roof beams" with "Everything Sally said is true." A characteristic *use* of simple claims that something is "true" is to express this kind of epistemic deference (Williams 2015). The content-determining clause includes specifying the material-inferential component given by the equivalence schema: that except in instances that generate paradox, the inference from "Snow is white" to "It is true that snow is white" and vice versa is always good. The content-determining clauses of the truth predicate enable it to fulfill its function. For the equivalence schema licenses us to introduce, in place of "p," a singular term for the proposition that p (<p>) and the predicate, "is true," so that we may generalize over all of the propositions by saying "every proposition expressed by Sally (or, more colloquially, everything Sally said) is true."

If we give this kind of analysis, we can avoid the embedding problem in a nice clear way: we keep separate the accounts of what *function* the vocabulary serves in our language from the account of what, in various cases, we are *doing in using* the term in simple indicatives, and separate both of these from the account of what the term *means,* which is given in the content-determining component.

Let us now turn to offer such an analysis for the metaphysical modal terms. The account I have given in Chapter 2 gives us the material for stating the functional clauses:

- Function: Having metaphysical modal terms fulfills several functions:

  1. "Necessarily" makes explicit that the expression has regulative status.
  2. Modal terms enable us to make explicit our ways of reasoning with rules.[7]

---

[7] A form of inferentialism along these lines is articulated by Brandom (2007), especially pages 656–60.

3. "Possibly" enables us to convey permissions as well as requirements.

- Use: Basic (unembedded) claims of metaphysical necessity are characteristically used to convey, enforce, and/or advocate for semantic rules or their consequences (while *using* those very terms in object-language indicatives).

3.2 The Content of Modal Terms

With the function and use clauses in place, we now need to give the content-determining clauses for metaphysical modal terms, along with a story about how a term with the relevant content could perform the characteristic functions.[8] To give the content-determining clause, I will specify what rules that concept follows—those that make evident its inferential role. I will take the inferential role quite broadly, as including introduction rules (rules that entitle us to introduce the relevant form of speech—whether from other forms of speech or from worldly circumstances of application) and elimination rules (consequences of appropriate application—whether inferential or in terms of other practical responses) as well as (other) intra-linguistic rules (connecting proper use of this term to others).

So how can we identify the basic inferential role(s) of our metaphysical modal terms? We can take a clue from the work of Greg Restall (2012), who treats modal concepts as fulfilling the distinctive role of regulating our reasoning across different suppositions.[9] As Restall

---

[8] To make inferential role a central part of the account of the meaning of "necessarily" is natural in any case, since "necessarily" is a logical term behaving (as has often been noted) in many ways like "all." Moreover, it clearly avoids needing to think of the meaning of "necessarily" as involving special modal properties or features that the term is to pick out. (Avoiding this is a good thing in many ways: externalists, for example, would have quite a hard time seeing how the meaning of "necessarily" could be determined by causal relation to a property.)

[9] Normally, asserting p and asserting not-p clash; our standard logical rules rule out asserting, say, "I am at home today" and "I am not at home today." But, as Restall puts it, assertions and denials may also be undertaken "under the scope of various assumptions"—so, for example, "I am at home today, but *supposing I had forgotten my laptop*, I wouldn't have been at home today" does not induce a clash. When we reason

points out, we can reason across suppositions in two different ways. First, we may consider *subjunctive* alternatives: ways the world *would have been, if things had gone differently*, or, second, we may consider *indicative* alternatives: different ways we might take the actual world to be (different ways it could be, for all we know). The first marks reasoning governing the metaphysical modal concepts; the second concerns epistemic necessity and possibility. It is the first that we are concerned with here.

We can articulate two basic rules governing the concept of metaphysical necessity. I will call them "I" and "E" (for "introduction" and "elimination"), for any claim p:[10]

> I: If p is an object-language expression of an actual semantic rule (or a logical consequence of actual semantic rules), then you are entitled to introduce *Necessarily p*, regardless of any subjunctive suppositions.[11]

Rule I licenses us to add on the necessity operator to "All bachelors are men," for example, to get "Necessarily, all bachelors are men." It also licenses us to add "necessarily" to any object-language expression of an ostensive definition. The ostensive definition "call stuff of this chemical kind 'water'" may be expressed in the object language as: "stuff of this chemical kind is water." We can add "Necessarily" to that, giving us: "Necessarily, stuff of this chemical kind is water." This rule enables

---

under the scope of different assumptions, in Restall's terminology, we introduce different "zones" of discourse (2012, 1613). Ordinarily, the zones of discourse are isolated from each other, as in that example. Nonetheless, some things "jump across zones": for example, "Asserting that something is not only true, but *necessarily* true, makes it the kind of thing that jumps across zones" (Restall 2012, 1613). On Restall's view, our modal concepts are governed by rules that tell us when assertions and denials cross zones. The present discussion is very much inspired by Restall's inferentialist treatment of modal notions, while trying to make it informal and system-neutral.

[10] These parallel Restall's rules □R and □L respectively (2012, 1614). Restall argues that from □R and □L, combined with the standard rules, we can derive all the features of S5 (2012, 1614).

[11] The necessity at issue here is metaphysical necessity. A neat consequence of this: all logical necessities are guaranteed to be metaphysically necessary, since the logical necessities are logical consequences of anything.

us to make the regulative status of our expressions explicit, fulfilling function 1.

A second rule tells us what use we may make of these rules in reasoning (now that they have been made explicit). Putting it informally, if we have a claim that is an object-language statement of a semantic rule available as a premise, we are entitled to carry it over and make use of it as a premise in our reasoning, under any suppositions (as long as those very terms are being used at all). So, if we have *Necessarily p*, then we may use p in reasoning under any suppositions we may make about ways in which the world might have been different:

> E: If you have *Necessarily p* as a premise, you may use p as a premise in your reasoning anywhere, under any subjunctive suppositions.

This rule enables "necessarily" to fulfill the second function, enabling us to make explicit our ways of reasoning with rules. So supposing we have: *All cats are furry*. If we change suppositions about ways the world might have been had things gone differently (e.g., had we shaved some cats), we may not retain this premise and use it to reason from *Taffy is a cat* to: *Taffy is furry*. But if we have *Necessarily, all cats are mammals*, then we may use that as a premise to reason from *Taffy is a cat* to *Taffy is a mammal*, regardless of any changes in suppositions about ways in which things might have gone differently.[12]

As long as "necessarily" is in a language involving negation, we may also fulfill function 3 of conveying permissions as well as requirements. For we can convey that p is permissible by denying that its negation is required. More succinctly, we can do this by adding to the above principles the standard definition of possibility:

> ◇Df: ◇p iff ~□~p
> (Possibly p, if and only if, it's not the case that (necessarily: not-P)).

---

[12] It may be worth pointing out that the thought that cats *could turn out to be robots* is a supposition about a different *indicative* alternative: a different way the world *might actually be*. It is not a different *subjunctive* alternative, about a way the world *would have been*. Had there been robots surrounding those who grounded the reference of the syllable "cat," some would say, that would have been a situation in which the syllable "cat" would have picked out robots—but it would not have been a situation in which *cats* (now using our extant term with its actual history of use) would have been robots.

This may be taken as a rule governing the meaning of "possibly," and enabling basic possibility statements to fulfill their function of conveying permissions (by making evident what is not ruled out by the requirements).

These informal rules articulating the inferential roles of our metaphysical modal concepts (of necessity and possibility) may of course be formally expressed in various different ways,[13] and combined with rules of various other formal systems—just as the equivalence schema governing "true" may be.[14] Here the core point is that we can meet the challenge of the embedding problem by distinguishing the *functions* that modal terms play in our language, on the one hand, from the *uses* to which such terms are put in various speech acts; and on the other hand, distinguishing both of these from the *content or meaning* of our metaphysical modal terms—understood in terms of the inferential role that enables them to perform those functions. Combining our modal normativism with this approach to understanding the meanings of modal terms enables us to retain our non-descriptive stand while avoiding the embedding problem by identifying a constant *meaning* for "necessarily" in whatever sort of speech act it may appear.

3.3 Modal Propositions and Modal Truth

The embedding problem does not just challenge us to identify a constant meaning of the key terms, however. It also challenges us to explain how they may be used to express beliefs, used in reasoning, and so on. So moral expressivists, for example, are asked to give some account of how we may have moral beliefs (if "p is good" were just a way of *commending* p, it is hard to see how it could be *believed*—since "yay, p" seems to lack propositional content), and how we may reason with moral claims (since again it doesn't seem that we can reason with commendations). (This is often thought to be the easier challenge than identifying the meanings of the terms in question [Sinott-Armstrong 2000].)

---

[13] See Restall (2012) for an inferentialist treatment of modal logic.
[14] See Ripley (2013) for an inferentialist logic including a transparent truth predicate.

Both of these aspects of the challenge are straightforward to deal with on the modal normativist view—especially when we combine the functional pluralist story with the deflationary meta-ontology I have advocated elsewhere (2015). On the pleonastic understanding of propositions defended by Stephen Schiffer (2003), for example, introduction rules license us to move from any indicative sentence: p to derive the singular term "The proposition that p," which is guaranteed to refer (whether or not the original indicative was true). Claims of the form "Necessarily q" are themselves indicative sentences, and so we may apply the same rules to derive: "The proposition that *Necessarily q*" (or, more colloquially, "The proposition that it is necessary that q"). As a result, there is no barrier to thinking that modal claims express propositions in just the same sense as any other sentence does. Given that they express propositions, there is also no barrier to thinking that modal propositions may be believed, may serve as the contents of thoughts, and so on, in just the usual sense. Modal normativism is not a form of non-cognitivism.

Adopting a deflationary theory of truth also enables us to classify modal statements as true or false[15] without their having to be made true by modal features of the world.[16] We can begin from "All bachelors are men," and (since that claim is an object-language expression of a semantic rule) rule I licenses us to add "necessarily" and assert "Necessarily, all bachelors are men." On the deflationary view, the concept of truth is simply governed by the equivalence schema: <p> is true if and only if p, so we can recognize the equivalence of this

[15] It is, of course, not unprecedented to simply deny that modal claims may be true: Wittgenstein denied that claims of necessity can, strictly speaking, be true. For discussion of Wittgenstein's denial, see Wright (1980, 375). Bueno and Shalkowski (2004) also deny, on rather different grounds, that modal claims need to be capable of being true.

[16] We needn't here decide among deflationary views of truth. Alternatives include following pro-sententialists (Grover et al. 1975) in taking the claim " 'Necessarily p' is true" to be just a matter of (re)asserting "Necessarily p." Then the standards governing saying " 'Necessarily p' is true" do not diverge from those governing saying "Necessarily p." The standards for saying "Necessarily p" are that p is an object-language expression of a rule or its logical consequence. Blackburn offers another route, suggesting that the quasi-realists take truth in the relevant domain (about which we are being quasi-realist) to be a matter of *correctness* according to the relevant standards—where these standards need not be those of correspondence to reality (1993, 55). For a helpful comparative evaluation of different deflationary theories of truth, see Horwich (2010, Chapter 2).

with " 'Necessarily, all bachelors are men' is true." The uncontroversial equivalence schema applies just as well to modal as non-modal indicatives, so there is no problem in allowing that modal claims may be true. Once we have allowed that basic modal claims may be true or false, it is clear that they may be used in standard forms of truth-conditional reasoning.

Now at this point some readers might get a slightly queasy feeling, recalling Jamie Dreier's (1996) arguments that truth minimalism does not help solve the embedding problem. But the upshot of his arguments is that it does not do so *on its own*; we must first solve the embedding problem, and then we may find it attractive to adopt truth minimalism (to make a clean and straightforward account of how modal claims, so understood, may be true, may be reasoned with, etc. [1996, 39]). That is precisely the way I have proceeded: first, offering an inferential role account of the *meaning* of "necessarily," and then using truth minimalism to make it clear how claims under the necessity operator may be true, may be used in reasoning, and so on.

Dreier raises another challenge to expressivists by noting that one cannot simply assert that we can begin by performing some speech act, introduce rules that allow us to transform it into propositional form, and go on to reason with it without worry. The case he raises is of "hiyo," where "Hiyo, Bob" is used in the speech act of accosting, but comes to permit transformation into propositional form, so wherever we are entitled to say "Hiyo, Bob" we are also entitled to say "Bob is hiyo" (1996, 43). Although we may make this shift to the predicative form, however, Dreier insists that that is no guarantee that the new expression ("Bob is hiyo") can be meaningfully embedded in conditionals and the like in ways that enable us to reason with it. If we try to embed it as "If a dingo is near, then Bob is hiyo," we still have no idea what this means:

> [T]here is no sense to be made of the idea that someone might use that conditional to infer "Bob is hiyo" from "A dingo is near." It is obvious that the idea of inferring is out of place when the conclusion is the speech act of accosting.

(1996, 43)

But while this problem is a legitimate one, it is not a threat for the relevant account of modality. The view here is that statements expressing metaphysical necessities give us ways of conveying rules in object-language indicatives. But rules (even in their more overt forms) are always usable in making inferences when expressed in indicative form (in imperative form they can't be embedded in the antecedents of conditionals, but they are in the consequents). We make inferences using rules when we say, for example, "If the white player must move first then Julie must move first," "If players must wear helmets then I'm not going to play," and so on. Expressions of rules (unlike acts of accosting) already are suited to figure in inferences, so there is no threat of failure here as there is in the "hiyo" case.[17]

3.4 Avoiding the Criticisms of Conventionalism

Given this account of modal truth, however, some might fear that the normativist view defended here falls back into the old problems thought to plague conventionalism. For some might think that it makes it a contingent matter that the relevant necessary truths *are* necessary by making the truth of "Necessarily, all seals are mammals" depend on our adopting certain conventions. Since it is a contingent matter that we adopted those conventions (rather than those for "car," say), the critic might allege it is contingent that this claim is necessary. Thus on the conventionalist view (the criticism goes), we must give up the axiom of modal logic S4 that if P is necessary, it is *necessarily* necessary ($\Box P \rightarrow \Box\Box P$) (Sider 2011, 268).

On the contrary, however, the normativist view gives us reason for *accepting* that $\Box P \rightarrow \Box\Box P$. For the introduction rule (I) tells us that where P is an object-language expression of an actual semantic rule, one may introduce: *Necessarily P.* This is itself an object-language expression of an actual semantic rule governing the metaphysical "necessarily." And so we are entitled to add "necessarily" again onto any metaphysical modal claim of the form "Necessarily P."

---

[17] Thanks to Mark Warren for helpful discussion of this point. For a response to the "hiyo" problem for the case of moral discourse, see Warren (2014, 112).

As we have seen in Chapter 1, the classic objections arise to conventionalism when it is thought of as the view that our linguistic conventions (or our adoption of these conventions) serve as *truthmakers* for our claims of necessity (making those claims turn out to be contingent). But basic necessity claims, on the normativist view, are not descriptions *of* semantic rules, nor are they descriptions that claim *that* certain semantic rules are in place or were adopted. We must not confuse (normative) *statements of* rules or ways of *conveying* rules in object-language indicatives with *descriptions of* what rules there are. We must carefully distinguish the claim "It is a semantic rule that 'bachelor' is to be applied only when 'man' may be applied," which is a statement *about* rules, from the object-language expression *of a* rule we find in the properly modal statement: "Necessarily, bachelors are men." The first has the adoption of linguistic conventions as a truthmaker; the second does not. The thought that adoptions of linguistic conventions, pronouncements, and so forth serve as truthmakers for our modal claims relies on confusing statements *about* rules (descriptions of what the rules are) with statements *of* rules (or, more particularly in this case, object-language formulations of rules), and misses the point of the non-descriptivist approach.

Where, then, does the critic go wrong? The critic gives us a conditional, claiming that on the normativist view: "If we had adopted different conventions, then 'necessarily all seals are mammals'[18] would have been false." But when we evaluate a counterfactual conditional, we must evaluate its truth at another world, *leaving its meaning fixed as the actual meaning at our world.* For we want to know whether this same *claim* ("Necessarily, all seals are mammals"), with the same meaning, would be true at another world, in other circumstances or given other suppositions. After all, it is *claims*, not typographical sequences, that are true or false. If we do leave the meaning fixed, though, then at another world—a world in which people had different linguistic conventions, or indeed in which there were no people or language at all—our actual *claim*, "necessarily, all seals are mammals" (meaning intact), would remain *true.*

---

[18] Taking this, of course, as a claim of metaphysical (not epistemic) necessity.

The truth of a basic necessity claim, on this view, does not require the adoption of any linguistic conventions. As with all sentences, the *existence* of the sentence requires the existence of language, and its *meaningfulness* (and so its existence as a *sentence*, rather than just as a typographical or sound sequence) requires certain conventional rules for use of certain marks or sounds. And the sentence must exist and be meaningful if we are to assess whether it is true. But that is no surprise—it is simply a truism. And it is a very different matter from its requiring the adoption of linguistic conventions, or the making of certain pronouncements, *as truthmakers*.

Another way to see why the standard criticisms of conventionalism don't apply here is by noting that the modal normativist is entitled to accept certain "independence counterfactuals"—for example: "Seals are necessarily mammals, *and this would be true even in situations in which speakers adopted different linguistic rules* (or in which there were no speakers)." For this itself is an implicitly regulative claim—that our term "seal" (in its current rules of use) is to apply to whatever is the same biological kind as the kind instantiated by these things at the actual world, and that this regulation (of our *actual* term) is to remain in effect even in contingencies in which speakers use language differently (or in which there are no speakers at all). (And this idea is no different than the regulation we draw on when we agree with Abraham Lincoln's quip that a dog would still have four legs, even if a "tail" were called a "leg.") Since the normativist is entitled to *accept* such independence counterfactuals, she is also entitled to *reject* accusations that, on her view, if our conventions were different, standard metaphysical necessity claims would be false.[19]

3.5 Conclusion

I have given the outlines of a normativist view of metaphysical modality, and aimed to show how we can develop a view along these

---

[19] The same form of reasoning may be applied to put to rest worries that, if (as I suggest we should in Chapter 8) we allow that the rules governing our terms are *revisable*, then *what is necessary* changes as well.

lines that clearly avoids the problems that plagued (or were thought to plague) its predecessors. I have tried to show why it would be a mistake to think that the standard criticisms of conventionalism apply to this view. I have also aimed to show how the view may avoid the notorious Frege-Geach problem by not only giving an account of the *function* of the metaphysical terms "necessarily" and "possibly," but also distinguishing this from the various *uses* to which the terms may be put, and distinguishing both of these from the *meaning*. I have also aimed to develop a view of the meaning of modal terms in a way that makes clear that this may remain constant even when the use of these terms changes in embedded contexts. I hope that in all of this I have given good reason for thinking that, despite the historical difficulties that have arisen, the difficult waters that surround non-descriptive accounts of modal discourse may after all be navigable, so that we can retain hope of getting the many benefits a non-descriptive approach promises.

Nonetheless, plenty of work remains to be done, for later barriers arose to the normativist approach, and a number of other objections and purported counterexamples must be handled. I turn now to show how we can avoid the barriers to the view apparently thrown up by Kripke's purported discovery of *de re* necessities and of the necessary a posteriori. Thereafter I will address some other recurrent objections. Once that work is done, I will come back to discuss the great ontological, epistemological, and methodological payoffs of adopting the normativist position.

4

Handling *De Re* and A Posteriori Modal Claims

In the previous chapters I have developed a contemporary non-descriptivist approach to modality, modal normativism, according to which metaphysically necessary truths are seen as object-language indicative expressions of semantic rules and their consequences. I have tried to show that, properly understood, the view clearly avoids the criticisms raised (often mistakenly) against classical conventionalism. I have also tried to show how it can avoid another important historical challenge to any non-descriptive approach: the Frege-Geach problem of showing how we may allow that modal statements have a constant meaning even across embedded contexts, and how we may treat modal statements as true or false and capable of being used in reasoning. If the work so far is successful, we will have good reason to think that modal normativism can overcome the challenges that pressed older forms of non-descriptivism into obscurity.

Yet in the current historical context, the view still will not be granted even initial plausibility until we can show how it can handle the major barriers that arose later, after the heyday of classical non-descriptive approaches. For Saul Kripke's work raised some notoriously difficult cases. The first such cases arise with the apparent presence of *de re* modal predications. *De re* attributions of modality can be made using names; for example, we may say of Kamala Harris, that she is necessarily a person. Where quantified claims are concerned, *de re* modal claims include a variable bound to a quantifier outside the scope of the necessity operator. So we may also say: there is something that is necessarily a person ($\exists x \Box Px$), making a true *de re* modal claim. (By contrast, in *de dicto* modal statements, the quantifier is within the scope of the modal operator, as in "Necessarily, for all x, if x is a bachelor, then x is male." It

Norms and Necessity. Amie L. Thomasson, Oxford University Press (2020). © Oxford University Press.
DOI: 10.1093/oso/9780190098193.001.0001

is a distinction that makes a difference: for while the *de re* modal claim "there is someone who is necessarily a person" seems true, the corresponding *de dicto* necessity claim "necessarily, there is someone who is a person" is false—assuming it is not necessary that any people exist.) Since *de re* modal truths use names (or variables bound to a quantifier outside the scope of the modal operator), the usual thought is that these simply *ascribe modal properties to individuals*, in ways that have nothing to do with semantic rules, and so can't be accommodated by modal normativism. On the contrary, the idea that such modal claims ascribe modal properties to individuals seems to fit most naturally with the heavyweight realist view that there are modal properties in the world, which our modal statements describe.

Even more worryingly, after Kripke it has become widely accepted that there are necessities that are knowable only a posteriori, including predications such as "Water necessarily has the microstructure H_2O" or "Alice Walker necessarily originated from Willie Lee Walker and Minnie Tallulah Grant," and identity statements involving natural kind terms ("Water is necessarily H_2O") or names ("Hesperus is necessarily Phosphorus"). These present other difficult cases.[1] For we might think that our knowledge of the semantic rules should yield something like a priori knowledge, or at least knowledge acquired in the armchair by extrapolation from our own linguistic competence, rather than from empirical investigation. And so, it might seem that if we accepted that metaphysically necessary truths are reflections of semantic rules, we could not hope to account for there being metaphysically necessary truths that are only knowable a posteriori. On the contrary, the presence of "discoverable" necessary truths seems again to give impetus to a heavyweight realist view that takes modal features to be discoverable parts of our world. As Hilary Putnam puts it, such cases suggest that "Human intuition has no privileged access to metaphysical necessity" (1975, 151).

---

[1] Of course any of these individual claims about what is necessary or contingent could be challenged (and many have been). I am not here concerned to defend or attack any of these particular claims about what is necessary or contingent. Instead, I only aim to show that *if we accept such claims*, they present no barrier to the normativist understanding of modality defended here.

Conversely, Kripke also raised cases of apparently contingent a priori truths such as "Stick S [the meter stick establishing the standard] is one meter long." Such cases might again be thought to undermine the idea that there is a close connection between semantic rules and necessities—for this might seem to give an object-language expression of a semantic rule (for "meter") and yet is not a necessary truth (as the stick could change length, e.g., if heated).

Causal theories of reference, which came into prominence after the heyday of non-descriptive approaches to modality, play a central role in pressing these problems. For the pure causal theorist holds that the meanings of our names and natural kind terms is given by their reference, not via any kind of associated conceptual content.[2] If there is no conceptual content to names or natural kind terms, it seems impossible to understand the necessities involved in claims such as "Kamala Harris is necessarily a person" or "Water is necessarily H_2O" as reflecting semantic rules governing these names or kind terms. Instead, the causal approach to reference encourages the idea that essences are out in the world, awaiting discovery.

To make the modal normativist view plausible in the contemporary context, I must show how to meet these challenges.[3] I will begin by directly confronting pure causal theories of reference. In section 4.1 I will argue that we *do* have reason to think that our names and natural kind terms are governed by some semantic rules—though we must broaden our understanding of the forms these rules may take. Then, I must go on (in sections 4.2 and 4.3) to show how the relevant forms

---

[2] Direct reference theories are traced back to Mill (1843/1875), but the modern form of a causal theory of reference, on which names are taken as mere "tags," was developed by Ruth Barcan Marcus (1961), and later popularized by Kripke (1980) and Putnam (1975).

[3] Many readers will note certain parallels between the approach taken here and responses to Kripkean examples developed in two-dimensional semantics, especially in the versions developed by Frank Jackson (1998) and David Chalmers (2006). Since the exposition of a two-dimensional framework usually relies on claims about possible worlds, I will not take that route here (in order to avoid any appearance of circularity), but rather will work directly in terms of arguing for relevant semantic rules, and showing how various modal claims may be seen as reflections of these rules. Nonetheless, I wish to acknowledge here the importance of that preceding work in this territory, and parallels in insisting that the classic Kripke/Putnam cases of *a posteriori* necessities are not inconsistent with accepting that there are various kinds of rules governing our terms.

of rules may be used to the normativist's ends: to show how even *de re* and a posteriori modal claims may be understood as object-language reflections of semantic rules and their consequences—thus showing how the normativist approach may be extended to handle these hard cases.[4]

4.1 Rules for Names and Natural Kind Terms

Direct reference theories, according to which a name just picks out its referent "directly," without any associated meaning other than their referent, make it seem impossible to think of *de re* necessities as reflections of semantic rules. For if (with Ruth Marcus [1961]) we think of names as mere "tags," we might think there just aren't the right kind of semantic rules to be reflected in object-language expressions as modal truths. And so we might naturally think that we can discover nothing about the referent of a name simply by making use of our semantic competence: we must go out into the world and discover its features, modal or otherwise. I suspect that something like this picture, combined with the popularity of direct reference theories, has been

---

[4] The basic framework for developing a solution to this kind of problem was developed by Alan Sidelle (1989). Sidelle aims to show how a conventionalist treatment of modality may be consistent with acknowledging *de re* and *a posteriori* modal truths. I would distance myself from both the term "conventionalism" and some of its commitments (e.g., there is no requirement on my normativist view that all of the rules be thought of as merely conventional, as I discuss in Chapter 5). I also reject Sidelle's way of expressing the metaphysical view that goes with his treatment of modality—he frequently claims that his view is one on which there is "no real necessity" and that there are no mind-independent modal features or objects; that we "make" or articulate essences, kinds, and individuals (1989, 57). But as will become clear through my treatment of simple realism in Chapter 6, I think it is a mistake to draw conclusions like these from the normativist view. Nonetheless, Sidelle's basic idea that *a posteriori* necessities may be accounted for through appeal to schematic rules ("conventions," in his terms), filled in empirically, and expressed in the "linguistic" mode, is the key to the account of *a posteriori* necessities developed in this chapter. His move to account for *de re* necessities by appeal to the idea that names are "introduced as terms of certain types" (1989, 50) also parallels the solution here (which for me is independently motivated by other work on reference). So, although it is done in somewhat different terms than I will use, Sidelle's work is an important predecessor of and inspiration for the work that follows here. For other approaches that show how one may understand modality by appeal to analyticity or (more broadly) meaning and yet accommodate Kripkean cases, see Ludwig (in progress) and Schieder (2016).

largely behind the revival of the idea that modal properties must be real discoverable features of our world.

The usual meta-semantic picture linked to a direct reference theory is a purely causal theory of reference, according to which what determines which object a name refers to is (roughly) whatever is linked to it by an appropriate causal chain. These theories have been similarly popular for natural kind terms—on such a picture, what determines the reference of "water" is not any associated conceptual content, but rather (roughly) appropriate causal links to samples of liquid in the environment.[5]

But pure causal theories of reference also face notorious problems (see Devitt and Sterelny [1999, 79–81] and Thomasson [2007, Chapter 2]). One of these is the *qua* problem. Simply put, causal relations alone cannot determine whether an introduced term is to refer to a statue, lump, time slice, mereological sum of particles, or something else. Another related problem is the problem of reference failure, for causal relations alone likewise cannot determine whether or not a term succeeds in referring at all. Our utterances are always causally connected to *something,* and yet we sometimes think our terms nonetheless fail to be properly grounded (see Thomasson 2010). So, the argument goes, we need to accept that even names and natural kind terms have at least certain kinds of conceptual content, in order to address the non-reference problem (disambiguating whether or not a term is successfully grounded, and comes to refer) and to address the *qua* problem (distinguishing which entity, of various empirically indistinguishable options, it is to refer to, should it succeed in referring).

What kind of conceptual content should this be? One common response is to suggest that names must at least be associated with a category of entity *to be referred to*—if the term succeeds in referring at all.[6] So, for example, "Kamala Harris" may be associated with the

---

[5] I will leave to the side details about how exactly to express these conditions, as it will not matter for the point to be made here: that modal normativism may be rendered consistent with central intuitions about *de re* and a posteriori necessities.

[6] Devitt and Sterelny argue that attempted reference groundings "will fail if the cause of the perceptual experience does not fit the general categorial term used to conceptualize it," and that as a result we should accept not a pure causal theory, but rather a hybrid

category *person*, in a way that enables us to say that the name refers to a person and not a mere physical body, time slice, or mereological sum. Michelangelo's "David," by contrast, may be introduced as a statue name (which is not to be reapplied after a drastic change in shape), distinguishing it from a lump name (which may be). Similarly, natural kind terms such as "water" may be introduced as names for a chemical kind. The presence of such rules might give aid and comfort to a modal normativist. For one might hope to account for *de re* modal truths such as that Kamala Harris is necessarily a person, that the statue "David" necessarily has a certain shape, or that water has its chemical composition necessarily, by appealing to basic rules that mark out "Kamala Harris" as a *person name*, "David" as a *statue name*, and "water" as a *chemical kind* name.[7]

Causal theorists, however, reject the idea that our names must come associated with conceptual content that gives a category of entity *to be referred to*.[8] For (they argue) these are both things we could "discover" to be *false*, while the terms still refer—and so it cannot be part of the *meanings* of the terms that "Kamala Harris" is *to refer to* a person, or

---

"descriptive-causal" theory (1999, 80). See also Thomasson (2007, 38–44). The association with categories simplifies the exposition, though I argued that what is really crucial is (frame-level) application conditions and co-application conditions: rules determining (respectively) when the term may be properly applied, and when it may be applied again and count as applying to the same thing. Ludwig (in progress, 19–20, 31) introduces a similar idea that some names may be "category names" that impose some requirements on their referent without purporting to uniquely determine a referent. (Ludwig, however, gives reference clauses for category names that rely on "non-description" [purely directly referential] names.)

[7] I softened the thesis somewhat (in ways that can matter), arguing that the *qua problem* and the *reference failure problem* give us reason to accept that reference to concrete individuals is determinate *only to the extent that* the term is associated with determinate application conditions and co-application conditions (2007, Chapter 2; see also Thomasson 2010). Even uses of demonstratives (I have argued) have determinate reference on a given occasion of use only to the extent that they are associated with such rules (even if these are vague, open-ended, or disjunctive in form, and are open to revision).

[8] I will leave to the side here controversies that arise from doubts that there are analytic truths—a view made unpopular by Quine's criticisms of the analytic/synthetic distinction. I won't discuss this here, as I have done so elsewhere (Thomasson 2007, Chapter 2), and of course others have given extensive responses to Quine as well (see, e.g., Strawson and Grice [1956] and G. Russell [2008]). I will also leave to the side Williamson's (2007) objections to the idea that conceptual competence may be a route to metaphysical knowledge, for I have also dealt with that issue elsewhere (Thomasson 2015, Chapter 7).

that "David" is *to refer to* a statue. Putnam's classic arguments, for example, purport to show that it "could turn out" that we are mistaken (given a massive hoax), and that Kamala Harris is really a robot; or that the (alleged) statue "David" is really an organism (with a very slow metabolism). Such intuitions are widely thought to show that these names could refer even if the basic category they were associated with were wrong.[9] And that in turn is thought to show that names like "Kamala Harris" and "David" can't really be governed by semantic rules that mark them as person names or statue names, in which case we cannot hope to understand the corresponding modal claims as object-language reflections of these rules. Thus the meaning of the name is nothing more than its referent, and we must discover what that is, and what sort of thing it is, with what modal properties.

Before we jump to such conclusions, however, we should consider what we would say in other imagined cases. Suppose that instead of there being one robot, a hoax was perpetrated by two dozen exchangeable robots, able to cover more campaign stops. In such cases, it's doubtful that we would say that it turns out that Kamala Harris is two dozen robots. Or suppose the hoax took the form not of an electro-mechanical impostor (or impostors), but rather of faked video footage of all sorts: hardly anyone would want to say that "It turns out that Kamala Harris is a bunch of video clips" rather simply saying "Kamala Harris doesn't exist." This suggests already that, in order to distinguish cases in which we would and would not accept that the term refers, we need to accept that there are *some* rules or conceptual constraints built into the term that help establish cases in which it does or does not refer.[10] These initial considerations already suggest that it would be a

---

[9] It is worth noting that it is entirely open to the modal normativist to deny that there are such rules, as long as she is also prepared to deny that there are such metaphysical necessities. The normativist is committed to there being a link between the semantic rules and the metaphysical necessities—but is not (simply in virtue of being a modal normativist) committed to any particular views about what the semantic rules are, or what the metaphysical necessities are. It thus remains open to a normativist to agree with causal theorists that there are no such rules, and go on to deny that there are the relevant necessities. This is not, however, the route I will take here. The intuitions that there are such metaphysical necessities are quite widespread, and so I think it would be better to show how we can accommodate them, while also accommodating the intuitions of causal theorists.

[10] I develop this line of argument in Thomasson (2010). See also Devitt and Sterelny (1999, 80).

mistake to move from intuitions that Kamala Harris could "turn out" to be a robot to conclude that our singular terms have *no* conceptual content at all. We can argue about how to articulate the relevant rules, but we once again seem to need *some* associated rules to address the problem of reference failure.

We also still need appeal to some rules to avoid the *qua* problem. What we have discovered in the (first) robot case is an empirical fact— we have encountered an empirical surprise. Neutrally described, we have discovered that where we thought there was a woman, all that was present was a complex electro-mechanical device. We have discovered that the interior was not flesh and blood, as we assumed, but chips and wires. But consider what we can't discover empirically: we can't make an empirical discovery that Kamala Harris is actually a mereological sum of cells rather than a person, or that she is "really" a time slice of a person rather than a continuant. For there are no empirically detectable differences among these situations. In short, no parallel situation would count as discovering merely that the *modal* facts of the world were different than we assumed, while no *empirical* mistake was made. As the *qua* problem suggests, disambiguating among these merely modally, ontologically (but not empirically) different potential referents can't come from the world. This gives us reason to take seriously the idea that such disambiguations must instead come from some associated rules of use.

In short, the right conclusion to draw from cases of surprising discoveries is not that our terms lack conceptual content—on the contrary, we seem to *require* appeal to it to distinguish situations in which reference succeeds versus fails, and to distinguish *which* thing is referred to where there are no empirical differences among the options. The question is what form we should understand these rules as taking.

If considering "what we would say" in case of surprising empirical facts doesn't tell us that we should reject the idea that there are any rules at all, then how should we understand these rules? One way to think of them is as often involving *conditionalization* on various (actual) empirical facts. Rules of all kinds can be conditionalized on empirical facts—they are, for example, when we say that *if there is a fire,* the elevator must not be used; *if you are a resident of Vermont,* you must pay sales tax; or *if you possess a type of card requested by another player,*

you must relinquish it. It seems equally plausible to think of the semantic rules governing names (for example) as conditionalized: if (or,
perhaps better, assuming) the empirical facts are as expected (no hoax;
application conditions for "person" fulfilled), then the name "Kamala
Harris" is to refer to a person (and not a mereological sum of cells, a
time slice, or any other *empirically* indistinguishable but *modally* distinct option).[11] This provides the needed disambiguation, while still
leaving it open what to do should the relevant empirical conditions not
turn out as expected.

What happens to our rule (and our name) in cases in which the
relevant empirical assumption fails?[12] Putnam's cases suggest that
we would allow that the term refers anyway to something of an unexpected kind—whatever is at the end of the causal chain. But, as we
have seen, things aren't as simple as that. Even if, in some situations,
we might (upon a strange discovery of a hoax) come to say that it turns
out that the name "Kamala Harris" refers to a robot, our intuitions are
not nearly as unified and stable as causal theorists and their followers
have supposed. For, as we have seen, other surprising discoveries (e.g.,
that there are only video clips) might lead us to conclude that the term
fails to refer. Moreover, even where the same discovery has been made
(the speaker at the podium is suddenly revealed to be made of silicon
chips and wire), in other contexts it seems we might deny that Kamala
Harris exists:

---

[11] Sidelle at one point similarly suggests that the conventions should be understood
as saying "that supposing certain actual conditions hold, we are constrained in our
descriptions of counterfactuals in a certain way" (1989, 46).

[12] One option I suggested elsewhere (Thomasson 2007, 50–51) is to allow that in
situations of extreme ignorance (where we aim to just introduce "Klut" to refer to "that
distant thing in the field"), we may have a hierarchical conditionalized intention, for example that it is to refer to an animal if application conditions for "animal" are fulfilled; if
not, then to an artifact if the application conditions for "artifact" are fulfilled, if not then
to a lump, and so on. So one could suggest that there is a hierarchy of fallback positions
(given our natural priorities and interests, say in people and artifacts) in the relevant
rules. Nonetheless, one might legitimately worry that it requires too much of our conceptual structure to think that there are such hierarchical "fallback plans" in place. It
now seems better to me to allow that cases in which empirical assumptions fail call for
decisions about what to do with the rules, rather than *discoveries* of what the fallbacks are
and what they entail.

"How many plausible candidates do the Democrats have now?"

"Three: Joe Biden, Elizabeth Warren, and Kamala Harris."

"Didn't you hear? It's all been an elaborate hoax. There is no Kamala Harris. What people took to be Harris was just a robot designed by Apple!"[13]

In cases of surprising discoveries, where the empirical condition fails, it may (given the rules) remain *open* whether we should characterize what we have discovered as a case in which Kamala Harris turns out to be a robot, or a case in which it turns out that Kamala Harris doesn't really exist. And the direction we take may depend on our interests—or, perhaps better, depend on the enduring interests of the language community in employing terms like these.[14] If our interests lie in tracking the path of a (single) speaker across Iowa, a robot or person will serve. If we're interested in identifying presidential candidates (or individuals with rights, who are biologically fragile, etc.) it won't. Accordingly, we might keep the idea that it was to be a person term and so reject it as non-referring, or we might reject the person requirement and adapt it as an artifact term (notice that we still must disambiguate it in its new use as a term for an artifact versus a term for a mereological sum if we hope to answer questions about whether Robo-Harris survived the replacement of its circuitry).

Imogen Dickie (2015, 168–69) raises an actual case that makes a similar point. The mathematics papers attributed to Nicolas Bourbaki were in fact authored by a group, not a single individual. So what would we do, if we were to make this discovery? Dickie suggests, if

---

[13] I draw out an analogous case in which we might say a species term fails to refer rather than that it refers to "little robots" in Thomasson (2007, 49–50).

[14] Coherently with this, Joseph Rouse argues that linguistic practices in using a term may be seen as continuous despite changes in particular norms governing them, given the sense that "something has been continuously at stake in the development of the practice in which they occur" (2014, 37). This seems to be a generalized version of the idea presented here: that our interests, or more broadly what is at stake communally in a practice of using a term (what its function is, what it does for us), may help determine which way the norms of a practice develop when the world throws surprises our way. (Rouse's examples include considering what we do with general terms like "gold" and "jade" when we find similar-looking substances—depending on whether our interests are in chemistry or crafting [2014, 29].) For further discussion of related issues see Jackman (1999) and Tanesini (2014).

it were a biographer who made the discovery, the biographer might aptly deny that the name refers and declare "There is no Bourbaki."[15] By contrast, if a mathematician made the discovery (and didn't care a whit about the personal history of the author, only about the mathematical contributions of the papers), she might not care, and might not treat the name as failing to refer, but rather as referring to the group (2015, 168–69).

Much the same goes for the causal theorist's examples involving natural kind terms. Putnam famously argued that it could "turn out that" cats are robots—and that has been thought to undermine the idea that it could be part of the meaning of "cat" that it is to refer to an animal kind (in a way that could be reflected in modal statements such as "Necessarily, cats are animals"). But in other cases, if we find that the supposed exemplars of a new kind of sparrow, Key Sparrows, were robots planted by a glory-hungry birdwatcher, we would naturally deny that Key Sparrows exist (see Thomasson 2007, 49–50). Our reactions to surprising diversity in what we took to be chemical or geological kinds likewise may tip either direction: we deny that iron pyrites are gold, for example, but accept that there are two kinds of jade (Rouse 2014). Peter Hacker develops a similar response to Putnam's arguments that "momentum" *turns out* to have always meant "what is conserved in elastic collision" rather than "rest mass times velocity" (1996, 330 n.46). As Hacker puts it (following Wittgenstein in Section 438 of the *Zettel*):

> Prior to Einstein, the meaning of "momentum" oscillated between "mass times velocity" and "whatever quantity is conserved in elastic collision," either of which could be taken as defining it. Since they seemed invariably to coincide, there was no need to decide which was a criterion and which a symptom. With the discovery that rest mass times velocity is not strictly conserved in elastic collision it became reasonable to define momentum as what is conserved in elastic collision, not as mass times velocity.
>
> (1996, 330 n.46)

---

[15] Dickie uses the case as grounds for thinking that we must reject a "match in kind" requirement for reference. For fruitful discussion of the Bourbaki case, see also Lefftz (2018).

Frank Jackson also makes this point quite clearly, arguing that often "surprising" cases (e.g., where we thought there were cats, there were little robots) are cases that are initially indeterminate, and call for decision:

> In practice you may not have made the decision about how you will use language that settles whether you'd use "Cats are not animals" to pick out the possibilities to which probability should be moved should some *very* surprising discoveries be made, or whether you'd use "There are some things that would count as cats except that they are not animals." The nature of the possibility is the same in either case; what is unsettled is how you'd pick it out in language—and the latter may be unsettled simply because the possibility is so exotic there is no point in expending energy in deciding ahead of time which way to jump should the need arise.
>
> (1998, 54)

I would add to this only (1) that observations of cases in which we would likely "jump the other way" further support the idea that these are cases that are indeterminate and call for a decision, and (2) that which decision we make likely depends on what interests are at stake.

In sum, the variations in all of these cases speak in favor of the idea that the relevant semantic rules may simply not tell us what to do if the empirical assumption fails—just as conditionalized commands like "if the sauce starts to burn, turn down the heat" don't tell you anything about what to do if the sauce does not start to burn, or as the rules of basketball might not tell you what to do in the unlikely event that the ball becomes stuck on a light fixture. The rules we live by and speak by (particularly where they are informal and tacit, rather than made explicit like the rules of games) are typically open-ended, have areas of indeterminacy, and are open to revision. I will have more to say about the revisability of rules (and the relevance of this to understanding metaphysical debates) in Chapter 8.

The point for the present is that the right lesson to draw from cases of empirical surprise is not that our terms are governed by *no* semantic rules, but rather that such rules are implicitly *conditional* on the assumption that certain empirical conditions hold, and that—as with other rules we live by—the rules are revisable and renegotiable, especially when we encounter empirical surprises that overturn our assumptions. In the face of such discoveries, we are pressed to *rethink what to do*, and this is often more a matter of *decision* than of *discovery*.[16]

By taking that thought seriously, we can accommodate *both* kinds of response to empirical surprises, in a way that the Putnam view cannot. This gives us a more natural and general response to the problem cases than a pure causal theory can. Allowing that there are such implicit rules, even if they are conditional (and open to revision), enables us to avoid the *qua* problem and the reference failure problem that plague pure causal theories. For a rule, say, that, if the relevant (empirical) application conditions are fulfilled, "Kamala Harris" is to be a person name, still enables us to disambiguate and say that (supposing no big empirical surprises) the name does refer to a person—rather than to a mereological sum, a time slice, or any of the other merely *ontologically* alternative candidates for referents. It also enables us to say why (supposing our interests were in tracking a speaker across Iowa) we might in some cases still allow that the term refers (to a robot— provided it's a single trackable object), and in others (if we are interested in identifying viable presidential candidates) we might deny that it refers at all.

The modal normativist is committed to there being a link between metaphysical necessities and semantic rules. But simply being a normativist does not commit one to a particular view about what the semantic rules (or correlated necessities) *are*. The idea that the semantic rules we adopt are often open-textured, so that we must decide what to do in surprising cases, is a welcome addition for a Carnapian like myself. Making this allowance doesn't interfere with the idea that where we think there are metaphysical necessities, they can still be seen as object-language reflections of the semantic rules—however schematic or conditionalized the rules may be. In some cases, if we think

---

[16] This idea is also put forward by Carnap, who writes that the change in meaning of "fish" brought about by zoologists "was not a correction in the field of factual knowledge but a change in the rules of language; [although] this change, it is true, was motivated by factual discoveries" (1950/1962, 6).

that the semantic rules are very open-ended, it may turn out that there is little we can say about what the correlated metaphysical modal facts are. I will return to this idea in Chapter 8, when I discuss the results of normativism for the methods and limits of metaphysics. But from a deflationary point of view, to entail that there may be such limits is a feature, not a bug, of the normativist approach.

4.2 *De Re* Modal Claims

I have argued thus far that the standard externalist arguments do not give us reason to deny that our terms (including our names and natural kind terms) have conceptual content. Instead, they give us good reason to think that the rules governing them often hold *conditional* on certain empirical assumptions, and that these rules are *revisable* in cases in which those assumptions fail.[17] What I aim to show now is that such conditionalized rules are still well suited to the modal normativist's task, and can enable us to handle claims of *de re* and a posteriori modalities on the normativist model.[18]

An important fact that is often left out of view in discussions of *de re* and a posteriori necessities is that the relevant necessity claims are always implicitly *conditionalized*. That is to say, they apply *given* that certain conditions in the world (actually) hold. Kripke's original discussion makes this clear again and again: it is only *given that the queen exists and originated from a certain sperm and egg* that she *necessarily* originated from that sperm and egg (1980, 113); *given that there is a unified natural kind exemplified by observed tigers* that tigers are necessarily of that kind (1980, 121); *given that water is H_2O* that it is necessarily H_2O, and so on. The supposition is often left out, as we go on to simply assume it in further discussions about necessity,

---

[17] If you want to know why allowing that the rules are *revisable* doesn't lead to changes in or contradictory claims about what is necessary, look back to the response to the problems for conventionalism in section 3.4. Note that allowing that certain rules are revisable is emphatically *not* a matter of denying that there are any rules (or any correlated necessities)—just as it would be absurd to suggest that, since the rules of chess have been revised over time, chess has no rules—or that in chess, anything is permitted.

[18] David Braddon-Mitchell considers the option of using similar conditionalized rules to analyze qualia talk. See Braddon-Mitchell (2003, 115ff).

and thus obscure the conditional form. Acknowledging the availability of semantic rules that hold *conditionally* (on assumptions about what facts are *actually* the case) enables us to understand such cases in normativist terms.

For the *de re* modal fact to be captured was really that *if* (or assuming) Kamala Harris is a person, it is necessary that she is a person. And that can be seen, by the normativist's lights, as a reflection of the relevant conditionalized semantic rule. For suppose (as I have argued) that the name "Kamala Harris" is a person name. And take that to involve (in part) its being governed by a conditional rule such as *if (or assuming) the relevant empirical application conditions (for a person name) are fulfilled*, the name is *to refer to* a person (not a mereological sum, a time slice, or any of the other *ontologically* but not *empirically* distinct alternatives). Then we can go on to understand the relevant *de re* necessity claim in normativist terms—as the object-language reflection of a semantic rule:

- Rule: (If the application conditions for "person" are fulfilled, then) "Kamala Harris" is *to refer to* a person.
- Semantic descent: (If the application conditions for "person" are fulfilled, then) Kamala Harris is a person.

And since the consequent is an object-language correlate of a semantic rule (which holds on the condition that the antecedent is fulfilled), we are entitled to add "necessarily," giving us:

- Modal: (If the application conditions for "person" are fulfilled, then) Necessarily, Kamala Harris is a person.

With this understanding of the rules, we can still treat the modal fact—that (assuming Kamala Harris is a person) it is necessary that Kamala Harris is a person—as reflecting a semantic rule (in this case, a conditionalized rule). But we also respect the intuition that it's epistemically possible that the relevant condition "turn out to" have failed. Accepting that rules may be conditionalized in this way doesn't interfere with the fundamental normativist idea that metaphysical modal facts are discoverable by extrapolation from conceptual competence and (in some cases) empirical knowledge (here: knowledge that the application conditions for a person name in fact are fulfilled, so that the term is indeed to be a person name). The normativist may certainly allow that modal knowledge may require empirical knowledge as well as extrapolation from conceptual competence, and still meet her demystifying goals.

Once we allow that names may be governed by rules of this form, we can also show how other *de re* necessities may be understood as object-language reflections of semantic rules. Consider, for example, a *de re* modal claim such as "Necessarily, Michelangelo's 'David' does not survive a drastic change in shape." "David" here can be understood as governed by a rule that—provided the application conditions for "statue" are met (say, a three-dimensional artifact is created by an artisan with suitable intentions in a suitable artistic context), the term is *to apply to* a statue (not a lump, mereological sum of particles, time slice, etc.). Another part of what goes into being distinguished as a name of a certain *sort* is that the name is associated with *co-application conditions* that establish when the name may (or may not) be *reapplied* to *the same individual*. So, since "David" is a statue name, the name is not to be reapplied after a drastic change in shape. Then we can once again account for the relevant *de re* necessity as a consequence of the rules:

- Rule: (If the application conditions for "statue" are fulfilled, then) "David" is *to refer to* a statue (it is a statue name).
- Rule: A statue name is not to be reapplied after a drastic change in shape.
- Consequence: (If the application conditions for "statue" are fulfilled, then) "David" is *not to be reapplied* after a drastic change in shape.
- Semantic descent: (If the application conditions for "statue" are fulfilled, then) David does not survive a drastic change in shape.
- Modal: (If the application conditions for "statue" are fulfilled, then) Necessarily, David doesn't survive a drastic change in shape.

By this route, we can see that the normativist has every prospect of showing central and plausible *de re* necessity claims to be object-language reflections of semantic rules—provided we accept that names and sortal terms are governed by certain kinds of semantic rules.[19] As I have argued, that is something that we have independent reason to accept.

4.3 A Posteriori Modal Claims

In addition to the *de re* necessities discussed so far, a modal normativist must also show how to account for the necessity of such a posteriori modal claims as:

- Necessarily, Alice Walker originated from Willie Lee Walker and Minnie Tallulah Grant.
- Necessarily, water has microstructure H_2O.

The key to seeing these as object-language reflections of semantic rules is again to notice the variety of forms our rules can take. I have argued in Section 4.1 that we should allow that names and kind terms can be governed by conditional rules that (assuming the assumed empirical conditions are fulfilled) the term is *to refer to* a person (or a statue, or a chemical kind, etc.). Part of what is involved in being a name of any of these kinds, however, can also involve being subject to certain rules that are *schematic* and *world-deferential*.

Let us consider the first of these. Let us begin from the idea (argued for in Section 4.1) that a name like "Alice Walker" is governed by the rule that (assuming the relevant application conditions are fulfilled) it is *to refer to* a person, and (to simplify matters) let us suppose the empirical assumptions hold—so that the rule holds that the name is *to refer to* a person. Suppose it is a rule governing person names (given the

---

[19] In an early response to Kripke, Mackie (1974) suggested a response along these lines. There he argues that the fact that *de re* necessities apply to certain individual things and natural kinds "is primarily a feature of the way we think and speak, of how we handle identity in association with counterfactual possibility. They reflect implicit rules for the ascription of identity, for the recognition of the same person or thing or stuff or species, in neutrally described merely possible situations" (1974, 560). "If this is correct," he noted, "then these *de re* modalities need not in themselves offend the empiricist" (1974, 561).

co-application conditions for "person") that any given person name is only to be applied to an individual (that is, applied in a way that entitles us to attribute identity) who derives from the same genetic origin—whatever that origin turns out to be. The rule is thus schematic, waiting to be completed and filled in by empirical information, which might be unknown to competent speakers.[20] Then we can begin from noting that "Alice Walker" is a person name, and that (as a general schematic rule governing person names), a person name applies only to whoever originates from (whatever origin the originally baptized individual has). Then we can see how the necessities are related to the empirical facts and the semantic rules as follows:

- Schematic rule: "Alice Walker" is to be applied only to whoever originates from (whatever origin the originally baptized individual has).
- Empirical fact: The originally baptized individual originated from Willie Lee Walker and Minnie Tallulah Grant.
- Filled-in rule: "Alice Walker" is to be applied only to whoever originated from Willie Lee Walker and Minnie Tallulah Grant.
- Modal: Necessarily, Alice Walker originated from Willie Lee Walker and Minnie Tallulah Grant.

The modal claim can still be seen as an object-language reflection of a semantic rule governing person names; but since it is only complete when filled in with the empirical information, the (filled-in) necessity claim can only be known a posteriori. In this way we can see the necessity claim as not knowable a priori (as indeed it shouldn't be). Nonetheless, it still can be known in a non-mysterious way that combines semantic mastery with straightforward empirical knowledge—and thus meets the goals of my meta-ontological deflationism.

---

[20] The idea that these rules may be schematic comes from Alan Sidelle, who expresses it in somewhat different terms, saying, "we have conventions that specify that *whatever takes a certain value* is to be necessary . . . but that leave it as an empirical matter just what it is that takes this value" (1989, 37).

A similar move can be made to account for "Water necessarily has microstructure H_2O." We can begin by noting that "water" is linked to a rule that (assuming the application conditions for a chemical kind name are fulfilled), "water" is to be a chemical kind name. We can also suppose that (as a general schematic rule governing chemical kind terms), a chemical kind name applies only to whatever has (whatever the microstructure the relevant sample has). Then (likewise assuming the empirical assumption is fulfilled) again we can arrive at the necessary truth via rules and empirical facts as follows:

- Schematic rule: "Water" is to be applied only to whatever has (whatever microstructure the relevant sample has).
- Empirical fact: The relevant sample has the microstructure H_2O.
- Filled-in rule: "Water" is to be applied only to whatever has the microstructure H_2O.
- Modal: Necessarily, water has the microstructure H_2O.

A similar approach can enable us to handle cases of necessary a posteriori identity claims such as "Hesperus is necessarily Phosphorus." In this case, the schematic rule is one that entitles us to move from any identity claim to the inter-applicability of names:

- Schematic rule: Where a = b, any name "a" that properly applies to a may be applied to b.
- Empirical fact: Hesperus = Phosphorus.
- Filled-in rule: "Hesperus" may be applied to Phosphorus.
- Modal: Necessarily, Hesperus is Phosphorus.

By methods like this, we can see that *de re* and a posteriori modal claims are no barrier to seeing metaphysical necessities as object-language reflections of semantic rules (and their consequences)— provided we allow that rules may take many forms, including rules that may be conditionalized, schematic, and world-deferential. The problems thought to arise for earlier views in accounting for such necessities were problems that arose from having too narrow a conception of the forms semantic rules could take.

I have left a lot open here. I have, for example, left it open exactly how we should understand the relevant application conditions, whether they must be fulfilled in some "baptismal" situations or through a critical mass of later uses, and so on. For the point here is not to develop a semantic or meta-semantic theory, but only to say enough to make it clear that those who accept that there are *de re* and a posteriori necessities need not reject a modal normativist approach.

These results also show that a modal normativist needn't and shouldn't be wedded to the idea that all necessities are knowable based solely on semantic competence. We may need empirical knowledge to know that the assumptions on which our rules are conditionalized hold. And given that the rules can be world-deferential, we should expect knowledge of some necessities to also involve knowledge of the worldly facts that feed into the schematic rules. But this does not at all undermine the goal of the modal normativist, of demystifying modal knowledge and the methods of metaphysics. For on this model, modal truths are still knowable without invoking anything mysterious—we just need a combination of semantic competence and ordinary empirical knowledge. In this way, our methods for knowing metaphysical modal facts are rendered non-mysterious, just as I have argued elsewhere (Thomasson 2015) that the methods for knowing existence facts are. (I will give a more detailed account of modal knowledge in Chapter 7.)

4.4 The Contingent A Priori

There is still one other sort of Kripkean case that might cause worry. For cases like those Kripke thought of as "contingent a priori" might be thought to be object-language expressions of semantic rules that are nonetheless not necessary. For example, if we introduce the term "meter" by saying " 'One meter' is to designate the length of stick S," it seems that the person has given a linguistic rule there, so that (on the modal normativist view) we should be entitled to add ."necessarily" to it, and so to conclude "Necessarily, stick S is one meter long." Yet Kripke (1980, 54–56) gives good reasons for thinking that it is contingent that stick S is one meter long: if it were subjected to heat or various other stresses, its length would be different, and its length *could* have been different, even at the time of the linguistic ceremony. And that seems right.

The trouble here is with the ambiguous way in which the rule is stated. The proper rule, it seems (as Kripke brings out), is one that introduces "one meter" to rigidly designate a certain *length*. And so the proper way to formulate the rule (put ambiguously before) is that *whatever length stick S actually has (now)*, "one meter" is to (always and under any suppositions) designate *that length*. From this more careful statement of the rule, we only get that it is necessary that *that length* is one meter (not that *that stick* is one meter). And that seems the right necessity to get.

4.5 Conclusion

Views that aim to understand modal truths by appeal to semantic rules have long been thought to be threatened by cases of *de re* and a posteriori necessities. I have argued, however, that properly understood, the modal normativist approach is not threatened by such cases. For it can easily accommodate them by accepting that there are more kinds and forms of semantic rules than has often been thought, including rules for names and sortal terms, and rules that may be conditionalized, schematic, and world-deferential. And we have independent reason to accept that.

Many have thought that *de re* and a posteriori necessities give reason for thinking of modal facts or properties or essences as discoverable features of our world—features it might take special metaphysical investigation or intuition to discover. But if the above is correct, then such modal truths do not at all support this view or the mystifying approach to metaphysics that has come with it.

5

Other Objections
to Modal Normativism

The key features of the modal normativist view laid out thus far include a functional thesis and a meaning thesis. The functional thesis is that the function of modal claims is not to describe or track features of reality (of this world or other possible worlds), but rather to give perspicuous ways of formulating rules and permissions, and of making explicit our ways of reasoning with and from rules. In the case of specifically *metaphysical* modal claims, I have argued, the rules at issue are *semantic* rules. The meaning thesis is that the meanings of the metaphysical modal terms "necessary" and "possible" can be given in terms of inferential rules, including the introduction rule (Rule I) that entitles us to move from an object-language expression of an actual semantic rule p (or logical consequence thereof), to infer: Necessarily p. The functional thesis and the meaning thesis are connected, given that the rules at issue are rules that enable these terms to fulfill their characteristic functions.

While I have dealt with hard cases involving *de re* and a posteriori necessities in Chapter 4, there are also other putative counterexamples to modal normativism. Since the modal normativist holds that basic necessary truths are object-language correlates of semantic rules, counterexamples to the view take one of two forms: either they identify (apparent) semantic rules that do not seem to have corresponding necessities, or they identify apparent necessities that don't seem correlated with any semantic rules. I will treat apparent counterexamples of each of these forms in turn. Thereafter I will turn to deeper objections that allege that, in virtue of its reliance on rules, the view is implicitly circular.

Norms and Necessity. Amie L. Thomasson, Oxford University Press (2020). © Oxford University Press.
DOI: 10.1093/oso/9780190098193.001.0001

5.1 Putative Counterexamples

5.1.1 Rules without Necessities?

There are various cases in which it seems that we have an object-language expression of a linguistic rule, but where it seems that we are not licensed to add "necessarily" to it, or where doing so would not leave us with a truth. So, for example, "I am here now" may seem like an object-language expression of a linguistic rule. Gillian Russell (2008) argues that it is analytic, since it is guaranteed to be true, whenever it is uttered, in virtue of the meanings of its constituent expressions. Yet clearly it is not necessary that I am here now—in this case we seem not licensed to add "necessarily" on, and if we did we would not get a truth. I could have been on campus if I had arranged to meet with my students now, or in Barcelona if I had accepted that conference invitation.

But on reflection this sort of case does not present a counterexample to the view that basic claims of metaphysical necessity are object-language expressions of semantic rules. For "I am here now" is not a *claim*, in my terms, at all; it is a context-sensitive sentence that may be used to make different claims in different contexts. The claim being made in this context is that Amie Thomasson is in Vermont on October 1, and that is most certainly not an object-language expression of any semantic rules. As a result, we are not entitled to add "necessarily" onto it, and if we did, we would not get a true necessity claim.[1]

---

[1] Similarly, "All actual professors are professors" seems analytic, yet it is not necessary that I, Peter Lewis, Susanna Siegel, and the rest be professors: any of us could have become accountants or doctors, or died in infancy. Put in my terms, these seem to be object-language correlates of semantic rules and yet not to be claims to which we can make this explicit by adding "necessarily."

Kirk Ludwig defends a view similar to mine, expressing it as the view that "necessary truths" (on the fundamental understanding of "necessary") are conceptual truths ("De Re Necessities," in progress, 7). And he provides an admirable response to such difficulties. Regarding "All actual professors are professors," Ludwig writes, "actual" does not serve as an adjective. Instead, it is a term with the function of shifting the attached noun to make it purely extensional (leaving aside the intension). If we understand it in that way, then we should take it as making the claim: "That individual and that one and that one are professors," which is clearly neither analytic nor necessary (8), and which, in my terms, is clearly not an object-language expression of any semantic rules.

5.1.2 Necessities without Rules?

The more formidable range of challenges for modal normativism involves cases in which there seem to be basic claims of metaphysical necessity, without any obvious correlated semantic rules. If these modal claims cannot be seen as object-language expressions of semantic rules (or consequences thereof), the threat arises again that we must see them as describing (or attempting to describe) modal features of the world. Several different sorts of case arise. In Chapter 4 I have shown how we can handle *de re* and a posteriori modal claims. Here I will consider cases involving claims of necessary existence, or of necessities holding without their being stated in language at all. Treating these in turn will give a far better idea of how the normativist view handles not just the basic claims of metaphysical necessity we have treated so far, but a whole range of modal claims.

5.1.3 Necessary Existents

One sort of case involves claims about (alleged) necessary existents—for example, some might object that "God exists" is necessarily true, but doesn't express a semantic rule. Now I don't think that *is* a true claim, so I shouldn't be obliged to account for its truth. My suspicion is that those who *do* think of it as true are thinking of necessity in a somewhat different sense than the sort of metaphysical necessity at issue here—something more like nomological necessity (that there must have been a God the creator). That question is left open by my account of metaphysical necessities.

An interesting contrast is with the case of other (alleged) necessary existents. Some objectors think the same point can be made without theistic presuppositions. And so, for example, it is said, "Necessarily, numbers [or sets or properties or other abstracta] exist" is true, and yet (the objection goes) *surely* it can't be analytic, or a matter of semantic rules, that anything exists (to think otherwise, it is often said, is to take the bizarre view that our adopting certain semantic rules could bring things into existence).[2]

---

[2] Thanks to Nick Stang for raising this sort of objection.

But my approach can actually handle these cases (of the necessary existence of numbers, sets, properties, and the like) very well—lending credence to the idea that something different is going on in the God case (that it may be something more like an alleged nomological necessity at issue). Addressing the claim of the necessary existence of various abstracta also makes it clearer why it is advantageous to combine modal normativism with the easy approach to ontology I have defended elsewhere (Thomasson 2015). For the deflationary easy approach to ontology is built on the idea that the introduction rules for terms like "number" guarantee that the terms introduced refer—regardless of any empirical facts in the world. For we can make transformations from, for example, "the cups and the saucers are equinumerous" to "the number of cups equals the number of saucers," from which we can draw the conclusion that there is a number (see Hale and Wright 2001). But we can equally draw this conclusion from the negation of the original sentence: from "the cups and saucers are not equinumerous" we can infer "the number of cups is not equal to the number of saucers," and conclude again that there is a number. A central point of the deflationary meta-ontological approach is that there *are* semantic rules—in this case, rules that serve to introduce new noun terms such as "number" into our vocabulary—that guarantee that the terms introduced refer, regardless of any empirical facts.[3] It is those rules, of course, with which the object-language expression "Necessarily, numbers exist" is correlated.

I have argued that we can, after all, see the necessities expressed in these claims of necessary existence as object-language reflections of a consequence of the semantic rules. However, that is not to say that our adoption of the relevant semantic rules *brings anything into existence.* No: according to those very rules themselves, there would be numbers even if there were no semantic rules adopted anywhere (for, after all, the rules guarantee reference independent of all empirical facts). Where we can get these sorts of inferences, from conceptual truths via

---

[3] Those concerned that there can be no such guarantee, given worries about magic, the bad company objection, or a variety of other problems are referred to Thomasson (2015), where I address these and other common concerns.

the rules of use that introduce the terms, to the existence of abstract entities such as numbers, sets, or properties, we can conclude that the existence of the relevant entities is not contingent on any empirical facts of the world—in that familiar sense, it is necessary. But the fact that it is necessary that the relevant entities (numbers, sets, properties, etc.) exist is nonetheless a reflection of the rules of use that introduce such terms to our vocabulary.

5.1.4 Modal Demonstratives

Another case in which there are alleged to be necessities without corresponding semantic rules is when we don't use a name or general term to refer, but merely ostensively point to something, saying, for example "That [thing] has its shape essentially." What is said in uttering this may, the objection goes, be necessarily true, but there is no semantic rule with which it is correlated (for "thing" is not governed by any semantic rule that ensures that co-reference requires shape constancy). But as I have argued elsewhere (Thomasson 2007), we can only single out an object in thought or reference to the extent that we associate the relevant term (be it a description, name, or demonstrative) with certain application and co-application conditions to disambiguate whether, and if so to what, the term refers (though, as noted in Chapter 4, these may be rules that are in effect *given the assumption* that certain empirical conditions hold). An utterance such as "*that* has its shape essentially" is true only if "that" decisively refers to something that has shape as an essential property—say, to a statue rather than a lump. But it only decisively refers to a statue *rather than* a lump if "that [thing]" is associated (perhaps conditionally) with co-application conditions that disambiguate the statue rather than the lump as *to be* the referent. (Causal relations alone can't disambiguate, as the speaker is equally causally connected to the statue and the lump.) So here again there is a corresponding semantic rule implicit in enabling the speaker to single out the relevant entity (as she must if what she says is to be clearly true), and it is that rule that the object-language claim "That [thing] has its shape essentially" reflects.

5.2 Circularity Worries

The goal, as I mentioned at the outset, is to find a way of understanding true claims about metaphysical necessity as reflections of semantic rules and their consequences. The most basic circularity worries emerge as worries about whether the semantic rules themselves have to be understood in terms of metaphysical modality, rendering the account circular.

Some might argue that we must presuppose a more serious, explanatory sort of modality at some level.[4] For consider the semantic rules, which (according to the normativist) are reflected in our object-language claims of metaphysical necessity. Are they simply arbitrary, or did they *have* to be this way? If we take the first option, the accusation goes, the normativist view seems to be too much like old-fashioned conventionalism. For it seems to leave us with the views that the basic necessary truths could have been different if we had adopted different semantic rules, and that the rules we have are completely arbitrary (when in fact they seem quite natural). On the other hand, if we say "no, the rules *have to* be this way," then we seem to be building modality in on the ground floor after all. The picture the critic seems to want at this stage is that the semantic rules *have to be* that way: that we have the semantic rules we do *for a reason*, namely to enable us to track the modal boundaries in the world. But in that case we must invoke the modal features to explain why we have the rules that we have, rather than starting from rules to (ultimately) explain object-language talk of modal features: the direction of explanation goes the other way up, and we must after all presuppose an explanatory modal realism, and a view of modal talk as describing those modal features of reality.

When I say that basic metaphysical necessities are object-language reflections of semantic rules, however, this is not tied to the idea that those rules are merely *conventional or arbitrary*. It is entirely open to the modal normativist to hold that at least some of our concepts are

---

[4] Thanks to Edward Halper for raising the objection in this form. Another circularity objection was raised by Jonathan Schaffer: you say we are to understand metaphysical modalities in terms of rules. But rules must be understood as telling you what to do at all possible worlds, so we again have to presuppose possible worlds in explaining metaphysical modality.

governed by basic rules that are innate or natural, and are built in for creatures like us. It is, of course, an empirical issue whether any such basic concepts are built in to human beings or other species, and if so what they are and what rules govern them—but there is no reason the normativist must deny that some such rules may "come naturally" and thus not be "merely conventional" or arbitrary in a sense that would see them as the products of groundless choice. Normativism is not conventionalism.

In fact, good psychological evidence has been amassed for the idea that there are certain basic concepts that are the products of natural selection, and are tied to what Susan Carey calls "core cognition" (2009, 71–72). Carey identifies these basic concepts as including concepts for middle-sized objects, agents, causation, and quantity (449). All of these concepts, Carey argues, are generated by innate input analyzers, which act on perceptual input *in accord with rules* built in as a product of evolution.[5] The object concept, for example, involves rules in which tracking spatiotemporal continuity plays a key role in object individ-uation and identification, as do features like perceived rigidity and cohesiveness. Thus, here we can see certain rules for identifying the presence of an object and for re-identifying the same object over time as built in to contemporary people via a long evolutionary process. For, as Carey writes: "All the work to date suggests that the core cognition of objects exhibited by young infants has a long evolutionary history" shared with cottontop tamarins (with whom our common ancestor reaches back more than 100 million years) and our closer relatives, the Rhesus macaques (96). If that's right, then many of the modal judgments we make, verbally or nonverbally, about object identity, continuity, and number may be seen as reflections of these rules: rules that are not arbitrary or conventional, but built in as the products of a long evolutionary process.

The idea that some concepts are more basic than others, and that some rules (and with them certain concepts) may be built in as the

---

[5] Thus, we shouldn't think of basic experience as merely involving perceptual primitives, and on that basis learning and constructing representations of objects, number, agency, or causality. Indeed, she says that there is no known proposal for how this learning could work (456).

product of evolution is certainly open to the modal normativist—whose claim is not that these are arbitrary, merely conventional, or anything like that, but rather that what is explanatorily basic is rules, and that our talk of modal features in the world is an object-language reflection of these basic rules.[6]

But if such basic concepts are built in for us as a product of evolution (the critic might ask), doesn't that give us reason to think that they are built in *for a reason*—that they track those categories and modal features of the world that *there really are*, leading us back again to an explanatory form of modal realism?

There is no need, however, to presuppose explanatory realism about modality to accept the view that natural selection is responsible for the most basic set of rules underlying our conceptual system. Natural selection doesn't care a bit about correspondence to a modal or categorical reality. It cares about the *success* of the organism: success at surviving, success at reproducing. All of this can be understood in perfectly pragmatic terms that simply appeal to the fact that these rules are very *useful* to have—more useful than rules that would track simply by property continuity or location or other ranges of perceptual features. The evolutionary usefulness of certain core category concepts no more provides evidence for a kind of explanatory modal realism than the usefulness of color perception in enabling us to avoid dangerous snakes and detect tasty fruit provides evidence for a sort of color realism that would say we have experiences with these phenomenal qualities because these qualities as we experience them are part of the world.

Ah, but if the normativist accepts that, given the way we evolved, we *had to* have basic concepts something like these to survive—even if she rejects the idea that it is because they reflect the true modal properties of the world—aren't we still bringing in a deep metaphysical necessity? For don't we then say that, given the laws of natural selection (perhaps plus facts about the environment and the mutations that occurred), we *had to have* concepts with these basic rules?

---

[6] One worry that might be raised is whether evolutionarily built-in rules can be normative. Clearly they can if we can treat evolution as involving norms. Even without that claim, if we retain and accept these evolutionarily built-in rules (or regularities) and tie them to overtly normative linguistic rules, rather than overriding them, they will attain normative status.

To the extent that laws are involved in making this sort of claim, they are not laws expressing metaphysical necessities, but rather *scientific laws* regarding the causal relation between possessing certain types of conceptual systems and surviving in various environments. What, then, can we say about claims regarding *causal* or *nomological* necessities?[7]

Understanding claims of causal or nomological necessity (such as we think of as being articulated in scientific laws) raises a different set of issues. First, (as I argue in Chapter 7), questions about how we could know claims about what's physically possible or necessary—or, more broadly, about how we could come to know dispositional or empirical counterfactual claims—do not seem to be as epistemologically intractable as questions of how we could come to know *metaphysical* modal truths.[8] So there would still be some progress, even if the view developed here about claims of *metaphysical* necessity did require a descriptive account of claims of *physical* necessity. It is beyond the scope of this book to adjudicate among competing views of physical necessities. But it is worth noting that there are available and plausible views of physical necessity claims that do not treat them as descriptive— indeed, non-descriptivist views of modality were first developed to address the status of scientific laws.[9] As I mentioned earlier, one attraction of normativism is the hope of unifying our understanding of different sorts of modal claim as all reflecting (different sorts) of norm. While metaphysical modalities are reflections of semantic or conceptual rules, the natural correlate view would take the nomological necessities expressed in scientific laws to reflect norms of reasoning on the basis of empirical evidence, or something along those lines. There is not space here to evaluate the motivations and prospects for such a

---

[7] Thanks to Michaela McSweeney for pressing me to say more about nomological necessity here—though I am sure I still have not said enough to address all of her concerns.

[8] Empirical approaches to understanding how we can come to know empirically grounded counterfactual and dispositional claims have been developed, for example, in recent work by Vetter (2015), Williamson (2007), Bueno and Shalkowski (2015), Leon (2017), and Roca-Royes (2017). I return to this in Chapter 7.

[9] For related views, see Sellars (1958), Brandom (2008, Chapter 4), Williams (2010, 323–29), and Price (1996). Compare also Ryle's early view that statements of scientific laws serve as inference tickets (licensing possessors to move from asserting some factual statements to others [1949, 121]), and Ramsey's (1929) arguments that causal laws express an inference we are prepared to make.

view, but others have developed important views in the vicinity, views that do not think of scientific laws as aiming to *describe* necessities. For example, as Michael Williams writes, "On a Sellarsian approach, causal talk is a special kind of normative talk" (2011, 324–25). If we take a normativist approach, we can, for example, roughly take causal laws as norms for making empirical inferences based on empirical evidence—not as descriptions of some sort of special modal properties in the world, or as universal generalizations requiring truthmakers (see Ramsey 1929). Nonetheless, where the function of a scientific law is to serve in forming generalizations that are predictive and explanatory, we can see that such norms for making empirical inferences are not at all arbitrary, but are rather based on empirical information regarding what sorts of inference succeed, which fail, and which inferential rules serve well in a general predictive and explanatory theory.[10] Exactly how to work out the details is beyond the scope of this book, but as long as some such treatment of claims of scientific laws is defensible, there is no need for the normativist to appeal to deep metaphysical *or* physical necessities in order to hold that the rules governing certain basic concepts are not accidental. In sum, then, it is entirely open to the normativist to embrace the empirical evidence that there are some basic concepts, complete with rules for individuation, that are built in for us, while denying that we have these rules because they map the metaphysical modal facts.

The move to avoid arbitrariness by appealing to the naturalness of certain built-in basic concepts, however, clearly won't work across the board. For it is just implausible that many of our social and culturally local concepts are built in. Clearly a great many more concepts are built from the most basic ones: concepts that are tightly tied to our linguistic sortals and their particular rules, and that vary across different linguistic and cultural groups. How can we respond to the arbitrariness worry in these cases? Well, for starters, the worry seems far less urgent.

---

[10] I develop parallel arguments elsewhere (Thomasson 2020) that our natural kind concepts are not arbitrary, but rather may be empirically justified given their purpose of serving in our explanatory and predictive theories. For adopting them may be justified by appeal to *empirical* evidence that some concepts (say, fish and dolphin) work better than others (say, sea creature) in supporting predictive and explanatory generalizations. See also Carnap (1950/1962, 6).

In many of these cases, it doesn't seem out of place to allow that there is some arbitrariness in rules—for example, for whether this counts as the same nation as that (is Latvia the same nation now as it was in 1920, before the period of more than 50 years of Soviet [and German] rule?) or whether this is the same literary work or festival as that. It does not seem terribly plausible to think that these terms are designed to "match" modal boundaries discoverable deep in the world. Instead, we seem to adopt precise rules as we need them to adjudicate legal or political disputes, or for other practical purposes.

Nonetheless, even in these cases, we needn't treat the rules that govern our particular sortal terms (and thus that are reflected in basic modal truths regarding the objects if any picked out by those sortals) as completely arbitrary, even if we don't say that they are designed to map the modal features of reality.

Considering the rules of games again may help: it would be absurd to suggest that the rules of checkers, say, are designed to map the facts about what really is obligatory and permissible in the game (facts that make the rules true). Yet even if we don't treat the rules as trying to map the facts, and correct to the extent that they do so, we also needn't say that the rules are completely arbitrary. It is not arbitrary, for example, that one player is permitted to control all of the red pieces and the other all of the black pieces rather than, say, one being given nine red pieces and three black, while the other has the converse. That would be confusing, and hard to track who was entitled to move which pieces—in short, it would be a disaster from a *pragmatic* point of view. Nor is it arbitrary that the players alternate moves rather than, say, the black player being permitted to make seven moves for every move the red player makes—that would lead to such accusations of unfairness that no one would want to play such a game, so such a game would not be taken up and survive in our culture. In short, that, too, would be a pragmatic disaster. Similarly, the rules defining what counts as a foul in basketball, football, or soccer are not arbitrary, but rather are largely designed with such pragmatic goals in mind as limiting player injuries.

So we can respond to the arbitrariness worry for such cases by saying that the rules governing our concepts and terms are not arbitrary to the extent that adopting these rules rather than their rivals is of *pragmatic* use to us. It may, for example, be of pragmatic use to individuate artifacts in part by their shape (rather than their color or location), since this is so often crucial to preserving their proper function (which is what we care about), while individuating mere lumps by quantity of matter rather than shape or color reflects their role in our practices of buying and selling basic materials—where we do not care about the shape. I have elsewhere (Thomasson 2020) worked to develop a pragmatic approach to understanding conceptual choice in a way that makes it clear that it is a false dilemma to think that such choices either must be determined by "metaphysical facts" or must be considered completely arbitrary.

5.3 Does It Rely on a Heavyweight Understanding of Logical Necessity?

A final line of objection puts pressure on us to get a unified account. The idea is that the normativist's story relies on a more basic understanding of logical necessity. But if we must make use of a heavyweight realist conception of logical necessities, the thought is, that will pretty much undo whatever good we might have hoped to gain by adopting a normativist conception of metaphysical necessities. The worry may be raised in various ways.

One way it may come up is with an extension of the earlier arbitrariness worry. For, the critic might say, even if the appeal to what is natural for creatures like us provides a route by which we might deny that the rules governing certain basic concepts are accidental or arbitrary, that is not enough to justify a stronger feeling that at least certain rules—not those governing our basic concepts, but those governing logic and mathematics—are non-optional in a stronger sense. For such rules, the critic may say, are not just built-in for us, but are obligatory for *any* sort of creature or thinker, *because they match the logical or mathematical necessities of the world.*

The worry about whether we must presuppose a heavyweight realist account of logical modality may arise even more directly, however. For our normativist account of metaphysical necessity relies on a notion of *logical consequence*—since, as I have argued above, the concept of metaphysical necessity is governed (in part) by the following introduction rule:

> I: If p is an object-language expression of an actual semantic rule (*or a logical consequence of actual semantic rules*), then you are entitled to introduce: *Necessarily p*, regardless of any subjunctive suppositions.

As a result, if we had to understand a relation of logical consequence as describing a modal relation holding among propositions (that: necessarily, if the premises are true the conclusion is true; or: that it is impossible for the premises to be true and the conclusion false), we would be requiring that certain modal relations hold in the world as a precondition for some claims of metaphysical necessity to be true. Worse still, if we understood logical consequence in terms of models, and models in terms of possible worlds, we would end up saying that the conclusion is a logical consequence of the premises if every possible world in which the premises are true is a world in which the conclusion is true: thus, at least on the face of it, understanding logical consequence in terms of possible worlds.[11] It would be far preferable to find a way to understand logical consequence (and logical necessity generally) that does not treat claims of logical necessity as attempts to describe modal relations among (Platonistically conceived) propositions, nor as functioning to describe possible worlds.

The thought that a normativist account of metaphysical modality would be no good unless we could give a parallel account for logical necessity is premature, however. For the target here was to understand debates in metaphysics concerned with metaphysical modalities. From an epistemological point of view, it is those that were most mysterious and contested. We have a far better idea how to go about answering questions about what is logically necessary or possible (at least given a particular logical system), using the methods of logic. So, even if we could only work out a normativist view for metaphysical modality, it would be of great use in helping resolve the epistemological problems

---

[11] I will return in Chapter 6 to discuss how a normativist may, in any case, come to understand possible worlds talk as arising from hypostatizations out of modal truths.

specific to metaphysical modal claims, and the corresponding problems in the methods of metaphysics.

But in fact I think that the prospects for extending a broadly normativist approach to cover claims of logical necessity are very good. The modal normativist needn't deny that in some sense or other we *have to have* at least certain of these rules—whether this is given the laws of nature, or in order to best fulfill certain pragmatic goals, or in order to count as a thinker or reasoner at all. All that is required is that these claims of necessity be understood in the same way all claims of necessity are on the normativist view: not as attempts to *report on* the modal facts of the world, but rather as implicitly *normative*. That is not circularity but thoroughgoing consistency.

Fortunately, there are plausible approaches to logical necessity that take that normativist route: inferentialist approaches such as those developed by Greg Restall (2005) and David Ripley (2013). On an inferentialist approach, those statements we take as logically necessary may be understood as ways of making explicit norms regarding assertion and denial. The inferentialist treats the meanings of our terms, including our logical terms, as "to be explained in terms of which inferences are valid" (Ripley 2013, 140). The bilateralist form of inferentialism, which I will be particularly concerned with here, in turn understands the validity of inferences as a matter of norms governing assertions and denials (Ripley 2013, 140). We can read a valid argument as "constraining a pattern of acceptance and rejection" (Restall 2005, 5). So, for example, $X \vdash Y$ tells us that it would be a mistake to assert X and deny Y; in Ripley's terminology, it tells us that asserting X and denying Y is "out of bounds" (2013, 141). In these terms, the meanings of the logical constants can be laid out as conditions governing assertions and denials, for example, we can explain the fact that it is valid to argue from: A, B to: A&B in terms of the meaning of "&," governed by the rule: If it would be a mistake to accept X, accept A, and accept B, and yet deny Y, then it would be a mistake to accept X, accept A&B, and yet deny Y (Restall 2012).

Restall (2005) shows how we can, using the sequent calculus developed by Gerhard Gentzen, understand logical consequence in terms of constraints on combinations of assertions and denials—regardless of whether one is using the notion of logical consequence in a classical or non-classical logic. Such a treatment of logical consequence is precisely what we need here, since it treats claims of logical consequence as expressions of norms regarding what may be (jointly) accepted and rejected—not as reports of relations among propositions or features of the world (its logical structure).

To say that it's logically necessary that if the premises of an argument are true then the conclusion is true, is just to say that the conclusion is a logical consequence of the premises, and so this treatment of logical consequence also gives us a normativist way of understanding logical necessities. A claim that it is a logical necessity that, if the premises are true, then the conclusion is true, on this model, is not a *description* of some feature of this world or of all possible worlds. Instead, it expresses a *norm* regarding acceptance and rejection: that one mustn't accept the premises and reject the conclusion. To say that a given proposition, all on its own, is logically necessary, can be understood as saying that, regardless of what else one accepts, one mustn't reject it. And, of course, as I have suggested, such norms need not be treated as merely conventional or optional.[12] I will leave that question open, simply noting that it is compatible with the normativist approach to take at least certain central norms as non-optional, perhaps even as constitutive of what it is to count as a thinker or reasoner at all.[13] As Restall and Beall describe it (without endorsing it), on such a view we may "take the formal rules of logic to be *constitutive norms* for thought, regardless of its subject matter" (2005/2016, section 2).

In short, as long as some broadly inferentialist treatment of logical consequence and of the related notion of logical necessity is available, there is no need to worry if the normativist account of metaphysical necessity presupposes an understanding of logical consequence. Nor need we worry that we must import a metaphysical understanding of logical necessity that will undermine the value of getting a normativist

---

[12] Nor need the norms be treated as "immediately [*coming*] *from* mind-and-language-independent reality" as McSweeney (2018, 3) describes a view (without endorsing it).

[13] And that's a good thing, too. Robert Barnard (2013) argues that we must take logical norms seriously—as they must be understood as categorical (not hypothetical), and cannot be reduced to convention. For, he argues, understanding logical norms as hypothetical itself presupposes their being categorical. Fortunately, this is an insight we can preserve without having to think of these logical norms descriptively.

treatment of metaphysical necessity. Quite the contrary: the availability of an inferentialist treatment of logical necessity makes a normativist approach to modality seem more plausible as part of an across-the-board understanding of modal claims.[14]

5.4 Conclusion

We come now to the end of the defensive portion of the book. Since the modal normativist view is contentious, and has hardly been on the radar in recent decades, it will no doubt continue to attract novel criticisms. I hope here to have shown at least that it can avoid the classic problems thought to bring down its historical predecessors, as well as to show how the view can handle the "hard cases" and apparent counterexamples that have helped keep non-descriptivist views off the table. If modal normativism can accommodate all of these cases and remain standing, we stand to gain very substantial ontological, epistemological, and methodological advantages.

Now we can turn to the fun part: showing not that such a view is defensible, but rather why one might want it. The ontological, epistemological, and methodological advantages I will showcase in Chapters 6, 7 and 8 give us the central reasons for taking seriously the normativist approach to modality as an attractive rival to the heavyweight metaphysical mainstream.

---

[14] There are also other factors favoring an inferentialist (rather than a descriptivist) approach to understanding logical consequence and validity. As Yablo (2000, sections IX–X) puts it, if we think of validity in descriptivist terms (as in absence of counter-models), we seem to leave "hostages to metaphysical fortune." "An argument's validity-status would seem to be a conceptually necessary fact about it. Surely we don't want the validity of arguments to be held hostage to a brute logical contingency like what model-like entities happen to exist!"

6

Ontological Advantages

In Chapter 1 I argued that there is a rather lost history of non-descriptivist approaches to modality that seem promising, and seem to have been unnecessarily abandoned. In Chapter 2 I tried to lay out in as clear terms as possible a contemporary non-descriptivist view of modality, under the name "modal normativism," and to show how it understands metaphysical modal claims, and in Chapters 3, 4, and 5 I responded to some of the main objections raised against views along these lines.

Over the next three chapters, I aim to highlight the tremendous potential importance and attractions of the view. There are three principal interrelated attractions of the modal normativist position: ontological, epistemological, and methodological. I begin here by trying to clarify its ontological consequences and advantages.

6.1 Modal Facts and Properties

Non-descriptivist views about a range of discourse are often presented as a form of anti-realism about the entities in question. Accordingly, the main advantage of such views is often presented as the *ontological* advantage of not having to say that there are such (weird) entities. Moral expressivism, for example, is sometimes motivated by the thought that there *are no* moral facts or properties in the world to describe.[1] Modal conventionalism is often presented as the view that

---

[1] It is *not* so motivated by Blackburn, however. For despite his use of the label "quasi-realism" (which might seem to suggest that something is held back from "real" realism), Blackburn is always clear that his quasi-realist view of ethical discourse does *not* mean defending our right to talk "as if" there are moral truths, when in fact there really aren't any. Instead, he insists that there isn't any coherent conception of moral truths (or necessities) except one on which it is true that there *are* moral truths and necessities.

Norms and Necessity. Amie L. Thomasson, Oxford University Press (2020). © Oxford University Press. DOI: 10.1093/oso/9780190098193.001.0001

modal facts or properties are not a real part of the world at all—Alan Sidelle, for example, glosses conventionalism as the view that "there is no necessity 'out there'" (1989, xi). Some present this as a great advantage: that we needn't posit these strange entities. Others treat it as a problem. Some critics, for example, object that the view implicitly denies that there are any modal facts or features of the world, and that this leads to troubles—either the straightforward absurdity of thinking that there just are no facts of the matter about what sorts of change a person or statue can or cannot survive, or even worse conclusions that there are no objects in the world. For, as Michael Rea (2002) and Crawford Elder (2004) have argued, for there to be, say, a person or a statue, is for there to be something capable of surviving some kinds of change but not others. As Rea puts it, to think that "there is such a thing as Socrates but literally *no fact at all* about whether Socrates could survive a trip to Macedonia or a trip through a meat grinder . . . is patently absurd" (2002, 82). As a result, being an anti-realist about modal facts or properties might also be thought to threaten realism about ordinary material objects.

However, the form of modal non-descriptivism developed here is not committed to or motivated by the idea that there are no modal facts or properties in the world. Instead, it is best put as a view about *what it is for there to be* modal facts or properties, and *what we are doing* in attributing them to the world. It is natural to develop the view in this way by combining the modal normativist view with the easy approach to ontology that I have argued for elsewhere across the board (Thomasson 2015). When the two are combined, we can see that modal normativism is a form of realism. Not a reduced or pseudo form of realism, but what I have elsewhere (Thomasson 2015, Chapter 3) called "simple realism." The simple realist view holds that there are modal facts and properties *in the only sense that these terms make sense*—in the only sense in which it makes sense to raise, and answer, the question of their existence at all. (But it does not, like certain

As he puts it for the latter case: "What then is the mistake in describing such a philosophy . . . as holding that 'we talk as if there are necessities when really there are none'? It is the failure to notice that . . . [we] . . . need allow no sense to what follows the 'as if' *except* one in which it is true" (1993, 57). In this way, his approach is entirely in harmony with that developed here.

more heavyweight realist views, take them to be "explanatory posits"—
they are not posited as part of a "best total theory" nor in order, say, to
"explain" what makes our modal claims true.) The deflationary meta-
ontological view I have defended at length (Thomasson 2015) holds
(following Schiffer 2003 and others) that we can derive singular terms
referring to properties and facts by way of trivial inferences from uncontroversial truths that involve no such singular terms. So, from "The
rug is blue" we can move redundantly to "the rug has the property of
blueness" and thus acquire reference to the property of blueness—
licensing us to say that there is such a property.

Similarly, easy arguments enable us to restate *modal* truths redundantly in claims that entail the existence of *modal* facts or properties.
All modal truths p may be restated redundantly as "It is a fact that p."
So, from "Necessarily, all bachelors are men" we may move to: "It is a
fact that it is necessary that all bachelors are men," and then to "there
is a modal fact." (One might want to require for the move from "p" to
"it's a fact that p" to be legitimate that we treat denials of p as genuinely contradicting assertions of p. So, for example, we might hesitate
to move from "strawberry ice cream is best" to "it is a fact that strawberry ice cream is best," if the first was an expression of preference that
we would not consider in real conflict with another person's uttering
"No, strawberry isn't best; chocolate is." But modal claims easily meet
this higher standard, and so again there is no barrier making the inference from a modal truth to talk of the modal facts.)[2]

Similarly, from a *de re* necessary claim, such as "Obama is necessarily human," we can move to "Obama has the property of necessarily being human" and thus assert that there is a modal property.[3]
So the normativist, as I see it, should say that there are modal facts and
properties—not in some reduced sense, but rather in the only sense
terms like "fact" and "property" have, a sense in part constituted by the
rules that introduce such noun terms into our vocabulary.

So understood, the deflationary meta-ontological approach leads
to a straightforward first-order simple realism about the properties
and facts in question. As Gibbard aptly writes of Blackburn's view,

---

[2] Thanks to Mark Warren for raising this issue.
[3] We can derive talk about essences in the same way.

"I suspect that the upshot is a realism not 'quasi' but sophisticated" (1996, 331).

6.2 Possible Worlds

I have argued that modal normativism results in a simple realism about modal facts and properties—but what about possible worlds? Talk of possible worlds was introduced in developments of possible worlds semantics, which proved useful in disambiguating modal talk, avoiding scope ambiguities, and precisely characterizing logical consequence. David Lewis showed that quantifying over possible worlds brought crucial philosophical advantages—for only by quantifying over worlds can we express claims of global supervenience (e.g., of the form "no two worlds could differ in their moral properties without differing in their natural properties") or speak of different *ways in which* something might be possible (e.g., "there are three ways we could have won the game last night") (1986, 13–17).

Lewis infamously suggested that we should interpret modal operators as quantifying over possible worlds (1986, 20)—where his possible worlds were supposed to be concrete worlds "like" our actual world, but causally and spatiotemporally isolated. It would, however, be a mistake (too easily encouraged by the terminology and by Lewis's own ways of presenting his view) to think of possible worlds talk as serving a function analogous to planet or galaxy talk—of tracking distant objects and reporting on their status. As Arthur Prior put it,

> To say that a state of affairs obtains is just to say that something is the case; to say that something is a possible state of affairs is just to say that something could be the case; and to say that something is the case "in" a possible state of affairs is just to say that the thing in question would necessarily be the case if that state of affairs obtained, i.e. if something else were the case . . . We understand "truth in states of affairs" because we understand "necessarily" not vice versa.
>
> (2003, 243–44)

To treat possible worlds as ways of modeling modal logic is not "to say that this logical structure is *explained by* modal models" (Restall 2012, 1612). Nor is to allow possible worlds talk thereby to treat it as describing, tracking, or reporting on other concrete worlds "like ours." In Kripke's famous phrase: possible worlds are "not *discovered* by powerful telescopes" (1972, 44). And so, we face the question Mackie insisted on, "what are we up to when we talk about [possible worlds]?" (1973, 90).

Looked at more closely, possible worlds talk lends itself perfectly to a functional analysis like that given in Chapter 2. What modal logicians showed, and Lewis added to, was that adding talk of possible worlds—including quantifying over them—added *expressive power* to our language, enabling us to express modal claims more clearly than before, and to express philosophical theses (e.g., about the relation between the mental and the physical, or the moral and the non-moral) we could not otherwise express. We can subject this to the same sort of functional analysis given of more basic modal terminology in Chapter 2: possible worlds talk serves the function not of tracking features of additional worlds and reporting on their features, but rather of adding these sorts of expressive power to our language.

Just as we can begin from modal discourse and make trivial inferences that entitle us to talk of modal facts and properties, so can we make trivial inferences that entitle us to speak of possible worlds. Even Lewis—particularly in his earlier work—sometimes suggests such trivial inferences as a way into speaking of possible worlds. Back in *Counterfactuals* (1973), Lewis puts the argument this way:

> I believe there are possible worlds other than the one we happen to inhabit. If an argument is wanted, it is this. It is uncontroversially true that things might have been otherwise than they are . . . But what does this mean? Ordinary language permits the paraphrase: there are many ways things could have been besides the way they actually are. On the face of it, this sentence is an existential quantification. It says that there exist many entities of a certain description, to wit, "ways things could have been." I believe that things could have been different in countless ways; I believe permissible paraphrases of what

I believe; taking the paraphrase at its face value, I therefore believe in the existence of entities that might be called "ways things could have been." I prefer to call them "possible worlds."

(1973, 84)

A few years later (1979, 182), Lewis reiterates this argument, in more or less the same words. Of course, Lewis's ultimate argument for "positing" possible worlds is not this—but rather the argument that the theoretical benefits of accepting possible worlds "are worth their ontological cost" (1986, 4). Nonetheless, the earlier argument provides the basis for what might be thought of as an "easy" argument (in the sense of Thomasson 2015) for the existence of possible worlds.

For we could make trivial inferences along the following lines:

1. There could have been talking donkeys.
2. There is a way the world could have been: a way in which the world contained talking donkeys.
3. There is a possible world in which there are talking donkeys.

Stalnaker (1976) accepts this form of argument but argues that it does not justify Lewis's development of the concept of possible worlds as being things "of the same sort as the actual world." Instead, Stalnaker defends what he calls a "more moderate form of realism about possible worlds" that might be justified by our "common modal opinions" (67)—in which possible worlds are "ways things might have been" (70).

Yablo (1996, 256) calls the earlier argument Lewis's "paraphrase" argument and goes on to criticize this sort of argument, in part by arguing that the phrase "ways the world could have been" doesn't serve a referential function (but rather is an answer to an indirect question— such as "how could farm animals have seemed more intelligent?").[4]

---

[4] Yablo also suggests that when we do introduce quantification over ways we should treat that as "feigned"—as pretending that the phrases have a referent of an ordinary kind (1996, 268–69). For critical discussion of Yablo's fictionalist program, see Thomasson (2013c). Also, unlike Yablo, I deny that these inferences have ontological *presuppositions*. For discussion see Thomasson (2014a).

But in any case, one needn't go via *ways* to make a trivial argument for possible worlds. As Alexander Steinberg has argued, one may take there to be valid trivial arguments of the form:

1. It is possible that p.
2. If it is possible that p, then there is a possible world at which p.
3. There is a possible world at which p. (2013, 770)

Steinberg takes this as the basis for developing a pleonastic account of possible worlds, along the lines suggested by Stephen Schiffer's pleonastic accounts of propositions, properties, and other entities. Such arguments perfectly fit the model of easy arguments I have defended elsewhere (Thomasson 2015): they are cases in which we move from an uncontested truth in the first premise, via a premise (2) that may be regarded as a conceptual truth—one that could be used to introduce the concept of a possible world—to a conclusion that there is an entity of a kind not mentioned in the first, uncontested premise. (Those who have reservations about easy arguments I refer to Thomasson [2015], where I give an extended defense of such arguments.) Such trivial arguments ensure that we are entitled to say *there are* possible worlds, but don't tell us much more about them. In particular, an argument like this will ensure that there is a possible world in which there is a talking donkey, but it won't tell us much more about what is true in that world, and it won't tell us when possibilities are identical and distinct. Steinberg shows how to do this by first introducing talk of a (proto-)possibility (that there be a talking donkey), and talk of what it *forces* (that there be a talking mammal) versus what it leaves open (whether there are any talking pigs). He then gives identity conditions for (proto-)possibilities according to which (proto-)possibilities are identical just in case they force the same things.[5] But more is needed to get full-blown possible worlds: possible worlds are supposed to be *complete, maximal* entities—so we need a way of understanding how one can introduce possible worlds talk in a way that gets us worlds with this feature. Steinberg does this by treating a "refinement" of a

---

[5] Readers interested in the technical development of the view are referred to Steinberg (2013).

proto-possibility P as one that forces everything P does (and more besides)—so the (proto-)possibility that there be a talking donkey and a talking pig is a refinement of the (proto-)possibility that there be a talking donkey. Possible worlds may be identified with worlds that are fully refined—as possibilities that leave no questions undecided (2013, 782).

Given that the normativist can accept not only that there are modal facts and properties, but even that there are possible worlds, we are perfectly entitled to quantify over possible worlds. This is advantageous, since it enables us to retain the expressive power that talk of possible worlds and quantification over possible worlds brings. Nonetheless, possible worlds, so conceived, are not the disconnected concrete wholes posited by Lewis.[6] Thinking of possible worlds on the pleonastic model brings an important advantage over the Lewisian model. For, as Steinberg points out (2013, 769–70), it avoids the notorious epistemological problems of Lewisian realism. Instead, we can have a plausible story about how we acquire knowledge of the possible worlds by appealing to the trivial inferences by which we become entitled to refer to them. We still, of course, need a story about how we get to basic modal knowledge (expressed in claims that certain propositions are possible or necessary). Such an account will be given in Chapter 7—but, preliminarily, it is not hard to see how the normativist could tell such a story by appealing to a move from conceptual competence (and sometimes also empirical knowledge) to entitlement to add a modal operator. With that basic modal knowledge in place, it is easy to see how we may come to acquire knowledge of possible worlds pleonastically considered—where this is not a matter of mysteriously acquiring information about concrete worlds with which we can have no causal contact, but rather of exploiting our conceptual competence and making trivial inferences to which we are entitled by the rules of use that introduce possible worlds talk.

---

[6] If Lewis's main argument were the "paraphrase" argument (rather than the theoretical benefits argument), then his inference to possible worlds, in which he also concludes that these possible worlds are *concrete*, would be an instance of what Simon Evnine (2016) has called the problem of "too much content." See also discussion of this problem in Thomasson (2015, 221–30).

Of course the advantage Lewis primarily sought by thinking of possible worlds as concrete was an ability to *reduce* the modal to the non-modal—whereas traditional ersatz views of possible worlds (e.g., as maximal consistent sets of propositions) had to tacitly rely on modal notions like consistency. It is this reductive ability that is supposed to lead to gains in ideological simplicity that make up for the "ontological costs" of accepting the worlds (Lewis 1986, 4–5).[7] Treating possible worlds as pleonastic entities in this way may not get this desired sort of reduction (Steinberg's notions of *forcing* and of [proto-] possibilities that *cannot* be refined any further might be thought to be tacitly modal). But I think there are real questions to be raised about the benefits of this sort of "ideological simplicity" and whether—particularly in this case—it is desirable or even plausible.

On the normativist view, we do not begin by "positing" modality as a fundamental feature of the world (losing ontological simplicity) or "positing" a fundamental modal operator, and saying no more about it. Instead, we begin from isolating *functional* differences in pieces of language—for example, between indicatives that function to *describe, track, and co-vary with* elements of our environment, and indicatives that serve other functions such as conveying *rules or norms*. We do require a fundamental distinction between language that is normative and language that is descriptive. But it is not at all clear that this distinction marks a failure in "ideological parsimony" that counts as a mark against the approach. On the contrary, failure to make and appreciate this distinction would lead to the old mistakes of psychologism, thoroughly demolished by Frege and Husserl more than a century ago. On my view, the sort of complexity we require to get normativism off the ground is not a cost to be lamented, but an essential feature of any adequate philosophical theory.

6.3 What We Gain

This quite naturally leads to the question: If both the normativist and the traditional modal realist say that there are modal facts and

---

[7] But see Shalkowski (1994) for arguments that Lewis's own view is not really reductive.

properties, and even possible worlds, what distinguishes modal normativism from those traditional modal realisms to which it was supposed to be providing an alternative? It seems like we could even say that modal discourse *describes* modal facts, properties, or other possible worlds in the deflated sense of giving us true indicatives—but if so, what remains of the alleged difference between this approach and traditional forms of modal realism?[8]

Speakers may certainly think of themselves as using (or aiming to use) modal discourse to *describe* the world when they make such utterances, in one sense: when one says, for example, "statues can't survive a drastic change in shape," one (wittingly or not) *shows* something about the semantic rules for the terms employed, but the literal semantic content *is* world-oriented content about statues, and may say something true about the world. In that sense, it is no mistake to call the discourse "descriptive."

But if we allow that this discourse may be used descriptively, don't all the same philosophical problems for modality arise again, as we ask about those modal facts and properties? And if so, what has been gained by insisting on the non-descriptive functional analysis of the vocabulary?

Actually, the problems don't all arise in the same way—on the contrary, we can make major new progress on these old problems. While we may speak in a simple sense of modal statements "describing" modal facts or properties, it is a philosophical mistake (though no mistake in first-order modal attributions) to think of such utterances as serving to track modal features of the world, which they must mirror to be true, and which serve to explain the truth of the modal claim. For if the functional analysis given in Chapter 2 is correct, metaphysical modal terms just are not in the business of tracking features of the environment in that way: their entry rules establish no such "link" between worldly features and the proper use of the term, and the success conditions for their use require no such link. One may use such metaphysical modal terms "descriptively" in the sense of aiming to use

---

[8] This is a problem that has been raised, and addressed, in various ways in the neo-pragmatist literature. See Dreier (2004), Price (2013, Chapter 8), and Chapter 3 of Thomasson (2015).

them to say true things about the world, but that doesn't mean that such uses appeal to or require the presence of modal facts or properties to *explain* the truth of what is said.

The real difference between the normativist view and traditional heavyweight realist views of modality lies not in whether each says there are modal facts, properties, or even possible worlds, nor even in whether (in an everyday sense) we can "describe" them. Instead, the difference lies in the meta-ontology behind the answers to those questions, and in the role the properties and facts play. In more traditional forms of realism about the modal, modal facts or properties (or other worlds) are "posited" as truthmakers for our modal claims: they are supposed to be what *explains* what *makes* our modal claims true, and are argued for on grounds of their indispensability to such an explanation.[9] By contrast, on the normativist view, modal facts and properties (and possible worlds) are not "posited" to "explain" what makes our modal claims true (in quasi-scientific manner). We can't explain why poppies make us sleepy by appealing to the fact that they possess the dormitive virtue: true though it may be that they possess the dormitive virtue, as long as "dormitive virtue" is just introduced as a fancy, hypostatized way of expressing the fact that they make us sleepy, it cannot be used to *explain* why they make us sleepy. So similarly, if talk of modal facts and properties is simply derived from hypostatizations out of modal truths, any attempt to "explain" modal truths by appeal to the existence of modal facts or properties would just yield a dormitive virtue explanation. This result, however, is not a liability for the normativist, since she does not require modal truthmakers to explain modal truth. On the contrary, the normativist denies that modal claims need truthmakers (in any sense that aims to be explanatory) at all. Instead, I say that there are modal facts and properties because we are committed to there being such, given the modal truths (which don't need truthmakers) and the rules of use for the very terms "fact" and "property" that license the trivial inferences—these ensure that the claims "there are modal facts" and "there are modal properties" come out as true, in the only sense these claims have. If we adopt the

---

[9] Phillip Bricker (2008) considers such a truthmaker approach to arguing for possible worlds, without endorsing it.

normativist functional view, we will no longer think that we "posit" modal facts, properties, or other worlds to "explain" what makes our modal statements true. On the normativist view, the entitlement to add "necessarily" to a basic claim arises from its giving object-language expression of a semantic rule (or consequence thereof). We don't need to appeal to a property of necessity in the world to explain the truth of the modal claim. On the normativist approach, talk of modal properties or facts is explanatorily downstream from modal truths.

Similarly, a contrast can be drawn between the sort of realism about possible worlds we get on the normativist view and Lewisian possible worlds realism. For Lewis treats his plurality of worlds as a theoretical posit to be justified by its theoretical utility, fruitfulness, and economy in primitives (see Lewis 1986, 133–35). By contrast, the normativist treats talk of possible worlds as simply derived by trivial inferences from talk about ways things might have been, or talk about what is possible. This talk does not require any such theoretical justification: the proper question is about the utility of the *form of discourse*, what function having it in our language serves, not about the theoretical utility of "positing" the objects. Possible worlds, on this view, are not a "posit" in the way that Vulcan or black holes were or are.

One way to put the difference in each case is to say that we get not an *explanatory* realism about modal facts and properties or possible worlds (that are "posited" as truthmakers or as part of a best "total theory"), but rather what we may call a *simple* realism. (You ask: "Are there modal facts and properties?" I answer: "Yes, there are").[10]

So the modal normativist cannot say that she has the ontological advantage of not positing modal facts or properties (since the version I have endorsed comes with the simple realism that says there are), or of having a "more parsimonious" ontology than rival heavyweight modal realist views. Nonetheless, the view does have ontological

---

[10] Of course "realism" about any sort of entity gets defined in a multitude of ways, but the core sense of "realism" is generally held to be what Plantinga (1987, 189) calls "existential realism": the view that there really are the things under discussion (modal facts and properties, in this case). Thus it seems most suitable to call this a realist view. The simple realist approach is of course in accord with the deflationary approach to existence questions I have defended at length elsewhere (see Thomasson 2015, especially Chapter 3, for more on "simple realism").

advantages. For various questions that may be pressed on the heavyweight realist (whether about modal facts and properties or about possible worlds) just don't arise here. If we assume descriptivism, we might become concerned with questions such as whether it is modal facts, modal properties, or other possible worlds that are the "real" truthmakers for our modal claims, and we face what Huw Price (2011, 187–89) has called "placement problems" about how these modal facts or properties relate to the non-modal facts and properties in the world: Do they "emerge" from them? They seem not to supervene on them. We might also be worried by puzzles about how the modal facts and properties of a statue and lump, say, could differ, given the sameness of their non-modal/sortal properties—puzzles that give rise to problems like the grounding problem: of explaining how entities with all the same non-modal/sortal properties (such as the statue and lump) could nonetheless have different modal properties—what could ground the difference?[11] But on the normativist view, it is clearly out of place to ask what the "real" truthmakers for our modal claims are (modal properties? modal facts or states of affairs? features of other possible worlds?). Moreover, this way of thinking of modal facts and properties makes evident why it is out of place to ask questions about whether we are justified in accepting these modal "posits," about what modal facts and properties *really* are, and about how they relate to non-modal facts and properties. For though "modal fact" and "modal property" are noun terms, they enter our language with an entirely different function than tracking some worldly feature such that we might want to investigate what it is really like or how it can arise out of lower-level worldly features.[12]

---

[11] Price notes analogously that philosophical concerns about the nature of moral facts may be dissipated once we distinguish the function of moral language from the function of "natural descriptions" that aim to track environmental features: "The question as to the real nature of a state of affairs referred to by a description is one that may properly be raised in naturalistic terms if the description concerned is a natural description [e-representation]—in this case it is a matter which may be investigated in scientific terms. But if all we have is a minimal description . . . then such a question involves a kind of category mistake" (2011, 68).

[12] For discussion of the grounding problem see Zimmerman (1995), Bennett (2004), Burke (1992), and Thomasson (2007, Chapter 4).

Thus certain ontological questions that present heavy burdens for the heavyweight realist are irrelevant from the modal normativist's view, since she does not "posit" modal facts, properties, or possible worlds as explanatory entities, and since talk of possible worlds and the like is merely a hypostatization out of ways of saying what is possible—not an attempted description of entities discovered, about which we might suppose there to be more to be revealed. In this way, the modal normativist approach does bring with it advantages of simplifying and demystifying various ontological issues, even though both the normativist and realist at the end of the day say "yes, there are" modal properties or facts or possible worlds.

Another virtue of the normativist approach is that (as Theodore Locke [2018 and in progress]) has argued) it is not just regarding traditional modal matters that it can provide a useful analysis. As Daniel Nolan puts it, "the twenty-first century is seeing a hyperintensional revolution" (2014, 149), in which claims about grounding, essences, and the like are becoming increasingly important in metaphysics. Such claims cannot be modeled merely in traditionally modal terms, as they introduce contexts in which terms that have the same extension across all possible worlds nonetheless cannot be substituted in a truth-preserving way. So, for example, "Socrates exists" and "{Socrates} exists"[13] are true in all (and only) the same possible worlds, yet the truth of the latter is commonly said to be grounded in the truth of the former, and not vice versa. As Locke (2018 and in progress) argues, the modal normativist is well positioned to account for such claims, by attributing the relevant asymmetries to asymmetrical relations between the concepts: "We need modal terms with these formal properties [of hyperintensional terms[14]] . . . because there are often important conceptual asymmetries or conceptual interdependencies between expressions in our language that bear on the competent and appropriate use of those expressions" (2018, 103).[15] For example, the

---

[13] That is: "The (singleton) set containing Socrates exists."

[14] Or at least those that are hyperintensional$_{GRND}$, in the disambiguating terminology introduced by Duncan, Miller, and Norton (2017).

[15] See also Locke (2019 and in progress). I have also done some work elsewhere to try to account for claims of relative fundamentality (level) and of constitution in terms of interrelations among rules of use for the terms involved. See Thomasson (2014b) and (2013b), respectively.

application conditions for "{Socrates}" appeal to, and must be given in terms of, those for "Socrates," but the reverse is not the case (2018, 139). I shall leave development and defense of this idea for elsewhere, but it is important to note, with Locke, that ultimately a normativist approach may be able to demystify not only modal but also hyperintensional, or "post-modal," claims in metaphysics.

6.4 Classificatory (and Other Forms of) Conventionalism

Before moving on to demonstrate the other benefits of modal normativism, it is worth pausing to compare it to similar recent views in metaphysics. Even among metaphysicians with generally realist inclinations, there has been a tendency to be suspicious of the modal. As a result, there has been a minor resurgence in positions inspired by conventionalism, while trying to avoid its hazards. The first of these was Alan Sidelle's neo-conventionalism (1989). As noted in Chapter 4, Sidelle's work was groundbreaking in showing a route for conventionalists to account for *de re* and a posteriori necessities. It also beautifully presents the epistemological advantages to be gained by taking something like this approach to modality. But it differs from the approach defended here in both its starting points in language, and its ending points in metaphysics. Sidelle does not give any sort of functional analysis of modal discourse, or provide a response to the Frege-Geach problem. Most importantly, the metaphysical conclusions Sidelle draws from his approach differ markedly from those I draw. Given the simple realist approach I adopt, I would not say, as Sidelle does, that "modality does not find its home in the mind-independent world, but rather in us, in our ways of speaking and thinking" (1989, 2–3), nor would I say that my view differs from (traditional) realists in terms of the "truthmakers" for modal statements (1989, 6), since I think one crucial point is to deny that such statements call for truthmakers—not to relocate truthmakers in our ways of thinking or speaking. Sidelle also takes his view to entail that "there is no real necessity" in the world, and so "nothing out in the world which is such that it has its microstructure necessarily" (1989, 38). Following an argument along the lines of Rea's given in Section 6.1, he then also concludes that his modal conventionalism should lead him to deny that there are any "fully independent" objects in the world (1989, 57). But (as noted in Section 6.1) these metaphysical consequences do not follow from the modal normativist view I defend.

But others who are inspired by conventionalism are more cautious in drawing out the metaphysical conclusions. Forms of what might be called "classificatory conventionalism" about the modal have recently been defended by Ted Sider (2011) and Ross Cameron (2010). Sider and Cameron both aim to avoid the commitments of traditional modal realism. But they do this not by denying that there "really" are modal facts or properties, but rather by denying that modality is fundamental (Sider 2011, 268), and by denying that the distinction between necessary and contingent propositions is a "deep" metaphysical division (Cameron 2010, 355) or denying that the term "necessary" carves at the joints of reality (Sider 2011, 269).

Instead, as Sider expresses the view, to say that a proposition is necessary is simply:

> . . . to say that the proposition is i) true; and ii) of a certain sort . . . What determines the "certain sort" of propositions? Nothing "metaphysically deep." For the Humean, necessity does not carve at the joints. There are many candidate meanings for "necessary," corresponding to different "certain sorts" our linguistic community might choose. Since none of these candidates carves at the joints, our linguistic community is free to choose whichever of these it likes. Perhaps the choice is arbitrary, in which case the facts about necessity are "conventional" . . . Perhaps the choice reflects something important about the role "necessary" plays in our conceptual lives.
>
> (2011, 269)

Cameron similarly expresses the general idea behind the view as that "in some sense we are responsible for the division of truth into necessities and contingencies, rather than us tracking a division the world makes" (2010, 354).

I call this view "classificatory conventionalism" because, on this view, conventions are explicitly not appealed to as anything like truthmakers of our modal claims; rather they are said to be responsible merely for *classifying* some truths as necessary, others as contingent. Which ones are classified as necessary? Sider suggests that (at least) mathematical and logical truths, as well as analytic truths and the true statements of fundamental metaphysics, count as "necessary," though he denies that this reflects anything deep about statements of these sorts. To the question "*Why* are logical (or mathematical, or analytic, or other) truths necessary?" he responds, "This is just how our concept of necessity works" (2011, 288). Though there may be family resemblances among many of the sorts of truths counted as necessary, such as *a prioricity* and being hard to conceive of as false, there need be no one feature that they all have in common because "The spirit of Humeanism, after all, is that the line between the necessary and contingent is not discovered, but rather drawn by us—perhaps somewhat arbitrarily" (2011, 289).

The classificatory conventionalist view is similar to the normativist view developed here insofar as both views accept that there are modal truths, but deny that the order of explanation is to "posit" modal facts or properties that "explain" these modal truths. The classificatory conventionalist says that there is nothing deep and metaphysical to explain why some truths are classified as necessary, others as contingent. But the natural question is to ask *why* truths of certain sorts get put in this classification, and others don't. What is the *point of* having such an apparently arbitrary mishmash of a concept? And why do we want to add "necessary" on anyway—what function does adding this terminology serve (if not of tracking some distinctive properties or facts)? Both Cameron and Sider show some sensitivity to this issue. Cameron writes:

> So what *are* our reasons for drawing this latter division [of truths into necessities and contingencies] the way we do? That's a good question; and to answer it we should also ask: why is it that we modalise in the first place? To help answer why we draw the division where we do we should first enquire as to why we draw such a division at all. Why engage in modal talk? What would we be missing if we didn't?
>
> (2010, 356)

This question, of course, is the starting point of the present analysis. I have reflected in Chapter 2 on why we need modal terminology in our discourse, as giving us crucially useful ways of expressing and reasoning with rules and permissions. This also gives the potential for a unified understanding of why we classify mathematical and logical truths, certain metaphysical truths, and the like all as "necessary"—if we can understand each as ways of conveying certain rules or norms (whether for use of certain terms, or for reasoning in general, and what follows from them) in the object language. But it is also important to note that generalizing the project in this way may require avoiding the label "conventionalism." For while the normativist holds that claims of necessity give ways of conveying and reasoning with rules in the object-language, there need be no implication that the relevant rules or norms are merely "conventional." Some may be (e.g., rules for use of particular social terms like "bachelor") but it is open to the normativist to hold that others are not (e.g., the most basic rules of reasoning conveyed in certain claims of logical necessity).

So while forms of classificatory conventionalism may share some of the ontological advantages of modal normativism, in accepting modal truths while denying that these call for modal facts and properties to *explain* what makes them true, the normativist view aims to provide a more satisfying and potentially unifying functional account of modal discourse. Moreover, classificatory conventionalists admit that their approach does nothing to help resolve the epistemological problems of modality. As Sider puts it, "The price [of his Humean account] is that no headway is made on epistemology: nothing in the Humean account of necessity sheds any light on the epistemology of logic or mathematics" (2011, 270). The focus here is on metaphysically necessary truths, not those of logic or mathematics. However, the normativist approach clearly does enable us to make good headway on the epistemology of modal statements of that kind. And it is there that its chief advantages lie, as I now turn to argue.

7

Epistemological Advantages

The clearest and most important advantages of the normativist view over its heavyweight realist rivals are epistemological.[1] The problems of accounting for our knowledge of modal facts have been familiar since Hume, and remain as forbidding as ever. As Graeme Forbes puts it, "no metaphysical account which renders it impossible to give a plausible epistemological theory is to be countenanced" (1985, 217). The problem of how we can come to know metaphysical modal truths is crucial. For the very thought that we can answer metaphysical questions about the identity and persistence conditions of things of certain sorts, about essences, or about existence conditions requires that we can know distinctively metaphysical modal truths. Without a plausible account of our knowledge of metaphysical modality, we are threatened with skepticism about metaphysics itself. Claims about what is possible also play a central role in other arguments in philosophy of language, philosophy of mind, epistemology, and elsewhere in philosophy. To the extent that these are best interpreted as involving claims about *metaphysical* possibility, skepticism about knowledge of metaphysical modality threatens to lead to a broader skepticism about knowledge in philosophy.

Those who aim to give an account of our knowledge of modality face two central challenges: the "integration challenge" and the "reliability challenge." The integration challenge, as Christopher Peacocke

---

[1] This chapter is based on my article "How Can We Come to Know Metaphysical Modal Truths?" *Synthese* (special issue: *New Directions in the Epistemology of Modality*) (2018): 1–30. https://doi.org/10.1007/s11229-018-1841-5. Reprinted here with kind permission of Springer.

Norms and Necessity. Amie L. Thomasson, Oxford University Press (2020). © Oxford University Press.
DOI: 10.1093/oso/9780190098193.001.0001

has called it, is the challenge of reconciling a plausible account of what is involved in the truth of statements of a given kind with a credible account of how we can know them (1998, 1). Most simply put, the integration challenge is a matter of insisting that we reconcile our views about the *metaphysics* and the *epistemology* of a given subject matter. Peacocke takes his integration challenge to be a generalization of the problem Benacerraf raised for mathematical knowledge, which he expressed as the problem of explicating the concept of mathematical truth in a way that would "fit into an over-all account of knowledge in a way that makes it intelligible how we have the mathematical knowledge that we have" (1973, 667).[2]

The second challenge is the "reliability challenge." Robert Nozick (2001) raises a version of the challenge for modal knowledge as follows: if we are to be justified in believing something in a given domain, we must have a reliable faculty for forming beliefs of that sort, the existence of which is best explained in terms of natural selection.[3] But, he argues, where modal beliefs are concerned, "we do not appear to have such a faculty, and it is implausible that evolutionary processes would instill that within us" (2001, 122). Since we have no good explanation of why we should have developed a reliable faculty for detecting metaphysical necessity, Nozick argues, we should be skeptical about claims that we have such knowledge—and even about the claim that there are such necessities (2001, 125). Nozick concludes that "there are no interesting and important metaphysical necessities" (2001, 120–21).

---

[2] There are controversies surrounding how to understand the Benacerraf problem (see Clarke-Doane [2016]). While Peacocke takes his integration challenge to be a generalization of the Benacerraf problem, Fischer (2017) takes the Benacerraf problem to be a more specific version of the reliability challenge. Nothing here is at stake in how to interpret the Benacerraf problem—and while it is clear that the integration challenge and the reliability challenge are related, it will be useful to be able to consider separately these two sides of the challenge for giving an account of modal knowledge.

[3] This challenge for modality in certain ways resembles Sharon Street's evolutionary debunking arguments in ethics (2006, 2011). Controversies abound, however, about exactly how one should interpret Street's arguments and about whether they can be answered. I will largely leave such controversies to the side here, to focus on the issues that have arisen specifically for the modal case. I will, however, return in sections 7.5 and 7.6 to discuss some potentially worrying parallels.

Both of these problems arise particularly vividly on a Lewisian approach to modality, but they do not arise there alone. The integration challenge is notoriously problematic for rationalist approaches to modal epistemology—at least if we combine these with a form of realism about metaphysical modal facts. For it is unclear why intuitions or conceivability should give us any evidence about mind-independent metaphysical modal facts.

In response to the difficulties of rationalism, there has been a recent surge of interest in empiricist approaches to modal epistemology. Barbara Vetter (2015) aims to solve the integration problem by treating modal knowledge as knowledge of modal properties of *this* world such as potentialities or dispositions—undercutting the feeling of inaccessibility. However, I will argue (in section 7.1) that this approach to modal knowledge does not solve the integration problem in a way that shows how distinctively *metaphysical* modal truths may be known. Similarly, Timothy Williamson aims to meet the reliability challenge with an empiricist approach. I will argue, however (in section 7.2), that his account is at best able to respond to the case of knowledge of empirically grounded counterfactuals. The moral is that, however promising these empiricist approaches may seem for accounting for knowledge of dispositions and empirically grounded counterfactuals, they cannot help resolve the problem of how we can come to know specifically the *metaphysical* modal truths that play a core role in metaphysical debates—and about which Nozick argues for skepticism.

We remain in need of a positive account of how we *can* acquire metaphysical modal knowledge. I turn to that task in sections 7.3 and 7.4. I argue that once we give up the assumption that metaphysical claims serve to describe or track modal facts, both the integration challenge and the reliability challenge show up rather differently—in ways that make them less insuperable. I go on to show how modal normativism opens up a clear and plausible route to respond to both of these remaining problems of modal epistemology.

Those sections lay out the basic story, while sections 7.5 and 7.6 go on to address lingering challenges that have arisen in the parallel moral case, including the need to give an evolutionary account of our ability to modalize well, and saying why our knowledge of metaphysical modal truths isn't an "unexplained coincidence." Overall, this chapter makes the case that the normativist approach gives us a clear response to the central problems of the epistemology of modality. This is a very substantial advantage.

7.1 The Integration Challenge

The integration challenge—of reconciling an account of what is *involved* in the truth of modal claims with a plausible account of how we can come to *know* them—arises in a particularly vivid form for David Lewis's (1986) modal realism. For Lewis thinks of modal knowledge (or, at least, knowledge of what is necessary and of what is possible but not actual) as knowledge *about* what is the case at spatiotemporally and causally disconnected worlds. But, given the inaccessibility of those worlds, he "arguably makes modal truth radically inaccessible" (Peacocke 1998, 3). And, indeed, if modal knowledge involves knowledge of worlds spatiotemporally and causally disconnected from ours, it is particularly hard to see why we would have any reason to think that our usual methods (of reasoning combinatorially, engaging in thought experiments, etc.) are any good at acquiring such knowledge.

Knowledge of possibility and necessity on Lewis's view, of course, amounts to knowledge about what is the case at some or all worlds. It is easy enough to acquire some knowledge of what is possible, via inferences from what is actual. Knowledge of what is necessary or *merely* possible is more difficult, however, since on a Lewisian view it would seem to require knowledge of what goes on at worlds other than the actual world. But given that these worlds are causally isolated from ours, there can be no causal account of our ability to know the facts in those worlds that parallels causal accounts of knowledge of the facts of this world. Of course, Lewis aptly notes that causal theories of knowledge founder on mathematical knowledge anyway (1986, 109)—but that is not to provide any positive account of how either *can* be known. Moreover, one might expect there to be important disanalogies in the stories to be told about how we can know mathematical truths versus truths about Lewisian worlds, given that the former concern abstracta (and so are more reasonably thought to be accessible via a priori methods) while the latter, by Lewis's lights, concern concreta. Indeed, as Brian Skyrms argues (1976, 326), if Lewis's worlds are supposed to be concrete, one might expect knowledge of them to require the same sort of evidence as one expects for knowledge of other concreta. By treating his worlds as entities of the same kind as our actual world, Lewis sets up the expectation that they should be knowable by the same sort of means—yet this option seems completely foreclosed by their spatiotemporal and causal isolation.

Lewis offers no general account of how we can acquire knowledge of modal facts, saying only that the problem of giving an analysis of modal knowledge is "a problem for everyone (certain skeptics and conventionalists excepted)" (1986, 113). He offers instead a story about how we *in fact* come to hold the modal *beliefs* we do—by way of general reasoning from principles of recombination, guided by imaginative experiments (1986, 113–14). The trouble is, however, that Lewisian modal realism makes it impossible to see why these principles of recombination, guided by imaginative experiments, should be any good whatsoever at revealing to us what is going on in these independent, spatiotemporally and causally isolated worlds. As Vetter puts it, "It seems like black magic that the epistemology of Recombination should just happen to get the metaphysics of possible worlds right, given that there is no connection by which the latter might have informed the former" (2015, 13).

Empiricist views provide a promising approach to solving the integration challenge, by bringing modality back to *this* world—enabling us to acquire knowledge of this-worldly modal truthmakers through something like standard empirical methods. Along these lines, Vetter (2015) argues that possibility is anchored in potentialities of (actual) individual objects, where potentialities include both abilities and dispositions of individual objects. Such potentialities might be thought to provide this-worldly truthmakers for modal claims, rather than appealing to isolated possible worlds. As Vetter puts it, like Lewis's view, "it anchors possibilities in objects. But its objects are just the ordinary objects of this, the actual world, with which we are in regular epistemic contact" (11). As a result, a chief advantage of the dispositional account is supposed to be its ability to demystify modal epistemology:

> Dispositionalism . . . avoids the drawback of a possible-worlds metaphysics by anchoring possibilities in the right kind of objects: actual objects, with which we have epistemic contact. By anchoring

them in the *dispositions* of such objects, dispositionalism promises a plausible story about the epistemology of modality. We clearly have a great deal of knowledge about the dispositions of the individual objects around us . . . We learn early on that glasses are fragile, that sugar is water-soluble, and that some people are irascible . . . we clearly *have* such knowledge, whatever exactly our account of it is; and . . . such knowledge is not a matter or philosophical speculation, but of both practical and scientific knowledge about the world.

(11–12)

Given that Vetter aims to ground all of modality in dispositions, this account provides hope of giving an empirical account of knowledge of modality; "[t]he epistemology of metaphysical modality may then just be a generalization of those empirical ways of knowing about dispositions" (12). And this, she claims, provides the basis for a good answer to Peacocke's integration challenge—far better than Lewis could give. For we can understand what is involved in modal truths as correctly describing the potentialities in the world, and also see how those can be known through our standard empirical ways of knowing about dispositions (Vetter 2015, 12).

Others have also tried to ease the integration challenge by treating modal properties as features of this world that could be known via broadly empirical methods. Otavio Bueno and Scott Shalkowski aim to develop an "empiricist-friendly approach to the epistemology of modality that does not rely on conceivability" (2015, 672). Their modalist view accounts for knowledge of the merely possible by appealing just to our knowledge of "the relevant modal properties of the objects under consideration" (680). They suggest that we can know, for example, that it is possible for the table to break, even though it hasn't broken, by knowing that it is made of wood, by knowing various claims about the relative strengths of bonds of both internal and external forces, and so on (679).[4] Similar empiricist views are developed

---

[4] Carrie Jenkins develops a different response, arguing that our concepts (say, of *vixen* and *female*) are empirically grounded in "structural features of the world" (say, that the property of being a vixen "includes" the property of being female) (2010, 268–69). By accepting this link, she aims to show how we can legitimately accept that conceivability can be a guide to modal knowledge, while retaining a broadly empiricist approach to modal knowledge (2010, 262). Her account, unlike Williamson's and Vetter's, is clearly

and defended by Felipe Leon (2017) and Sonia Roca-Royes (2017). Leon argues that the modal knowledge we have (which he limits only to "nearby" cases) traces "back to our knowledge of the actual world" (2017, 255). For example, one may know that a desk can be moved or a car painted blue via inductive knowledge of similar cases in which such changes are actual. Roca-Royes only aims to give an empiricist epistemology of *de re* possibilities for concrete entities—not the full range of relevant metaphysical necessities and possibilities. In such cases, she argues, as knowing that this table can break, or that Kennedy could die of a heart attack, our knowledge of unrealized possibilities arises via "extrapolation from knowledge about some other, similar entities' realized possibilities" (2017, 233).[5]

Views that take modal properties to be features of this world, which we can come to know through broadly empirical/scientific means, certainly have the potential to ease at least some of the problems of modal epistemology Lewis leaves us with, and so have seen increasing popularity in recent years (see, e.g., the various essays in Fischer and Leon [2017]).[6] But it is important to notice that the focus of these

directed toward knowledge of metaphysical modalities (including those we think of as reflected in conceptual truths), not just attributions of dispositions. But it is hard to see how these "structural features of the world"—the "containment" of one property in another, for example—could be thought to be empirically detected. These are not observations of concreta at all, but seem much closer to discoveries of truths about essences, which seem not to be simply sensorily detectable and to raise the problems of modal knowledge all over again.

[5] Bob Fischer defends a somewhat different empiricist approach, which takes our modal knowledge to arise from our theories: "if you have reason to believe that a theory is true ... you have reason to believe that certain models correspond to genuine possibilities" (2017, 274). As Fischer acknowledges, the approach seems to work less well for "mundane modal claims" (e.g., that my shirt could be striped, not plaid) than for scientific modal claims. While he tries to show how it can be extended to knowledge of counterfactuals like "if my wife weren't at home she'd be at work," it again is unclear how it could be extended to more purely philosophical modal claims about when we have the same person, or to whom our terms refer. And the thought that it would work for these cases relies on the controversial claims that theoretical virtues (apart from empirical adequacy) are truth-conducive (Fischer 2017, 278), and that ontological claims are confirmed with our scientific theories. See Thomasson (2017b) for doubts about both of these claims.

[6] Such empiricist views of the epistemology of empirical counterfactual and dispositional claims also fit quite naturally with a normativist view of these counterfactuals as *explaining* a state of affairs or *justifying* an assertion on empirical grounds (see Sellars [1958]), and so might be able to form part of a combined epistemological approach for modal non-descriptivists.

accounts is on ascriptions of dispositions (the glass has the potentiality to break, the sugar is soluble in water, etc.) and empirically grounded counterfactuals (if I were to drop the glass, it would break). Such dispositions and counterfactuals are the modal properties of interest to *science* more than to *metaphysics*—and are crucially different from the modal claims typically at issue in metaphysical and other strictly philosophical debates.

It is much less clear that anything along the lines of an empirical account of modal knowledge can be of use for specifically *metaphysical* modal claims. Roca-Royes is admirably upfront on this point. She argues directly that the empirical method she defends for coming to know certain *de re* unrealized possibilities for concrete entities does not extend to give us knowledge of whether essentialist claims (about, e.g., the essentiality of origin or essentiality of kind) are true (2017, 239). Indeed, she argues that gathering empirical evidence in favor of or against such claims is impossible (239). "What I am suggesting as epistemic grounds for basic and simple modal facts cannot constitute grounds for or against the long-controversial essentialist claims" (241–42). Similarly, she limits her results to unrealized possibilities for concreta, and suggests that "an epistemology of modality for abstracta requires a very different treatment" (243). One important feature Roca-Royes identifies is that possibility claims for concrete entities are testable—we can test the claim that wooden tables are breakable, say, by attempting to break some (232). These possibility claims also, we might add, come with *predictions* about what will happen if we try to break it (or things like it)—it is because there are such predictions that the claims are testable.

Leon develops a similar approach for cases such as knowing that a desk can be moved or a car can be painted blue, but aims to extend it to certain "nearby" philosophical cases, such as knowledge that there can be justified true belief without knowledge. But these seem fundamentally different types of case, in a way that should give us pause. In the desk and car cases, we have inductive reason to believe that such changes are possible, and the view has predictive consequences that we can test out: there is prospect of mistake, if we push as hard as we can and the desk won't budge, or if the paint constantly changes to silver when applied to the car, we may have reason to revise our judgment of possibility. But there is no such prospect in the philosophical cases: there is no predictive content to assessing whether there could be justified true belief without knowledge in certain cases. These cases tell us nothing about what we should expect to happen, and seem to be entirely untestable. The issue is rather whether in certain cases the observer is *properly described as* having *knowledge* (see Leon 2017, 257–58).

There are still more decisive reasons to think that—even if observation or perception (and/or the similarities and generalizations we come to learn on that basis) enables us learn that sugar cubes are disposed to dissolve in water, that glasses tend to break when subjected to certain forces, or that this table could collapse—this method doesn't generalize to enable us to know metaphysical modal truths. For we cannot in the same way come to know that a statue cannot survive a change in shape while the lump of clay that composes it can. Nor is it plausible to think that we can learn in that way whether personal identity depends on psychological continuity or the survival of the particular organism, or whether one can have the same ancient work of art after conservators replace some of its parts. For unlike dispositional claims, here the disputants can agree about all the empirical facts, and agree about all predictions of "what will happen" (couched in neutral terms), and yet disagree in their modal conclusions.

As the grounding problem[7] makes evident, the distinctively *metaphysical* modal features at issue in characteristic metaphysical debates are cases in which we have *the very same empirical information, and same physical laws and properties,* and yet come to different modal conclusions. For example, there is no difference in the physical properties of the statue and the clay, yet the statue and clay are commonly thought to have different modal properties: the first being incapable of surviving a squashing, and the second being capable of surviving it. We might be able to empirically discover differences in the dispositions of sugar versus sand for solubility by throwing each sample in its own beaker of water and observing what happens. But there is no parallel prospect for empirical discovery of differences

---

[7] For discussion of the grounding problem, see Burke (1992) and Bennett (2004).

in the modal properties of the statue versus the clay of which it is constituted: we can't just throw the statue in one beaker (or under one steamroller) and the lump in another and observe the differences in what happens. Nor can any empirical observations or scientific laws alone tell us whether a painting can survive replacement of certain parts, or whether a work of music must be created. Similarly, there are typically no differences in the *empirical* information available to the defender of psychological-continuity versus animalist views of personal identity: defenders of these views are not working from different data sets that lead them to different conclusions on the basis of different empirical information. As Derek Parfit puts it, in many difficult cases, where people go different ways on questions of personal identity (such as borderline cases of psychological and/or physical changes, or cases of division), we "could know the full truth about this outcome without choosing one of these descriptions" (1984, 260).

For these reasons, however plausible an empirical or modalist view might be of knowledge of dispositional properties or even of empirically grounded counterfactuals, it cannot be the solution to the epistemology of *metaphysical* modal disputes. Much the same seems to go for many other modal claims used centrally in philosophical debates. Whether, in Kripke's (1972, 83–84) famous case, the name "Gödel" *would* apply to Schmidt, if it turned out that Schmidt were (unbeknownst to the world) the true discoverer of the incompleteness of arithmetic, is not something we can determine by attending to empirical information. Whether Swampman could think of or refer to objects in the world, or one can have knowledge of a perceived (real) barn while traveling in fake barn country, similarly, are not issues to be decided by empirical or scientific means. Moreover, those who have different views about such cases generally have no differences in their empirical information or predictions (neutrally described). This is precisely the point according to many metaphysicians: that no simple observation, test, or prediction can resolve deep metaphysical disputes, in the way such tests could resolve disputes about what is soluble or fragile.

In sum, even if we try to diminish the integration challenge by appealing to modal features of this world rather than other worlds and thinking of them as knowable in broadly empirical ways, we still do not solve the challenge for the sorts of modal properties at issue in the debates of metaphysics, and many of those that play a role elsewhere in philosophy (as opposed to, say, those of chemistry). For there does not seem to be the prospect of an empirical route to explaining how we could come to know these distinctively metaphysical modal properties. In each case, our empirical information could be the same, and yet our modal beliefs differ. This is just the grounding problem, arising in a new, epistemological, guise. The integration challenge remains for accounts of *metaphysical* modality.[8]

7.2 The Reliability Challenge

The reliability challenge Nozick presents for modal knowledge is the challenge of giving a naturalistic story about how we could have evolved to have a reliable faculty for coming to know modal truths. In one form (paralleling the original form, which Benacerraf [1973] presses for mathematical knowledge), the challenge arises given the fact that other possible worlds or modal features of this world seem incapable of having causal impact on our beliefs. If we think of a causal relation as what, in other cases, ensures reliability, then the lack of causal commerce with modal "truthmakers" seems to undermine our claim to have reliable knowledge of modality. But, as Clarke-Doane (2016) and Fisher (2017, 270) make clear, a general challenge remains even for those who reject causal theories of knowledge. As Fischer puts it, "the critic can reframe the problem in terms of a demand for an explanation of our reliability about modal matters, and abandoning the causal theory of knowledge won't help with this version of the problem" (2017, 270).

Nozick's challenge may be seen as arising given two assumptions: first, that a belief is justified only if we have a reliable belief-forming mechanism about that domain, and second, that natural selection gives the best explanation of which reliable belief-forming mechanisms we

---

[8] Of course, if one denies the existence of one or both of the statue and lump of clay, no distinct modal properties need to be accounted for. For responses to several such eliminativist arguments, see Thomasson (2007a).

have. This seems to be the form of the challenge that Nozick is concerned with for modal truths, for he suggests that the debates about what's possible "would be avoided if we possessed a faculty of reason that could directly assess the possibility of general statements and of their denials," but goes on to say, "However, we do not appear to have such a faculty, and it is implausible that evolutionary processes would instill that within us" (2001, 122).

Like the integration challenge, this reliability challenge arises in a particularly vivid form for Lewisian modal realism. As Nozick puts it, "Since our ancestors evolved in the actual world, there were no selective pressures to reward accuracy about all possible worlds, and there was no handicap to being right only about the actual world" (2001, 122)—so it is implausible that we would have evolved a faculty to reliably assess whether something (non-actual) is possible or necessary.

Williamson responds to Nozick's reliability challenge by arguing that we do not need to posit a separate faculty for detecting metaphysical necessity, or to give an explanation of how we might have evolved a separate capacity. Instead, he aims to show that "the ordinary cognitive capacity to handle counterfactual conditionals carries with it the cognitive capacity to handle metaphysical modality" (2007, 136). The capacity to evaluate counterfactuals, he argues, can be given an evolutionary explanation, since it is of great use to us in facilitating learning from experience, in improving future performance in various tasks, and in discovering causal connections (140–41). And metaphysical modal thinking, he argues, is logically equivalent to a special case of counterfactual thinking, since a proposition is necessary if its negation counterfactually implies a contradiction (157). So, Williamson argues, there is no special problem in accounting for metaphysical modal knowledge. We need posit no special faculty of intuition, just a capacity to evaluate counterfactual conditionals.

But this just pushes the question back: How do we come to know counterfactual conditionals? Williamson is upfront in accepting that "there is no uniform epistemology of counterfactual conditionals" (2007, 152). Nonetheless (though he notes that this is neither always necessary nor always sufficient), he suggests that the most distinctive means of evaluating them involves imaginative simulation, in a way that makes use of our background knowledge and experience of "how nature works":

> · We can . . . schematize a typical overall process of evaluating a counterfactual conditional thus: one supposes the antecedent and develops the supposition, adding further judgments within the supposition by reasoning, offline predictive mechanisms, and other offline judgments . . . Some but not all of one's background knowledge and beliefs are also available within the scope of the supposition as a description of the counterfactual circumstances, according to complex criteria (the problem of cotenability). To a first approximation: one asserts the counterfactual conditional if and only if the development eventually leads one to add the consequent.
>
> (2007, 153)

So, for example, if we are evaluating the truth of the counterfactual "If the bush had not been there, the rolling rock would have ended up in the lake," we can know its truth by imaginatively rolling back history to a time shortly before the rock started to roll, and then (using our expectation-forming capacities "offline") rolling forward again, to imagine what would happen if the bush weren't there, while keeping patterns of development "as close as possible to the normal ones" (2007, 150).

This imaginative rolling forward of scenarios, using our predictive capacities "offline," may give an acceptable account of our knowledge of empirically grounded counterfactuals such as whether the rock would have fallen into the lake. But Nozick was not expressing a skepticism directed at our ability to know that the rock would have fallen in the lake. Instead, he was arguing for skepticism about our knowledge of claims about distinctively *metaphysical* necessities and possibilities. Williamson acknowledges that his account does not generalize to knowledge of all counterfactuals. Counterfactuals such as "If twelve people had come to the party, more than eleven people would have come to the party" seem to involve inference rather than imaginative simulation, while others such as "If twelve people had come to the party, it would have been a large party," he suggests, are neither involved in offline prediction nor in pure inference (2007, 151–52).

The problem from our point of view is this: the claims of metaphysical necessity and possibility typically at issue in arguments in metaphysics and elsewhere in philosophy are *not* analogous to claims about whether the rock would have rolled into the lake.[9] When we ask, "If Mary's brain were successfully transplanted into another body, would Mary survive?," "If 'Kubla Khan' were translated into Chinese, would it be the same poem?," or "If Schmidt were the true discoverer of the incompleteness of arithmetic, would the name 'Gödel' refer to Schmidt?," we are not rolling back a scenario in time and predicting, offline, its further development. The counterfactuals involved here are (if anything) most analogous to the one about whether, if twelve people had come to the party, it would have been a large party. It is claims to know the answers to these sorts of modal questions that Nozick is concerned about—for his target is to call into question philosophical arguments by intuition: "Philosophers who give great weight to intuitions need to offer some account of why such intuitions are reliable and are to be trusted; at least, they need to sketch how we would have acquired a reliable capacity of this sort" (2001, 125). But Williamson says very little of a positive nature about how a counterfactual like "if twelve people had come to the party, it would have been a large party" can be known—he merely insists that it cannot be known simply by applying general rules of inference (for it might involve knowing if the party was larger than average, which requires knowing what the average size of a party is).

Nozick's skeptical challenge was to explain how we could come to know specifically *metaphysical* claims of necessity and possibility, but Williamson does nothing to answer this challenge. Whatever its fate in defending knowledge of empirically grounded counterfactuals, a Williamson-style account does not solve the problem for knowledge of the kinds of modal claims centrally at issue in metaphysics, and often at issue elsewhere in philosophy. Once again, despite recent new efforts at demystifying modal knowledge, the classic epistemological problems remain in full force for understanding our knowledge of *metaphysical* modality.

---

[9] As Malgren (2011, 311–12) aptly insists, the capacities we use in evaluating counterfactuals may vary, depending on the *content* of the counterfactual involved.

7.3 Meeting the Integration Challenge

Both the integration challenge and the reliability challenge originally arose as problems for traditional approaches to metaphysical modality, which assume that modal discourse serves a *descriptive* function. The candidates for what is described vary of course, with some suggesting that there are modal features or properties of this world, or modal facts, or that the truthmakers involve possible worlds; and others suggesting that in the absence of good truthmakers we should be eliminativists or fictionalists about the modal. Anand Vaidya describes the integration challenge explicitly in terms of truthmakers: "The integration challenge for modality is to reconcile the mind-independence of modal claims with an epistemology that shows how we can know modal claims even though human thinkers do not bear causal relations to the relevant truth-makers for modal truths" (2017, section 2.3).

It is easy to see how the integration challenge becomes a problem if we assume that metaphysical modal statements have a descriptive function: of tracking and co-varying with features they describe, which can serve to explain their truth. To the extent that the descriptivist assumption informs our thinking, we are prone to think of our claims about metaphysical necessity and possibility on the model of claims aiming to track, co-vary with, and describe features of distant planets, or features of our actual environment. Despite their crucial differences, the views of both Lewis and Vetter fall into this pattern: both "posit" entities (possible worlds, in the case of Lewis, potentialities in this world in the case of Vetter) such that our modal knowledge must consist in knowing facts about these other worlds, or the potentialities in this world. In Lewis's case, however, there seems to be no prospect of giving a credible account of how we know these other worlds—for there is no prospect of any kind of causal connection to the other worlds. Vetter's work seems like a clear improvement in this regard, for we seem to have fewer barriers to knowing this-worldly potentialities, and we might be thought to have the basis for empirical knowledge of dispositions such as solubility. But as I have argued, even if we can get empirical knowledge of potentialities, that doesn't provide any account of how we could come to know the sorts of *metaphysical* modal truths that are centrally at issue in the debates of metaphysics and (often) elsewhere in philosophy (rather than those modal truths that are relevant, say, in chemistry).

On the other hand, if, with the normativist, we think of metaphysical claims as serving a fundamentally different function, the integration challenge shows up very differently. Once the option of treating modal discourse non-descriptively is on the table, the integration challenge can no longer be thought to arise in part because modal truthmakers do not bear a causal relation to human knowledge. For we no longer assume that modal truths require truthmakers with which we'd have to come into contact in order to acquire modal knowledge. This is not to say that no problems in the vicinity remain once we give up the descriptivist assumption—we still want a *positive* account of how we *can* acquire modal knowledge. Along those lines, we still face the most basic (and neutrally expressed) form of the integration challenge: reconciling a plausible account of what is involved in the truth of statements of a given kind (whatever that might be—not presupposing a truthmaker account) with a credible account of how we can know them.

How can a normativist reconcile an account of what is involved in the truth of a modal claim with a credible account of how we come to know the truth of modal claims? The normativist can give an account of what is involved in the truth of a modal claim: where a statement p is an object-language expression of an actual semantic rule (or consequence thereof), one is entitled to say "Necessarily p"; and from "Necessarily p," one is (by the T-schema) entitled to say "<Necessarily p> is true." Here we have an account of modal truth that enables us to distinguish true from false claims of metaphysical necessity without treating what it is for a claim of metaphysical necessity to be true as involving being *made true* by features of all possible worlds, or special features of this world.

How, on the normativist view, can we come to know such necessary truths? Once we give up the descriptivist assumption, and give up assuming that there are analogies between knowledge of modal properties and knowledge of natural properties detected in the environment, we also lose the assumption that there must be a causal relation to the relevant facts or features to legitimate the claim to have knowledge of them. The normativist doesn't think of acquiring modal knowledge as a matter of coming to see new, different features of the world, still less of perceiving some other possible worlds or a platonic world of essences. Instead, the normativist demystifies modal knowledge by considering the move from *using* language to knowing *basic* modal facts to be a matter of moving from *mastering* the rules for properly applying and refusing expressions (as a competent speaker), to being able to explicitly *convey* these rules (and what follows from them) in the object-language and indicative mood (though of course you may not be able to *recite* the rules even if you have *mastered* them, just as one may master grammatical rules without being able to recite them).

Competent speakers demonstrate tacit modal knowledge in their ability to properly use (apply, reapply, refuse) ordinary (non-modal) terms. But to acquire explicit modal knowledge we must gain an explicit understanding of the rules that most competent speakers may lack despite their ability to follow the rules. We can acquire a more explicit grasp of the underlying semantic rules by considering the multiplicity of actual or imagined cases in which the terms may properly be applied or refused, and analyzing their commonalities. By using that sort of thought experiment, one may gain a more systematic and explicit grasp of what the rules are. When we come—via this appropriate route from semantic competence—to express these rules in object-language indicatives, adding "necessarily" to make explicit the regulative status, and so to state modal truths arrived at via the appropriate route, we can be said to have modal knowledge.[10]

While this is the way of coming to know the most basic truths about what is metaphysically necessary, it is not the only way to come to know metaphysical modal truths. One may also consider what follows from the rules, either as combined with each other or with empirical facts. Empirical discoveries, moreover, may contribute to knowledge of more detailed, *derivative* modal facts. For example, it may be a conceptual

---

[10] This is the paradigmatic route to basic modal knowledge. Could one also count as having modal knowledge based on testimony from other competent speakers, say, without being a competent speaker oneself? I will leave that question to the side here. Some might worry that there is an implicit circularity, since this sort of analysis involves determining when the relevant terms *could be applied*. But that is an optional way of describing the task: better to think of it as working out when the term *may* and *may not* be applied, exercising one's *mastery* of the norms for using the term (not a *discovery* of *metaphysical possibilities* of applying it).

truth (knowable via semantic competence) that whatever microstructure the baptized sample has, water necessarily has that microstructure, while it is a derivative, empirically discoverable truth that water necessarily has the microstructure H_2O. But we can acquire knowledge of this derivative modal claim by way of empirical investigation (into the microstructure of *that* stuff) and knowing the more basic modal truth that, *whatever* microstructure water has, it has necessarily.

In any case, the normativist has available a plausible and fitting way of reconciling what it is for modal claims to be true with a credible account of how we come to know modal truths. What it is for a claim of metaphysical necessity to be true is for it to give an object-language expression of an actual semantic rule (or consequence thereof). And we can come to know the truth of basic claims of metaphysical necessity by starting with semantic competence and coming to gain explicit knowledge of the actual semantic rules involved, and/or by reasoning through their consequences, perhaps as combined with empirical truths. This gives an entirely fitting match of our account of what it is for metaphysical modal claims to be true, and of what it takes for us to know them.

The account provided of metaphysical modal knowledge here falls closer to the traditional rationalist camp than to quasi-empirical and counterfactual approaches to modal knowledge. Yet rationalist views of modal knowledge classically come up against the question: Why should our ability to conceive or imagine certain scenarios have anything to do with modal facts, which are supposed to be mind-independent and objective? As Wright puts it, if we cannot conceive of something, then "that is just how things are with us; it is a further, tendentious step to inflate our imaginative limitations into a metaphysical discovery" (1980, 439–40).[11]

The normativist approach provides a nice route through this issue. For on this view, our justification for asserting a claim of metaphysical necessity comes from our mastery of the semantic rules, much as our standard justification for judging a sentence of our native language to be grammatical comes from our mastery of linguistic rules. A basic

---

[11] Jenkins (2010, 261) also cites this point approvingly. For a response to Wright's worry, see Blackburn (1993).

claim of metaphysical necessity is true if it does actually have the status of an object-language expression of a semantic rule (or as following from that). Given the truth of a basic claim of metaphysical necessity, we are then entitled to say that there are the relevant modal facts. These links ensure that our modal judgments and the modal facts will tend to be in sync (and non-accidentally so), at least for easy and central cases.

One question commonly raised is how a given approach to modal epistemology can account for our relative confidence in what Peter van Inwagen (1998) has called "everyday" versus "remote" modal truths. One point that I aim to make clear is that we should distinguish types of modal truths—separating empirical dispositional or counterfactual claims from metaphysical modal claims. Where the former are at issue, a story such as that given by Roca-Royes (that it is a matter of how close the imagined case is to experienced cases) may be suitable (2017, 234). It is the latter that the normativist is concerned with, and here again an account can be given: those "nearby" or "everyday" truths in which we are confident of our modal knowledge—say, that a person typically retains her identity after moving a few feet to the left—are those in which the rules governing our concept are determinate, and apply to the case. Those in which we feel uneasy, in which the cases are remote (such as Parfit's [1984] cases of teleportation, division, gradual complete psychological or physical replacement) are cases that push the limits of our concepts, presenting cases that our concepts do not give a determinate answer to, and so cases that call for decision rather than simple application of the concept.

7.4 Meeting the Reliability Challenge

Like the integration challenge, the reliability challenge—in its classic form—relies on the descriptivist assumption, thinking of our claims about metaphysical necessity and possibility on the model of claims aiming to track, co-vary with, and describe certain features of our environment: as if they were detecting features of distant planets, or ordinary properties or facts of our immediate surroundings. This challenge is often presented as asking that we give reason for thinking that there is a reliable module for "detecting" metaphysical necessities (Vaidya

2017, section 1.2.4)—assuming that modal discourse should serve a kind of tracking function, so that (if it works properly) we can detect and keep track of the modal facts we aim to describe. The realist about modality is said to owe an explanation of how we could have evolved a reliable capacity to "track" the modal truths posited by traditional (heavyweight) realists. Street makes a similar argument for the *moral* case, arguing that the moral realist must aim to understand the evolutionary causes as "having *tracked* the truth; we may understand the relation in question to be a *tracking* relation" (2006, 125). Modal knowledge taken on that model must be conceived as analogous to knowledge of what predators are in the vicinity: having beliefs that reliably track the facts about what predators are in the vicinity might readily explain why we would have evolved a capacity for reliably tracking predators, and in general for forming reliable beliefs about certain relevant features of our environment.

The challenge for the modal realist is then conceived of as giving a parallel story for our beliefs about metaphysical necessity that shows why an ability to track these modal truths would be evolutionarily advantageous. And that is a formidable demand. Moreover, as I have argued in Section 7.1, even if we think of modal facts or properties as features of this world, our causal relations to the statue and the lump are the same—so it is hard to see how any causal story could be given of how we come to detect one set of modal properties rather than the other.

In short, the reliability problem arises in its most formidable form when we make the descriptivist assumption: thinking of the knowledge expressed in true modal statements as aiming to describe some other worlds, or modal features of this world, which we must then be able to detect and track in such a way that our modal beliefs can come to reliably co-vary with them. For then we can identify two in-principle barriers to giving any account of how we could have acquired modal knowledge. First, there are barriers to thinking that we could have any appropriate causal connection or other kind of access to the features of other worlds, or of this world, that are supposed to be known. Second, there are barriers to thinking that, even if we had such access, there is room for a story about why such knowledge would be selected for, why the ability to detect these merely metaphysical modal differences could aid our reproduction or survival.

However, as I have been arguing throughout, we needn't—and shouldn't—assume that modal discourse has a descriptive function. If we question the descriptivist's functional assumption, the demands of the reliability challenge again show up very differently. For we then give up the assumption that, if we know modal facts, we must think of ourselves as having evolved a special faculty for tracking features of other possible worlds, or special modal features of this world. And we come to think of the very search for a "tracking" account of modal knowledge as wrong-headed. Again, on this view we give an account of what it is to come to know modal truths that is not a metaphysics-first account, which begins by "positing" other worlds or features of this world, and then tries to show how we can come to know them. Instead, we begin from an account of what it is for a claim of metaphysical necessity to be true, and a parallel account showing how we can come to know these truths via extrapolation from our semantic competence, reasoning, and (sometimes) empirical knowledge.

On the normativist approach, of course, we still owe a naturalistically respectable account of how we *can* acquire modal knowledge. But this will no longer be put as a problem of how we could have evolved a faculty to detect features of isolated worlds, or modal properties of this world. Once the descriptivist assumption is dropped, the reliability challenge should not be thought of as a demand to explain why it would be an advantage to evolve reliable modality detectors, but rather of what the advantage is of being able to modalize (well): to speak modally, be responsive to, and express modal truths. All we need at bottom is room for a good evolutionary account of how we could have come to modalize as we do: of why it would be evolutionarily advantageous to be able to make, understand, and be responsive to modal judgments, and to do so *well* (in ways that ensure our judgments tend to be non-accidentally true).

The question of how we evolved the capacity to make metaphysical modal claims is an empirical one. Even work on how language in general could have evolved is in its infancy (Bickerton 2007); we certainly cannot provide a more specific account of how the use of metaphysical modal claims evolved. Nonetheless, what we can do is to insist that the two in-principle barriers to such an account that plague those who retain the descriptivist assumption fall away for the normativist.

First, there is, on the normativist view, no need to suppose that we could have any appropriate causal connection or other kind of empirical access enabling us to "track" the modal features or other worlds, in order to acquire modal knowledge. For on this view we acquire modal knowledge via extrapolation from our semantic competence (sometimes combined with reasoning and/or ordinary empirical knowledge)—not via access to disconnected worlds or to special modal facts or properties of this world. The difficulties of positing such a connection or tracking ability are thus no difficulties for the normativist.

Second, there is no need to give a story about why the ability to detect these modal properties would bring a selective advantage. There is only the requirement to explain how the ability to make true metaphysical modal judgments could have been useful—and the normativist is in a good position to do that. As I have described it in Section 7.3, the ability to acquire modal knowledge relies on three capacities: the ability to master semantic rules and to make explicit what is involved in that tacit mastery, empirical knowledge (at least sometimes), and reasoning abilities (in order to be able to figure out what follows from these rules—sometimes, as combined with the empirical facts). Let us assume (as seems reasonable) that there are respectable evolutionary explanations of why natural selection might have favored those capable of acquiring ordinary empirical knowledge, and of employing reasoning skills. All that remains to be given, then, is a naturalistically acceptable story of why it might be useful to be able to master semantic rules and convey them explicitly (in the form of object-language indicatives)—and respond appropriately when others do so.

On the normativist view, a central function of metaphysical modal discourse is to enable us to convey and reason with and from semantic rules in particularly advantageous ways—for example, enabling us to convey semantic rules in the object-language, in ways that enable us to also make explicit our ways of reasoning with rules, and to express permissions, and enabling us to publicly renegotiate the rules. Why might it be evolutionarily advantageous to be able to do these things?[12]

---

[12] I am indebted to Mark Warren for helpful discussion of this question.

Think of the advantages an individual has by being part of a community of users of a common language. Such individuals can only fully participate in those linguistic practices that benefit the whole community if they use language in ways that enable them to communicate, to understand others, to engage in joint planning, joint activities, and information sharing, and so on. But these evolutionary advantages come about only if such individuals can indeed *communicate* with others in the community, which requires that they use terms with at least closely resembling or overlapping rules of use. For such a communicative community to survive—one that uses a full rich natural language—it is undoubtedly useful for its members to have the capability of mastering the rules, and to have some way of instructing in the rules of use, communicating the rules of use, and policing (mis-) uses. Moreover, for the language of the community to be responsive to our changing circumstances and interests, there must also be ways of pressing for innovations of various kinds, (re-)negotiating the rules of use. Having metaphysical modal language enables speakers to do all of these things, thereby better enabling them to develop and retain a common language within the community, as well as one that is flexible and responsive to changing environmental conditions and to the changing needs and values of the community. Individuals who cannot master the rules of use, or grasp the import of modal vocabulary, are more prone to fail when others attempt to linguistically guide and instruct them, and to make more mistakes—mistakes that could prove costly, given the costs that can come from misunderstanding others and from the social ostracism and isolation that come from failure to be a full part of a linguistic community.

In short, if mastering a common public language, governed by largely shared rules that are teachable and open to innovation, can be shown to be useful from an evolutionary perspective, it is not difficult to see how the ability to modalize well (in ways relevant to expressing and responding appropriately to metaphysical modal truths) would be useful. There is certainly no in-principle barrier to there being a plausible evolutionary story about why it is useful to be able to modalize— nothing that parallels the principled problem that Nozick raises for Lewisian views.

7.5 Does the Challenge Arise Again?

Thus far I have aimed to show that recent empiricist accounts of modal knowledge do not sufficiently answer the integration challenge or the reliability challenge, where knowledge of metaphysical modality is concerned. I have also argued that both challenges show up differently once the descriptive functional assumption is dropped, and that the remaining form of each challenge is addressed well by modal normativism.

Nonetheless, those familiar with the parallel problems in the meta-ethics literature might worry that the answer can't be that simple. Street has famously pressed an evolutionary debunking argument in meta-ethics. Street's argument, at least on one widely shared interpretation, is a particular form of the reliability challenge.[13] In her later work, however, she makes clear that she does not think that the underlying problem is avoided by avoiding a tracking account of moral knowledge. For she acknowledges that Simon Blackburn, Allan Gibbard, and other quasi-realists reject tracking accounts, holding that "the *truth* of our values figures nowhere in the best evolutionary explanation of why we should hold them" (2011, 13). Yet nonetheless, she argues that "quasi-realists are in no better shape than ordinary realists" regarding epistemological worries (2011, 6). For, she argues, a problem arises for any view that aims to combine a naturalistic explanation of the nature and origins of moral judgment, with accepting that there is an "independent moral truth as such."

The normativist view of modality is similar in various ways to quasi-realist meta-ethical views. Both insist that the relevant area of discourse (modal/moral) has a "non-descriptive" function—that is, that it functions differently from standard empirical discourse that aims to "track" or "report" certain facts of the world. Both aim to give a naturalistic explanation of why we make certain moral/modal judgements, in a way that doesn't appeal to their truth. Both nonetheless hold that there are (modal/moral) truths, and that there are (modal/moral)

---

[13] Dreier (2012) and Schechter (2018) interpret Street's challenge as a version of the reliability challenge. For an alternative interpretation of where the challenge really lies, see Berker (2014).

facts. Perhaps most importantly, both accept that these moral/modal facts are—in a relevant and important sense—mind-independent. For both accept certain independence counterfactuals. The moral quasi-realist accepts, for example, that it would still be wrong to kick dogs for fun, even if it were the case that I (and others) approved of it. For, as Gibbard puts it, to say this "might amount to planning to avoid kicking dogs for fun, planning this even for the contingency of being someone who approves of such fun, and who is surrounded by people who approve" (2003, 186).

The modal normativist can tell a parallel story, entitling her to accept independence counterfactuals. For example, as I have argued in section 3.4, the normativist is entitled to accept, for example, that (assuming no empirical surprises, and so that the conditions for "seal" being an animal kind term are met)[14] it is necessary that seals are mammals, and that this would still be the case even in worlds in which there were no speakers or thinkers (and so in which we don't use the relevant terms) at all. Indeed, it is crucial that the modal normativist be able to accept this kind of independence counterfactual in order to avoid the classic objections to modal conventionalism, to the effect that it makes the truth of necessary statements contingent on our adoption of certain linguistic conventions.[15] Modal normativists can and do accept such independence counterfactuals, since while the *existence* of a claim (or the *meaningfulness* of the relevant piece of language) "Necessarily, seals are mammals" may depend on human language, its *truth*, on the normativist view, does not so depend. As I have argued in Section 3.4, we evaluate the truth of counterfactuals (whatever they are) in ways that *hold the meaning of the claim intact* while we conduct the evaluation. So, in this case as with others, when we ask whether "Necessarily, seals are mammals" would be true in other circumstances, we do so without changing the meaning of "seal," "mammal," or the other terms in the sentence. How do we determine (on the normativist view) whether any statement P is necessary? As always, when we ask whether

---

[14] The need for that assumption is made explicit in Chapter 4. I will leave that assumption implicit in what follows in this chapter, to make the exposition more straightforward.

[15] For criticisms along these lines, see, for example, Sider (2003, 199–200) and Boghossian (1997, 336). For response see Chapter 3.

□P, we ask whether P is an object-language expression of an actual semantic rule (or follows from such rules). Imagine we started from the non-modal statement: (a) "Seals are mammals." By the normativist's lights, since this is an object-language expression of what follows from an actual framework-level rule of use (combined with the empirical fact that seals are actually mammals), we are entitled to add "necessarily." That is why we are entitled to (b) "Necessarily, seals are animals." But (b) itself is an object-language expression of semantic rules—this time, adding the rule for "necessarily" that entitled us to add it onto our original claim (a). So, we are entitled to iterate the modality (adopting axiom 4 of modal logics) and conclude that the claim "Necessarily, seals are animals" is itself necessarily true. (If it's a rule, it's a rule that it's a rule.) But if (b) is necessarily true, then its truth is not contingent on the existence of minds, languages, and so forth (although the existence and meaningfulness of the relevant piece of language of course may be mind-dependent).

So, the modal normativist, like the quasi-realist, aims to give a naturalistically acceptable account of the relevant (modal/moral) judgments, while still accepting independence counterfactuals. Given all that ethical quasi-realism and modal normativism have in common, one might then wonder whether Street's arguments carry over to suggest that modal normativists have the same epistemological problems as traditional modal realists do. Let's see.

Street (2011) argues as follows. The quasi-realist wants to imitate what the realist can say, for example, about moral facts being mind-independent. But if quasi-realists want to do that, she argues, they must "admit as intelligible talk about the independent normative truth *as such*" (9). For two people might disagree about what the moral truths are (say, whether it's morally permissible to eat meat) and yet agree that, whatever the truth is here, it is mind-independent. The quasi-realist needs to capture the idea that there is something they agree about, Street argues, and to do so, the quasi-realist needs to accept that it makes sense to talk about "the independent normative truth as such." What does she mean by that phrase? She means "talk about the independent normative truth which does not presuppose any substantive views on what that truth is" (9). But once they admit that such talk is intelligible, she argues, quasi-realists (like traditional realists) owe an answer to the question

What is the relation between [the] evolutionary influence on our normative judgments, on the one hand, and the independent normative truth considered as such, on the other? . . . The following possibilities are exhaustive: either the evolutionary influence tended to push our normative judgments *towards* the independent normative truth, or else it tended to push them *away from* or *in ways that bear no relation to* that truth.

(12)

So, given that a "tracking" account that could explain how evolution pushed us toward the independent normative truth is "scientifically indefensible" (13) (and rejected by quasi-realists anyway), she argues, quasi-realists are left with the options that evolutionary forces pushed us in ways that led our normative judgments away from or in ways that bear no relation to the independent normative truth (13–14).

Street emphasizes that, in talking about the "independent normative truth considered as such," we must be completely neutral about what the independent normative truths *are*, such that, "for all we know as a conceptual matter . . . what's ultimately worth pursuing could well be hand-clasping, or writing the number 587 over and over again, or counting blades of grass" (14). Thus, she rejects responses that would explain, for example, how evolution pushed us toward believing that staying alive and developing one's capacities are worth pursuing independently of anyone's attitudes, or any explanations that take the form "what's ultimately worth pursuing is such-and-such, and here is why we were selected to think so," since these presuppose substantive views about what the independent truth is (17–18). For "as a conceptual matter, the independent normative truth could be *anything*" (14). Taking this into account, she insists that it would be an extraordinarily unlikely coincidence if the values we evolved to have happen to hit on the things that "are independently really worth pursuing" (14).[16] And so she concludes that "all standard epistemological worries about realism may be transferred to the case of quasi-realism" (27).

---

[16] In this way, Street's argument against quasi-realism certainly follows the form identified by Vavova (2015): of not merely presenting a skeptical challenge to show how moral knowledge is possible, but rather of raising targeted, empirical reasons to doubt claims of moral knowledge.

Let us put to the side the issue in meta-ethics of whether Street's argument is fair to meta-ethical quasi-realists or effective against them.[17] The key question here is whether arguments like hers show that *modal normativists* can't answer the reliability challenge as easily as I suggested, making their problem with modal epistemology as difficult as that facing traditional modal realists.

If we were to reconstruct the argument in those terms, it would go something like this. Modal normativists like myself accept that there are modal truths, and that these modal truths are mind-independent. But as long as normativists accept that there are mind-independent modal truths, they face Street's question "What is the relation between [the] evolutionary influence on our modal judgments, on the one hand, and the independent modal truth considered as such, on the other?" (12).

Whatever may be the case for quasi-realists, modal normativists certainly do not purport to (or need to purport to) remain neutral about what the first-order metaphysical modal facts may be. It is the very starting place of the view to say that metaphysical necessities are object-language expressions of semantic rules, or what follows from them. And so (assuming one also, in using a language, has substantive [if implicit] views about what the semantic rules are), the normativist will be committed to some views about what the modal truths are. Thus, although the modal normativist accepts independence counterfactuals, she is certainly not committed to the view that we can go completely wrong with our modal judgments—and if this is part of some heavyweight realist views of modality, there is no need for the modal normativist to mimic the realist in that (compare Street 2011, 17). Thus, the challenge for the modal normativist cannot be properly put as the demand to say, "What is the relation between [the] evolutionary influence on our modal judgments, on the one hand, and the independent modal truth considered as such [staying neutral on what these modal truths might be], on the other?"

---

[17] Blackburn (unpublished) denies that quasi-realists are, or need to be, committed to anything like Street's "independent normative truth considered as such," in which they must remain entirely neutral on what the normative truths are.

Instead, the fair epistemological challenge is to say: suppose the modal normativist is roughly right about what the metaphysical modal truths are, and right in thinking that basic true claims of metaphysical necessities are object-language formulations of semantic rules. What explanation could the normativist give of the reliability of our modal judgments—of why we don't go too far off track? That is the sort of explanation I have given.

7.6 The Unexplained Coincidence Problem

I have argued that modal normativists are under no obligation to give an account of how our modal beliefs may *track* modal truths, and have tried to show how they can give a naturalistically acceptable account of why the ability to make metaphysical modal judgments is useful, and why such judgments tend to be true. I have also argued that Street's attempt to show that there is a difficulty for quasi-realists in combining a naturalistic explanation of moral judgments with a view that moral facts are mind-independent (whatever its plausibility against quasi-realists may or may not be) does not carry over to present a problem for modal normativists. For while modal normativists are justified in accepting independence counterfactuals to the effect that metaphysical modal truths aren't contingent on our adoption of certain linguistic rules, they do not accept anything like the "independent modal truth as such" that Street uses to formulate her argument against the quasi-realist. But perhaps we still are not done.

For some formulate the challenge in a way that doesn't rely on saddling the quasi-realist with commitment to an "independent normative truth *as such*." Jamie Dreier takes the challenge to be simply to: "give an explanation of why we reliably form normative [/modal] beliefs" (2012, 271) or "how is it that we have a belief-forming mechanism [about modality] that is reliable?" (272). But Dreier does not interpret Street's challenge as arising from the requirement that quasi-realists accept talk of the "independent normative truth as such," *taking this to require no substantive commitments about what the normative truths are.* Dreier takes it to arise just given that the quasi-realist accepts certain independence counterfactuals (IC), such as:

(IC): Even if we were to approve of kicking dogs for fun, it would still be wrong to do it.

(274)

As noted in Section 7.5, the modal normativist does accept parallel independence counterfactuals—indeed, she must if she is to avoid the standard objections to modal conventionalism. So, she accepts:

(IC): Even if there were no linguistic creatures at all, it would still be necessary that water is H_2O.

On Dreier's interpretation of Street, however, accepting such independence counterfactuals leads to the problem of unexplained coincidence. Making the needed replacements to fit the modal case, we can read Dreier's version of the problem as follows:

> Once a theory takes these [independence] counterfactuals on board, it loses the capacity to explain the match between our [modal judgments] and the [modal] truth. For it cannot appeal to counterfactual dependence of [modal fact] on [modal judgment], and . . . there is no good explanation to be had by appealing to counterfactual dependence of [modal beliefs] on [modal facts]. Without any sort of counterfactual dependence to appeal to, the explanation for the happy match between our [modal judgments] and the [modal] truth is an Unexplained Coincidence.
>
> (adapted from Dreier 2012, 275)

Put in terms that bear on the modal normativist's position, the argument would be that as long as the normativist accepts that there are mind-independent modal truths (which I insist upon), she owes an explanation of the relation between the evolutionary influence on our *modal* judgments and the independent modal truths. But if we cannot give a tracking account to explain how evolution could have pushed us *toward* the independent modal truth, we are stuck with thinking they pushed us away from it or in irrelevant directions—leaving our success an unexplained coincidence. And so, without *some sort* of explanation we might be thought to leave it as an unexplained coincidence that the core modal propositions we believe after reflection and discussion tend to be true, and those we disbelieve under similar circumstances tend to be false.

Dreier gives an ingenious argument to show that quasi-realists in fact have no unexplained coincidence problem: he takes us from a language without evaluative predicates and builds, step by step, a (quasi-realist) moral language, complete with moral predicates, a truth predicate, and a claim of objectivity, and argues that there is no way an unexplained coincidence could enter at any stage (2012). Nonetheless, Dreier himself still considers the argument to be somewhat unsatisfying since, if successful, it shows *that* there can be no unexplained coincidence problem for quasi-realists, but does not tell us *why* no explanation is needed for the match between normative facts and our beliefs about them (2012, 286).

Can the modal normativist discharge this debt, for the modal case? I think the modal normativist is in a good position to answer this challenge—perhaps not head-on, by saying why *no* explanation is needed of the relation between modal facts and our studied modal judgments, but instead by explaining why we should expect an entirely different *sort of* explanation than that given in cases of perceptual knowledge, given the crucial differences in the function and rules governing the discourse. Dreier, following Gibbard, says one might try to say why there is no demand for explanation in the case of fit between our normative beliefs and facts by distinguishing robust facts, which are such that "our best (or, the correct) account of our thoughts and talk is partly in terms of it," and moral facts, where the "best account of our normative and evaluative thoughts never mentions the right or the good" (2012, 286–87), giving us a picture on which normative facts "do no explanatory heavy lifting, they are metaphysically lightweight, so phenomena involving them do not create real explanatory gaps," though even this he takes to be no more than a suggestive picture that doesn't give a straight answer to the question of why no explanation is called for here (2012, 287).

I have argued elsewhere (Thomasson 2015) that we should not excuse the lack of explanation by appealing to a metaphysical difference between "lightweight" and "heavyweight" facts, or anything along those lines. (Instead, I have argued that we should accept that there *are* the relevant facts in the only sense these terms have [Thomasson 2015, Chapter 3]). The relevant difference, on the normativist view, is not in the *metaphysical status of the facts*, but rather in the *function of, and rules governing, the discourse*. And that difference accounts not for why we need *no* explanation of the broad match between moral or modal beliefs and the correlative facts, but rather for why we should expect an entirely different *kind of* explanation. (Given the quarry here, I will draw out the response only for the modal case, leaving it to others to determine whether it is a model that could help in the moral case as well.)

The normativist holds that modal discourse has a fundamentally different function than discourse that aims to track and report on features of the external environment and co-vary with them. There are no doubt a great many different functions that areas of discourse can serve, but we can at least begin by drawing, following Price (2011, 20–21), a distinction between those areas of discourse that are e(xternal)-representations, in the sense that they put "the system-world link on the front foot," giving "priority to the idea that the job of a representation is to *co-vary* with something else—typically, some *external* factor, or environmental condition" (2011, 20)—and those that are not. Where the function of an area of discourse is e-representational, questions about how we are able to track the relevant facts, what perceptual or quasi-perceptual faculty we have for detecting them, and how that might have evolved in ways that enable our beliefs in the area to co-vary with the facts, are entirely appropriate.

Such questions, however, are not appropriate for areas of discourse that do not have an e-representational function. In the case of modal discourse, I have argued, the function is not to report on or track features of the environment—so the discourse can get along perfectly well without positing any such connection to justify a claim of co-variation. The idea that those engaged in Therapeutic Touch can detect human energy fields with their hands is debunked by tests showing no correlation (Rosa 1998). But where tracking external facts is not a function of an area of discourse, no such debunking of an area of discourse is appropriate. The function of metaphysical modal discourse (I have argued) is to enable us to convey, reason with, and sometimes renegotiate semantic rules (and their consequences) in the useful form of object-language indicatives. Modal discourse serves its function if it enables us to do that task well—it does not have as a success condition the ability to track features or this or other worlds.

But how, then, can we address the unexplained coincidence problem—giving some explanation (if not a tracking/fact-detecting explanation) of why our reflective metaphysical modal beliefs tend to broadly "match" the modal facts—or, more neutrally put, of why our reflective metaphysical modal beliefs tend to be true? While the normativist rejects the demand for a "tracking" explanation, she is able to say why evolutionary pressures might lead to development of a shared public language, with shared rules (yet rules that are also flexible and up for renegotiation in the face of changing circumstances or needs). She can also say why pressures on an individual for being a full member of a linguistic community (with all the associated benefits for survival and reproduction) tend to push them toward mastering those rules along with mastering ways of enforcing and responding to enforcements of those rules. Given all that, as I have argued in Section 7.4, we can give an evolutionary account of why speakers will tend to have the needed mastery of the rules, and ability to communicate those rules through the expression of modal truths.

Now we can ask, with Dreier: What explains the "broad match" between our most basic (metaphysical) modal beliefs and the basic (metaphysical) modal facts, if not the counterfactual dependence of one on the other? Where do our basic metaphysical modal beliefs come from? On the whole, when all goes well, they come from our linguistic mastery: first, from our mastery of the rules of use for ordinary terms ("bachelor" and "unmarried"); and second, from our mastery of the introduction rules for modal terms like "necessity," which entitle us to stick "necessarily" onto an object-language expression of a rule of use, and so can bring us to reject a statement that there is a married bachelor, and to believe that it's necessary that bachelors are unmarried. Why do these beliefs tend to "match" the modal facts? Talk of modal facts just involves hypostatization out of modal truths. On the normativist view, we can legitimately introduce a claim of metaphysical necessity by adding "Necessarily" onto any statement p that is an object-language expression of an actual semantic rule. And, using the T-schema, we are

entitled to infer from "Necessarily p" to "it is true that [Necessarily p]."
Where we have a true claim of the form "Necessarily p," we can also engage in trivial truth-preserving inferences that entitle us to infer from
the true claim "Necessarily p" to "It is a fact that p is necessary." Talk of
modal facts just involves hypostatization out of necessary truths, and
necessary truths just are object-language formulations of rules of use.
The question of why our metaphysical modal beliefs tend to be true
can be reduced to the question of why we tend to be able to accurately
express rules of use in object-language indicatives, and that can be
explained by our linguistic competence (including competence with
the term "necessarily").

In short, the needed explanation can go via understanding the
way the discourse about modal facts is introduced—not via the metaphysical standing of the relevant facts, or an appeal to a counterfactual dependence of modal beliefs on modal facts or vice versa. Given
that most of us are competent speakers of our native language, we can
expect native speakers to be pretty good (though certainly not infallible) at determining what is and is not an object-language expression
of a semantic rule, and so at distinguishing those necessity (and possibility) claims that are legitimately derived from those that are not.
On the normativist view, that fully entitles us to say that there is the
relevant modal fact in the only sense that has sense—there is no danger
of a "slippage" that might make us worry that, while we have blithely
engaged in this redundant inference, we have failed to match the *true*
modal facts of the world.

There are of course dangers that we (even competent speakers)
may fail to correctly judge what is/is not an object-language expression of a semantic rule of our common public language, or what is a
consequence thereof (particularly when we plug in empirical truths).
Our modal beliefs are not infallible. Moreover, the rules of our public
language may sometimes or even often be vague, indeterminate, contextually variable, and/or open to renegotiation—often leading to
difficulties in saying definitively what the modal truth *is*. But the point
here is that the modal normativist is in a position to give a perfectly
adequate explanation of why we needn't worry that most of our central
and reflective basic metaphysical modal beliefs might "fail to match"
the facts—an explanation that relies not on positing a tracking faculty

but rather on understanding the function and introduction rules for the discourse that enable us to speak of "modal facts" at all.[18]

So, the normativist is in a good position to give an evolutionary account of our modalizing. And she can also give an account of why, given our ability to use basic modal language, basic metaphysical modal beliefs tend to be *true*. On the normativist approach there is no danger of a kind of massive slippage that debunking arguments warn of between our modal beliefs and modal facts. For competent speakers, who have mastered the semantic rules, should typically be capable of acquiring the ability to convey those rules in object-language indicatives, adding the useful modal terminology. And when they do, the claims of metaphysical necessity they make will be true, and will entitle them to make trivial inferences about what the modal facts are. On this view, seeking to know modal truths by working from our semantic competence in this way is not at all like trying to get to Bermuda by "letting the course of your boat be determined by the wind and tides" (Street 2006, 121).

The modal epistemology we get out of the normativist view thus also brings the advantage of avoiding skepticism about modal knowledge. We might become skeptics about modal knowledge if we think it proper to expect and demand a causal connection to link the properties or facts known with our beliefs about them—and find none plausible in this case. Or we might become skeptics about modal knowledge if, with Nozick, we think it apt to demand an evolutionary story about how we could have evolved a faculty enabling us to correctly detect the modal facts and properties—but doubt whether any could be forthcoming. But I have argued that once we drop the descriptivist assumption these demands (so expressed) seem otiose. Moreover, once we adopt the normativist approach to metaphysical modality, we can see the route to a clear and plausible account of metaphysical modal knowledge that meets both of the classic challenges in the form in which they might be thought to remain, and avoids leaving the "broad match" between basic modal facts and our beliefs about them an "unexplained coincidence."

---

[18] The story, of course, will be somewhat more complicated for the acquisition of derivative modal knowledge, since that also involves knowledge of the relevant empirical filler facts, which is subject to the usual kinds of empirical error.

7.7 Conclusion

One important lesson that we can draw from this chapter is that it can be important not to assume that the problems of modal epistemology may all be treated together. A plausible story about how we can come to know the truth of empirical counterfactuals or dispositional claims may run very differently from the sort of story we need to account for our knowledge of the truths of metaphysical modal claims, and many of the other modal claims that play a central role in philosophy.[19]

A second lesson is that we should not simply assume that all forms of discourse have a descriptive, tracking, e-representational function. The epistemological problems appear most insuperable when we assume that modal discourse functions in ways that parallel ordinary empirical discourse. Similar epistemological problems are known to arise for other areas of discourse, including the mathematical and moral. And in both of those arenas, there are plausible views that reject the descriptivist assumption. Whether doing so also makes the parallel problems show up differently in those cases, and opens the route to a positive solution, I will leave for others to investigate.

The point I have made here is specific to metaphysical modality. I have argued that adopting the modal normativist position makes both of the classic epistemological challenges to modality show up differently. I have also argued that the modal normativist can meet the positive epistemological challenges that remain—providing a plausible account of our knowledge of metaphysical modality that meets the general integration and reliability challenges and avoids the unexplained coincidence problem.

The fact that the normativist view can give a plausible account of how we can come to know modal facts in a way that avoids the classic epistemological difficulties is a very significant advantage. In response to David Lewis's claim that the problem of modal knowledge "is a problem for everyone (certain skeptics and conventionalists

---

[19] This echoes a conclusion of Roca-Royes, who notes that her work "suggests very strongly that a sufficiently comprehensive epistemology of modality cannot look uniform" (2017, 243).

excepted)" (1986, 113),[20] we can now say that the time has come for another exception. As I have argued, the key to avoiding the traditional problems of how we can come to *know* the metaphysical modal facts, is avoiding the traditional descriptivist assumption about what metaphysical modal discourse functions to *do*. To build a positive modal epistemology, we must also work from there to give a plausible account of what the function of metaphysical modal talk is, how it is introduced, and what rules it follows. These can form the basis for explaining how we can come to know metaphysical modal truths, and why we might have evolved in a way that enables us to be pretty good at modalizing. And that, in turn, can help us not only to avoid skepticism about metaphysical modal knowledge, but also to avoid a despairing skepticism about a good portion of work in metaphysics and other areas of philosophy.

Related to these epistemological results are methodological results. For, as I shall argue in the next chapter, the normativist account also has the advantage of being able to vindicate our traditional methods for answering metaphysical modal questions—including methods along the lines of conceptual analysis, consulting intuitions about imagined cases, and the like—at least when such questions are taken in the mode of "internal" questions.

This of course does not mean that there is no room for indecisiveness, uncertainty, or error in our modal beliefs. Nor does it mean that we can't have valid grounds for *revising* our modal beliefs—particularly when we take modal questions in the mode of *external* questions. For there is another common use of metaphysical modal vocabulary—one that can do a great deal to account for the diversity of metaphysical modal opinions that remain even in a roomful of metaphysicians, all of whom are undeniably competent speakers. That is a use not in conveying or enforcing the rules of use for our shared terms, but rather in negotiating for changes in how these key terms are to be used, where these often go along with changes in our other (often nonlinguistic)

---

[20] Compare Sidelle (1989, 110–11), who argues that conventionalism is the only way to explain why intuition is a guide to modal truth. For reference to be determinate, we must associate the relevant modal conditions, but then we have the grounds to know what its modal properties are.

practices. In the next chapter I shall also discuss how understanding these uses of modal terms can help us understand the persistence of modal debates in metaphysics and what methods we should use in addressing them.[21]

[21] I would like to thank David Plunkett, two anonymous referees, and the audience at the University of Toronto for extremely helpful comments on an earlier version of this chapter, which led to substantial improvements.

8

Methodological Advantages

The major problem that motivated me in this study, as well as in *Ontology Made Easy* before it, was working out what metaphysics can and should do—and how we should do it.[1] It is a problem made visible by the proliferation of unresolved debates, where even the participants have no clear or shared conception of what *would* resolve them. These are problems in the methodology of metaphysics. I have discussed existence questions elsewhere (Thomasson 2015); here I will limit myself to discussing the methodological problems that arise for debates about what is metaphysically possible or necessary.

What kinds of methods *do* we use, and what kinds of methods *should* we use, in resolving these questions and adjudicating these debates? A central methodological problem that has arisen is: What could *justify* using those methods that are standard fare in metaphysical modal debates? Traditionally, debates about what is metaphysically possible or necessary appeal to intuitions or thought experiments. So, for example, when addressing questions about personal identity or the persistence conditions for works of art, we ask *what we would say* if someone underwent memory loss, or brain transplantation; or if some work of music were transposed or altered in various ways. Much the same goes for debates about questions of metaphysical possibility in other arenas—for example, when we ask whether we would count a speaker as referring to Schmidt with the name "Gödel," or whether a traveler in fake barn country could know that there was a real barn before her. Yet if one thinks of modal discourse as aiming to *describe*

---

[1] Portions of this chapter draw on Thomasson (2012) and are used here with kind permission of the *Monist*.

Norms and Necessity. Amie L. Thomasson, Oxford University Press (2020). © Oxford University Press.
DOI: 10.1093/oso/9780190098193.001.0001

mind-independent facts, properties, or worlds, it is hard to see why intuitions or thought experiments should have any relevance to such discoveries. The problems for modal epistemology become problems for the methodology of metaphysics—and, more broadly, for the methodology of philosophy, wherever other issues implicitly rely on questions about what is metaphysically possible or necessary.

I will argue here, however, that adopting the normativist approach to metaphysical modality brings enormous methodological benefits. First, the normativist approach provides a much-needed way of justifying the standard practice of appealing to intuitions and thought experiments in metaphysical modal debates—of seeing why that should, after all, be relevant. It also gives us a way of seeing how to proceed in addressing metaphysical modal questions, and how to resolve these debates. At least when we see them as asking these questions in what Carnap would have thought of as an "internal" sense, non-mysterious methods akin to conceptual analysis can play a central role in addressing metaphysical modal questions.

Yet many remain suspicious of conceptual analysis. Some worry that our terms may just not have sufficient conceptual content to do the job, or that it is not precise enough to answer all the metaphysical modal questions. Others worry that whatever conceptual content our terms do have may not be widely enough shared to do the job—that individuals or communities may have differing and idiosyncratic associated concepts. As a result, if we can't see disputants as aiming to track real metaphysical modal facts in the world, it seems their proposed answers to metaphysical modal questions turn out to be just a matter of "verbal disputes." But then, it is said, we can't do justice to the apparent depth and seriousness of the relevant debates, or to the feelings among all disputants that they are really disagreeing. More generally, many think of conceptual analysis as inherently incapable of preserving the sense that metaphysics is a deep, worldly enterprise—not just a shallow concern with our language or concepts.

Nonetheless, these concerns, too, can be met by a normativist understanding of modal claims. First, nothing in the normativist view as such commits us to specific views about how much shared conceptual content (in the form of shared rules of use) our terms have—only that the rules of use and the metaphysical necessities go together. Second, even where the rules do vary, we needn't be left thinking that the disputes are "merely verbal," nor need we deny that metaphysics is a deep and worldly enterprise, once we attend to the different ways in which we may *use* claims about what is necessary or possible. In Chapter 2 (in order to focus on the functional question) I put aside the "use" question, of what the point is of our uttering a metaphysical modal claim (on a given occasion). But now it is crucial to come back examine the various typical uses to which metaphysical modal claims are put. Crucially, such claims may be used not only in aims to *convey or reinforce* (in the object language) what (the speaker thinks are) the *actual* rules of use for terms, but also to *renegotiate or press for changes in the rules*—engaging in what David Plunkett and Tim Sundell (2013) have called "metalinguistic negotiation." Fully acknowledging the prominent *uses* of metaphysical modal claims in engaging in the *normative* work of negotiating for what linguistic/conceptual scheme we *should use* (and what rules our terms or concepts *should* follow) provides the basis for a deeper view that enables us to overcome these criticisms of traditional work in conceptual analysis. The methodological benefits of adopting a normativist approach, thus, include not just defending the relevance of traditional methods such as conceptual analysis, but also showing the way to a broader, deeper, and more worldly view of at least some of what we can do in metaphysics—without losing the epistemological benefits of deflationism.

8.1 Justifying the Use of Intuition in Metaphysical Modal Debates

Traditional descriptivist views of metaphysical modal discourse face a problem. On the one hand, they think of modal discourse as aiming to describe a range of modal properties, modal facts, or other possible worlds. On the other hand, standard arguments used in debates in modal metaphysics appeal to intuitions or thought experiments to justify claims about what sorts of change a person could or could not survive, under what conditions we would or would not have the same work of art, and so on. The standard approach to resolving metaphysical modal questions is to appeal to *intuition*. David Lewis suggests that we in fact often acquire our modal opinions by way of imaginative experiments (1986, 113). Ernest Sosa defends the view that intuition plays an "indispensable" role in metaphysical inquiry, in which "intuitions are supposed to function like observations" (2008, 239). Sosa (2008, 233) argues that intuitions can provide evidence for the truth or falsehood of modal propositions.

But the idea that we have some faculty of "intuition" analogous to perception that can provide evidence about extra-mental modal facts only raises more difficult questions. First, why should we think that our intuitions provide any evidence about modal facts, especially if we think of these as parts of the world (or the pluriverse) awaiting discovery, much as non-modal facts and properties are? As Alvin Goldman and Joel Pust put it, "The question facing a philosopher . . . is how and why to treat spontaneous mental judgments . . . as evidence for a philosophical hypothesis" (1998, 179). Certainly untutored intuitions about, for instance, what bridges will and won't stand, at what rate objects will fall, or what one's chances are of winning a bet, are notoriously inaccurate about these worldly issues. If we do think of modal claims as attempting to describe features of this or other possible worlds, why should we think our intuitions about their truth are likely to be any better? The idea that intuitions could provide us with knowledge about other worlds spatiotemporally and causally isolated from ours is equally obscure (Jubien 2007, 105–6).

Those who defend the use of intuition and thought experiments are often quick to say that intuition is a valid source of evidence only for issues involving *modal* facts. But why should we think that intuition provides knowledge *only* of modal propositions? Sosa himself doesn't give much of an answer to this question, writing, "One might quite properly wonder why we should restrict ourselves to modal propositions. And there is no very deep reason. It's just that this seems the proper domain for philosophical uses of intuition" (2008, 233).

In short, for those who take a descriptive view of metaphysical modal discourse, the appeal to intuition and imaginative experimentation seems badly in need of justification. We need a good story about why intuitions should be thought to be a guide to, and only to, modal facts, how the quasi-observational faculty is supposed to work, what to do in the many cases where intuitions conflict, and so on. Without that, the justification for methods commonly employed in answering metaphysical modal questions remains as mysterious as ever.

8.2 A Defense of the Relevance of Traditional Methods

Once again, the modal normativist can do better. On the normativist view, while there is something right about the idea that intuition plays a role in acquiring knowledge in modal metaphysics that it doesn't play elsewhere, there is a problem with the idea that our intuitions provide some sort of "evidence" or "data" (maybe imperfect and defeasible) about some deep, extra-mental philosophical facts. This is far from the view that I defend, and once the alternative view is made clear, the issues show up quite differently.

On the normativist view, we are not to take "intuitions" as a source of "evidence" or "data" about metaphysical modal facts. Consider debates about the existence or persistence conditions for things of a certain kind, K. On the normativist view, talk of what it takes for Ks to exist *is just* the object-language correlate of talk about when the concept or term "K" applies, and talk of when a K persists is the object-language correlate of talk of when "K" may be *re*-applied. So there is no worry that there might be slippage or inaccuracy between the rules of use for our term and the modal features of the objects (if any) referred to.

This provides a straightforward way to answer the general question: Why should people's intuitive conceptual judgments about whether a painting has survived or perished, or whether songs are identical or distinct, be thought to tell us anything about the existence, identity, or persistence conditions of works of art? To the extent that these judgments are reflections of people's competence in wielding the relevant concept, they are also reflections of the rules of use for the relevant concept and term. These rules of use can "tell us" about the conditions under which a painting or song exists, persists, is identical to a(nother), and so on, not because they provide some kind of relevant *evidence* or *data* based on some special insight into the modal facts, but rather because they fix what ontological sort of thing, if any, we are talking about, when we talk about paintings and songs.

This position can answer the question Sosa gave up on: why the proper role of intuitions should be restricted to *modal* propositions. The short answer is that modal facts are not to be understood on analogy with facts about color, size, charge, or other empirical matters of fact (about which intuitions might be worryingly fallible). Instead, as I have argued in Chapter 6, the modal facts that metaphysics seeks to uncover are hypostatizations out of modal truths: to say "it is a modal fact that paintings cannot survive the destruction of the canvas" is just a hypostatization out of the modal truth "paintings cannot survive the destruction of the canvas." And stating modal truths is just a way of making semantic rules (or their consequences) explicit, while using the object-language—in this case, of the rule that a painting name is not to be reapplied after the destruction of the canvas (even if, say, a similar pattern of colors appears on a poster). Speakers master these rules insofar as they are capable of judging correctly (in accord with these rules) whether a given noun term is to be applied or refused, reapplied or not, in various actual and imagined circumstances. As a result, we have reason to think that conceptual analysis, understood as elucidating these semantic rules, has relevance to discerning basic metaphysical modal facts that it lacks for empirical facts.

This gives a much cleaner and more compelling answer to the question of why we should care about our concepts, thought, or intuition about the subject: there's no appeal to a special "faculty" providing "evidence" about a special realm of properties. Instead, talk about the relevant properties and facts involves hypostatizations out of modal facts, which are expressions of semantic rules (and their consequences) made in the object-language. Thus on this view it is no great mystery how our concepts or intuitive judgments guided by those concepts may provide a "guide to how things stand" modally.

Moreover, we can show the relevance of conceptual analysis to grasping modal facts and the ontological facts that come along with them, without having to explain what this special "faculty" providing modal knowledge is, or how it manages to "detect" the modal facts, which seem not to be empirically detectable. The ability to give a clear and principled justification for the use of traditional methods of imaginative variation, thought experiments, and the like for addressing metaphysical modal questions is one clear methodological advantage we gain by taking the normativist approach.

8.3 Resolving Internal Metaphysical Modal Disputes

What does this tell us about what methods are to be used in answering and adjudicating disputes about metaphysical modal questions? Following Carnap, I distinguish two modes in which these questions can be asked and answered. The first is the straightforward "internal" mode, in which the speakers aim to simply *use* the terms in question in accord with their standard public rules. The second mode, addressing them as "external" questions, I return to in Section 8.6.

Speakers master these rules insofar as they are capable of judging correctly (in accord with these rules) whether a given nominative term is to be applied or refused, reapplied or not, in various actual and imagined circumstances. Thus the metaphysician (seeking to address the question considered as internal) must have mastered the rules, having an ability to follow them in properly applying and refusing expressions. This much any competent speaker does. But the work of the metaphysician also requires an explicit understanding of the rules that most competent speakers may lack despite their ability to follow the rules. In this respect, the metaphysician's work is analogous to the grammarian's work of discerning the syntactic rules competent speakers follow but may not be able to articulate (though the grammarian *states* the syntactic rules in a *metalanguage* while the metaphysician *conveys* the rules in the *object*-language). As Ryle notes, "Showing what to do is a more sophisticated performance than doing it ingenuously" (1950/1971, 248). Those who wish to know what is metaphysically possible or necessary may consider the multiplicity of cases in which the terms would properly be applied or refused, in hopes of acquiring an explicit understanding of the underlying rules governing proper application and reapplication of the term. They may also seek to uncover the *consequences* of the rules of use for our terms, either taken on their own, as combined with one another (sometimes in great systems), or in combination with empirical facts, and ultimately convey these semantic rules and their consequences in the object-language (though that is not all we may legitimately do—more on this below).

I have suggested that (internal) questions about the conditions of existence, identity, or persistence for things of a given kind K can be answered by moving from mastery of the application and co-application conditions for "K" to the ability to explicitly convey these (and what follows from them, perhaps as combined with empirical facts) in object-language indicatives. Such questions have long been central to metaphysics, including questions about the identity conditions for artifacts (think of "ship of Theseus" cases), about constitution (relying on issues about the relevant modal properties of statues versus lumps of clay), about personal identity, about the identity and persistence conditions for works of art, for social groups, and so on. But it is not only such questions that may be addressed using this method.

Wherever a question concerns what is metaphysically possible or necessary, the method for answering it (taken internally) will naturally rely on the ability to move from mastery of the rules of use for the expression, to communicating these (and their consequences) in the object-language. I have already suggested (in Chapter 5) how examination of the rules of use, say, for our number terms, may enable us to answer the question of whether numbers exist necessarily. A similar approach may also enable us to assess questions about the "natures" of entities of various kinds, to the extent that such questions are straightforwardly answerable at all. Consider, for example, questions about the "natures" of properties, such as whether properties are Platonic entities or *in rebus* universals. This question hinges on whether or not a property *must be instantiated* (at some time) in order to exist. If property talk permits inferences not only from "the shirt is red" to "the shirt has the property of redness" to "there is a property of redness possessed by the shirt," but also from the negation of the original sentence (or all sentences of that form), say from "the shirt isn't red" to "the shirt doesn't have the property of redness" to "there is a property of redness (lacked by the shirt)," then we may be able to conclude that there is a given property P regardless of whether it is instantiated—and, in that way, side with the Platonist. Of course, it may be that the rules of use for property talk are indeterminate in this regard, or that the fan of *in rebus* properties thinks that property talk *should not* be conducted in this way—perhaps because it leads to certain alleged "metaphysical problems" or mysteries.[2] In such cases, the debate about the nature of properties may shift to an external debate about how we *ought to* conduct property talk. (For more on debates considered as external, see Section 8.6.) I aim to remain neutral here about how exactly our property talk *does* work, only making the *methodological* point about how these questions may be addressed.[3] Other classic debates that appeal to metaphysical modality, such as debates about whether to be free you must be able to do otherwise, or whether knowledge requires more than justified true belief, may be similarly approached—again, as long as we ask these questions, internally construed.

This approach to metaphysics strongly resembles that undertaken in ordinary-language philosophy and phenomenology under the heading "conceptual analysis." As ordinary-language philosophers often emphasized, conceptual analysis requires a prior ability to properly *apply* (and refuse) the concept, so that we can (at the first stage) say of the various imagined cases whether or not each is a situation in which the term or concept may be applied, and proceed to generalize from these cases.[4] As Grice writes,

> We may notice that in reaching one's conceptual analysis of E, one makes use of one's ability to apply and withhold E, for the characteristic procedure is to think up a possible general characterization of one's use of E and then to test it by trying to find or imagine a

---

[2] As, for example, Armstrong worried that the Platonist view that allowed properties to exist uninstantiated would require a "Platonic heaven" to put them in (1989, 76), and would give a too "promiscuous" view of properties (1989, 79).

[3] Further questions about whether properties are *really* universals or tropes, for example, are rendered false dilemmas, if we accept the easy approach to ontology. For given that approach, we may allow that there are universals *and* that there are tropes—and in different contexts we may have reason for talking of each, if we wish to speak sometimes of what the various shirts have in common (a property of redness), and at other times of a particular *redness of this shirt*, which has changed in the wash. Given the easy approach to ontology and the abandonment of a neo-Quinean approach, there is no pressure to choose between these on grounds of parsimony.

[4] Chalmers and Jackson (2001, 320–24) give a similar picture of conceptual analysis as proceeding via consideration of what we would say in various actual and hypothetical scenarios while not requiring explicit analyses in other terms.

particular situation which fits the suggested characterization and yet
would *not* be a situation in which one would apply E.

(1989, 174)

This point is echoed by Moore (1966, 166), and Strawson (1992, 6–7).

So there is a sense in which, if we accept a normativist view of modality, the methods of answering metaphysical questions—taken
internally—are closely related to those of conceptual analysis.
Nonetheless, it may be misleading to say that the basic methods of metaphysics are those of conceptual analysis. For this might suggest that
metaphysics is merely a study *of* our language or concepts, undermining
the idea that metaphysics is telling us *about the world*.⁵ The claims of
metaphysics are not claims *about* our language or *about* our concepts,
and so we shouldn't say that the metaphysician is "looking for a general
characterization of the types of case in which one would apply E rather
than withhold it" (Grice 1989, 174). A general characterization of when
a term is to be applied and when withheld would be a *statement of* the
rules (in the metalanguage) or a *description of* what the rules are.

We can avoid this mistake by reminding ourselves that the claims
of modal metaphysics are not descriptions or statements *of* rules of
language (made in a metalanguage) but rather are made in the object-
language, *using* the terms in question. Since the terms are *used* in
making the claims of metaphysics, the literal semantic content of the
metaphysical modal claims is *about* the things, if any, our terms and
concepts refer to—not about our terms or concepts themselves. So,
while the study of metaphysics is correlated with a study of language
and concepts, it involves a semantic descent that enables us to speak
about the world by *using* the terms and concepts in question, and it
says something about the entities, if any, our terms refer to.⁶ Claims

---

⁵ I have myself said in various places (e.g., Thomasson 2007a) that the methods
of metaphysics involve conceptual analysis, and still would point out the parallels
in approach. Nonetheless, for the reasons discussed here I now think that this way of
describing what metaphysics is up to may be misleading. I have argued in Thomasson
(2007b), however, that there are ways of understanding traditional conceptual analysis
that avoid this problem (e.g., taking it to be an analysis performed *with* concepts, not *of*
concepts).

⁶ Husserl was always quite clear about keeping separate but noting the interrelations
among these levels of analysis; as he put it: the task of "clarification of *all* concepts" has as

about the relevant modal facts and properties are likewise made in the object-language and in that sense are likewise about the world. Since it is conducted in the object-language, metaphysics is world-oriented and can be said to result in knowledge about the modal features of objects.

Some might worry about this method, however, on grounds that a speaker might not know whether or not she has mastered the rules of a term: she may think she has mastered them, and yet it may turn out that her use is idiosyncratic, theory influenced, or just out of date. Indeed it is just that kind of mistake that is often uncovered by work in experimental philosophy, which may show that an individual philosopher's use of a term is at odds with the common public use (see Thomasson 2012 for further discussion of the relevance of results in experimental philosophy). If we want to talk about the ontological status of *symphonies* as we know them, as they are covered in copyright law, as we care about them in our acts of aesthetic creation, criticism, or appreciation, it seems that we must be concerned with the *common* rules of use for the term in a public language. Finding that one's own use is far out of line with the common use may give some reason for hesitating to make general judgments presented in the public language, and so experimental results may provide a useful corrective to the uses of a lone philosopher. That philosopher might still provide a true analysis of what *symphonies** are, using her own idiosyncratic concept, and she might be right about what things, if any, *her* concept refers to. The only trouble is: no one will care, or need care, if she's not talking about *symphonies*, the objects commonly discussed by musicians, conductors, fans, and the like. That is: no one need care *unless*, of course, she can convince us that there are reasons we *should* adopt her conception. More on this below.

Nonetheless, the possibility that the metaphysician turns out not to have mastered the rules does not undermine the idea that conceptual analysis (as conceived of here) is an appropriate method for addressing modal metaphysical questions—to the extent that they can be answered, taken as internal. As I have argued, competent

its "correlative task . . . the eidetic analysis and eidetic description of *all* objectivities and *all* kinds of unity pertaining essentially to them" (1989, 328).

users of a sortal term "N" can acquire modal knowledge about Ns by making use of their semantic competence in considering actual and hypothetical cases, and may thereby come to acquire a general and more explicit understanding of what the rules are, as well as reasoning through the consequences of such rules, including those that come from plugging in the needed empirical truths. On this picture, speakers who have mastered the rules of use for a term are in a position to acquire an explicit grasp of the rules, and with it to acquire metaphysical modal knowledge. They may of course not know *that* they have mastered the rules of use for a term—experimental results may undermine that assumption. If they don't know *that* they have mastered the rules of use for a term, they may not know *that* they have modal knowledge—but that is a separate issue. As long as we are willing to allow that one may know something without knowing *that one* knows it, we may still allow that competent speakers who *have* mastered the rules may make use of that mastery to acquire modal knowledge—even if they don't yet know *that* they are competent speakers, or even if the belief that they are competent could potentially be undermined by empirical results.

8.4 Objections to Conceptual Analysis

As I have argued so far, modal normativism brings us methodological advantages insofar as it can enable us to give a justification for the use of intuition and thought experiments in addressing metaphysical modal questions, and can lay out a clear methodology for addressing such questions (considered in the internal mode)—a method that centrally involves something close to conceptual analysis.

Yet some would think this is hardly an advantage. For the thought that we may use (something akin to) conceptual analysis in answering internal metaphysical modal questions faces various forms of objection and skepticism. Confidence in conceptual analysis ain't what it used to be. Some of the large-scale background objections I have addressed in detail elsewhere—for example, Quinean objections against analyticity (see Thomasson 2007 [Chapter 2]), and Williamson's attack on analyticity (see Thomasson 2015 [Chapter 7]). Other suspicions, say, of the ability to offer necessary and sufficient conditions simply do not apply to efforts to engage in conceptual analysis that are conceived in terms of what Strawson (1992) called "connective analysis"—aimed at understanding the inferential relations and connections among our concepts, not at giving reductive analyses of one concept in terms of necessary and sufficient conditions. I have also argued elsewhere for the need to accept that our terms have some conceptual content and have addressed objections to that (Thomasson 2007, 2015, and Chapter 4 in this volume). It would be redundant to repeat those discussions here.

Here, I want to speak to a different audience: not to those who would deny that there is any conceptual content at all, but rather to those who doubt that there is *enough* in the way of determinate, shared conceptual content to do the work needed in modal metaphysics. There are at least two independent dimensions of worry here. One is that, even if one allows that our terms (or, more narrowly, our sortal terms) have some conceptual content, they often do not have enough precise, or determinate, content to answer all of the questions we care about addressing in modal metaphysics. The other is that, even if speakers associate some conceptual content when they use their terms, there may be little that is *shared* across speakers or communities—leaving modal metaphysics on this model a parochial matter, and turning what looked like robust disagreements into nothing more than verbal disputes among those speaking different idiolects. Beyond these is a broader and more diffuse worry: that appeal to conceptual analysis just can't do enough to preserve the idea, shared widely among metaphysicians, that metaphysics is deep, worldly, and difficult—so that its debates cannot be resolved by the "shallow" process of appealing to our language or concepts.

The truth of the matter is that nothing in the modal normativist position commits one to any substantive position about exactly *how much* conceptual content there is (standardly, or in any given case), nor about *how widely* that content is shared. What the normativist *is* committed to is the claim that there is a *link* between what metaphysical necessities there are, and what semantic rules there are (as well as what follows from them), so that there is *no more* to be "discovered" modally about people, say, than what is implicitly contained in our conceptual system, or entailed by that when combined with empirical facts.

Nonetheless, as I will argue next, by combining the modal normativist approach with a view that semantic rules are typically open-textured and revisable, we get a package view that is very strong and attractive. For the resulting package view is able to turn both of the above concerns into strengths, and makes room for a view on which metaphysical debates can be deep, difficult, and of worldly relevance— but can do so without giving up the epistemological advantages of deflationism.

8.5 Limits to Detail and Precision

Since the normativist view commits one to the idea that modal truths and conceptual content are linked, it does entail that, where our concepts are not fine-grained enough, certain metaphysical modal questions (taken in the internal mode) may turn out to be "unanswerable" in the sense that there is no answer to them to be discovered (cf. Thomasson 2009). So if one is pressed to address detailed questions, such as how many words may be changed while the same work of literature remains, then, presuming that our concept just does not draw a line in such a fine-grained manner (nor defer to any worldly facts capable of doing so), there may be no fact of the matter to be discovered. As a result, the correct response is not to defend some arbitrary answer. Nor should we be embarrassed at the failure to give an answer. Similarly, it just may be that our traditional concept of death—which served well enough when death tended to occur at home and merely required burial within a matter of days—simply did not come with criteria precise enough to always determine the time of death to the minute (Gert et al. 2006). Where our concept is not precise enough to give an answer, the proper response may be to give no answer. Of course, it may happen that we come under pressure to give one. We might be pressed to give more precise identity conditions for works of literature or music in order to apply copyright law, and we might be pressed to give criteria that will yield a more precise time of death for purposes of organ transplantation and cessation of the use of expensive medical interventions (see Gert et al. 2006). But even when we are under such pressures, we do far better if we are upfront about the fact that we are not "discovering" covert worldly modal facts, but rather *proposing* ways in which our terms or concepts might be precisified to cope with new social, legal, or technological situations, or to serve new practical purposes.

As a result, there are also pragmatic advantages to be gained from adopting the modal normativist approach, and combining it with the view that our concepts are often open-textured and revisable. For adopting this combination of views can enable us to avoid the pressure to answer those who demand precise answers to questions about the survival or identity conditions of various entities, but then would dismiss any answer we might give as being arbitrary. Instead, we can show that such questions are problematic precisely because they are instances in which our conceptual structure is not detailed enough for us to be able to extract any answer through the usual process of mastery and hypostatization. When there is a real need, however, we can approach such questions in a more clear-headed fashion by recognizing that the nature of the problem is how to re-engineer and precisify our concept to serve a new purpose, or to serve an old purpose in a new situation. This kind of approach enables us to lay our cards on the table, and make public our reasons for choice in a way that disguising answers as "metaphysical discoveries" could not do. I have aimed elsewhere to lay the groundwork for a methodology for pragmatic conceptual engineering along these lines (Thomasson 2020).

In short, properly seen, the thought that often our concepts may not be precise enough to answer all of the questions we care about in modal metaphysics turns out to be a virtue rather than a vice. For this, combined with the modal normativist view of metaphysical modality, can help explain the feeling that, for certain metaphysical modal questions, straightforwardly giving any precise answer would be arbitrary. As a result, the fact that it would feel arbitrary for a realist about artifacts or works of art to give any answer to questions about their precise identity conditions should not count as a mark against these views, or a reason to deny realism about the objects. It can also explain the apparent irresolvability and endlessness of central debates in modal metaphysics, such as debates about personal identity. For there may simply be different, imprecise, concepts of *person* at work in different arenas, say in the legal arena versus the medical or biological arena, or in the relationships that govern our lives. But while our package view can explain the feeling that there is no precise answer to be given, and that certain debates are irresolvable, it does so without a hopelessness that treats these facts as just "too hard" for us to get a grip on. For it goes naturally with the idea that, where such questions really call for an answer, we must undertake it by way of a form of conceptual re-engineering—where we can make use of appropriate standards to ensure that such re-engineering is done well, in ways that serve the needs that prompted the questions.[7]

8.6 Understanding External Metaphysical Modal Disputes

This brings us to the second point of hesitation many feel about the prospect of engaging in something akin to (object-language) conceptual analysis as a central method in addressing questions in modal metaphysics. I mentioned in Section 8.5 the possibility that, for example, in debates about personal identity, there may be different concepts of *person* at play. The problem may be even worse—if content in general is not widely shared; if, as Peter Ludlow has argued (2005), there simply is little in the way of a "common coin" of shared conceptual content across competent speakers, who engage continually in a kind of renegotiation of micro-languages in particular conversational contexts. The modal normativist, as I have insisted, is not committed to any particular view about how much conceptual content there is (though of course some assumptions may be needed to account for some putative necessities), nor about how widely it is shared across speakers.

Nonetheless, the prospect of variation might be thought to threaten modal normativism in two ways. First, if there is very little shared content, it might be that there is very little that can be *said* in a public, shared context about modal metaphysical issues. While this might help explain the persistent lack of agreement and feelings of irresolvability, it might also be rather disappointing. Second, wherever the concepts

---

[7] The standards governing this re-engineering of course must not be standards that require a match with the metaphysical modal facts. See Thomasson (2020).

of speakers (or groups of speakers) do vary, the normativist position might then threaten to turn their disagreement into a mere verbal dispute, in which they simply talk past each other. For it looks like, on this view, the normativist must take disputants in arguments about personal identity, say, as merely talking past each other. If one disputant thinks that a person can survive the loss of all memories, and another thinks a person can't, are they just laying out the consequences of different conceptions of "person" each works with, so that nothing is left to be said except that each is correctly laying out the modal facts that follow from the rules that govern her own (or her community's) use of the term, and so both are right? Perhaps some (following lines suggested by Eli Hirsch [2002]) would allow that we can resolve that dispute by distinguishing which of them (if either) is really *speaking English*—or by noting that if they use the term in a way that is deferential to the community's use, at least one of them may be mistaken in their grasp of the meaning assigned by the community. But even that might seem a small consolation to metaphysicians who see themselves as involved in genuine and deep disputes. More broadly, many think it would make the relevant debates shallow and uninteresting to think of them as engaged in just explicating our linguistic or conceptual scheme, and leave us unable to account for their apparent difficulty, depth, and worldly importance.

I have so far been explicating the methods and limits of addressing metaphysical modal questions *taken as internal*. There are, however, other options for what one can legitimately do—and ways of interpreting what metaphysics often has done—that involve considering these questions in what Carnap would have thought of as an "external" mode. Once we see the prospects for addressing *external* questions in this way, I will argue, there is no need to see the debaters as simply engaged in shallow verbal disputes, and we can do far better at accounting for the apparent difficulty, depth, and worldly importance of classic modal debates in metaphysics.[8]

David Plunkett and Tim Sundell (2014) argue that individuals may be involved in a genuine disagreement without that disagreement

[8] For further discussion of these ideas, see Thomasson (2017a, 2017b, 2018, and 2020).

being "canonical" in the sense that speakers literally express incompatible semantic contents. Instead, they suggest, a great many ordinary disputes can be understood as disagreements that involve what they call "metalinguistic negotiation"—advocating for how a word *should* be used (or perhaps for which word should be used) relative to a context (2014, 3). Take, for example, arguments (in a radio show discussing who should be listed among the best athletes of all time) about whether or not the racehorse Secretariat is an athlete (2014, 16–18). One disputant may use the word "athlete" in such a way that it may be applied to non-human animals; the other may not. In that case, they are in a sense talking past each other, and each may be uttering truths in her own idiolect. Nonetheless, they are involved in a genuine disagreement about how the word "athlete" *should* be used, and "their metalinguistic dispute reflects a genuine disagreement about how to use the word 'athlete'" (2014, 17). For though the literal semantic contents they express may differ (and not genuinely conflict), each may pragmatically communicate that we should/should not single out non-humans for the sorts of praise and rewards (and responsibilities, etc.) bestowed on athletes.

As Plunkett and Sundell argue, seeing a dispute as a metalinguistic negotiation isn't a last-resort analysis. Instead, it follows from independently motivated observations about ways speakers routinely express disagreement—metalinguistic negotiation is ubiquitous (2014, 4). Moreover (as they point out), disagreements that take this form needn't be superficial or uninteresting—a great deal can hinge on these metalinguistic disagreements. For many of the words we care about, how we apply the terms is tied up with other norms about how we should act, who we should praise, and what we should do. Consider, for example, another case they discuss: disputes about whether waterboarding is torture. If one disputant is employing the former U.S. Justice Department definition, while the other uses the United Nations definition (when the first says waterboarding isn't torture and the second says it is), each may be seen as saying something true. But they can be seen as communicating incompatible propositions nonetheless, for example, about whether waterboarding should be seen as morally problematic, should be treated morally and legally as acknowledged cases of torture are, etc. Clearly something very serious is at stake in how we resolve the metalinguistic negotiation about how we are to use the word "torture," since this is centrally tied up with how we evaluate it morally, whether we permit or prohibit certain kinds of activities, and so on. And such disputes reflect genuine disagreements. So the modal normativist isn't constrained to see metaphysical disputes as either "mere verbal disputes" in which they are talking past each other (but not really disagreeing) or as superficial disagreements to be resolved simply by determining who is really "speaking English." These disputes also are not mere "verbal" disputes in the sense that we shouldn't really care about them, and would give them up if we recognized them for what they were. In at least some cases (and perhaps these are the cases that really matter) they may be seen as engaged in a kind of metalinguistic negotiation about how the term in question *ought to be* used. And in these disputes, a great deal may be at stake *beyond* the usage of terms.

The thought here, then, is that many disputes in modal metaphysics can be seen as external, in the sense that they are (whether explicitly or implicitly) engaged in metalinguistic negotiation regarding how certain key terms or concepts *ought to be* used—in a way that does not have to merely involve analyzing how the terms or concepts *are actually* used. This may take many different forms: in some cases, it may simply involve proposals to *precisify* an open-ended term, as perhaps with some work on death (Gert et al. 2006) or on persons. In other cases, it may involve proposals to implicitly *broaden* criteria (think of the recent ways of broadening criteria for "what marriage is," or Clive Bell's way of broadening what art is, beyond the mimetic); in other cases it may involve more deep or thorough proposals for revision.

In any case, this analysis gives us new hopes of accounting for the felt depth, seriousness, and worldliness of many debates in modal metaphysics. It also enables us to acknowledge that revisionary views may be of interest, rather than just discarding them as either misusing English or saying something obviously false. When one philosopher says works of art don't survive any acts of attempted restoration that involve replacing even the smallest part (Sagoff 1978), and another says they do, they need not be seen as just talking past each other or as engaged in an argument that can only be resolved by asking who is really speaking English (a case the revisionist is bound to lose). Instead, we can see their dispute as a genuine one, in which the first pragmatically expresses the view that such restorative practices should be suspended; and the second conveys the contrary view: that such practices are unobjectionable or even recommended. These views are plausibly tied to broader views about the value of works of art in our lives: whether we ought to treat them as inviolable but perishable historical relics, or to value them for the access they provide us to aesthetically valuable experiences, or access to grasping the intentions of the creator (access that might be lost as the work gets dirty or degenerates). Such disputes are very much worth having, and are not resolved just by determining which disputant is speaking English.

Such disputes, so conceived, are onto something deep—they are not concerned with how our parochial terms or concepts happen to work. Instead, they are about how we should live. This enables us at last to do justice to the feeling of "depth" in these debates—that we are not just aiming to find out about our concepts of persons (when we investigate personal identity), or freedom (when we enter the free will debate), or even works of art—but to find out something deeper, beyond parochial investigation of whatever our own concepts happen to be. But on this conception, what it is that we are arguing about is best understood normatively—in ways that are intimately tied up with large normative questions about how we should arrange our moral, legal, and other institutions and practices (governing medical care, inheritance laws, legal rights and responsibilities, punishment, museum exhibition and conservation practices, etc.). In this way, the modal normativist view can lead to a kind of metaphysical normativism—that sees some of the most important work in metaphysics as involved in a normative project of working out what conceptual scheme we *should* be working with; both at the level of asking what rules of use we should adopt to meet goals that are important to us, and at the level of asking what goals we should be pursuing (see Thomasson 2017b and 2020).

The idea that metaphysics is, or perhaps should be, involved in a kind of normative conceptual work has been powerfully advanced before. Carnap acknowledged a useful role for philosophy not just in conceptual analysis, but also in what he called "conceptual engineering"—working out what system of concepts is, or would be, most useful for science. In normative terms, these are questions about what concepts we *ought* to adopt and work with—for a given purpose, in a given context. And the project of "conceptual engineering" can be understood more broadly, concerning more purposes than just those of the sciences, and more concepts than the logical and scientific. Even in standard metaphysics, we need not ask simply "What is freedom?" or "What is a person?" and try to work out what follows from our standard concept—whether by traditional analysis or experimental philosophy (though that may be interesting enough). We may do better to step back to see what function these concepts need to serve for us—why we want such concepts, what role they are to play in our attributions of praise and blame, of legal and moral responsibility, of rights and duties.

Sally Haslanger has argued persuasively that work in the philosophy of race and gender, particularly, should be concerned not so much with attempting to analyze our actual concepts (whether we think of these as those we see ourselves as using, or as whatever is actually guiding our practices), but rather with getting at the "target concept"—the one we *should* be employing (2012, 388). How do we work that out? Not by just looking to patterns in the actual usage of the concept (or engaging in introspective reflection), but rather by engaging in what she calls "ameliorative conceptual analysis," which involves working out the point of having the concept in question, and then in figuring out what would do that work best (2012, 386). Or perhaps in certain cases, we might need to step back still further and ask not what the term (say, of race, or gender or class) *has* done socially in the past (consider critiques that such terms have largely served insidious functions of preserving privilege or legitimating inequities), but what we *should*, now, employ it to do. (Or, indeed, if we should simply give up the terms, or replace them with some other set.)

This way of understanding the modal metaphysics in normative terms also has the potential for rehabilitating certain revisionary metaphysical views—which can (now taken externally) be seen not as misdirected attempts to give object-language expression to the semantic rules of our extant concepts, but rather as engaged in metalinguistic negotiation—perhaps lobbying for new rules for certain key terms. We can do a far better job at both developing and evaluating such revisionary views if we are clear-headed about the nature of our project and don't deceive ourselves into thinking we are discovering some metaphysical reality that others were mistaken about. Moreover, we must have our eyes open to questions about what the benefits are that are to be gained, or purposes to be fulfilled, from the change in rules: perhaps they are rules that would better fulfill the purposes of the term, or (stepping back a level) that would better fulfill the purposes for which the term *ought to be* employed (say, in the case of race or gender terms). In some such cases, from the normativist point of view, there might well be a good case to be made. In other cases, where the perceived benefits have more to do with fulfilling the demands imposed by a neo-Quinean conception of metaphysics, or avoiding alleged "metaphysical problems" than with fulfilling any of the purposes for which the term is employed in its ordinary uses, the case may be less compelling.[9] At any rate, such revisionary proposals must be evaluated individually, and with a clear sense of the benefit supposed to be gained.

8.7 Conclusion

The conception of modal metaphysics that results from the normativist approach, then, is more multifaceted than it at first appears. And it is very much a Carnapian picture. I have argued elsewhere (Thomasson 2015, 36–45, following Huw Price 2009) that Carnap's "internal" questions are best interpreted as questions asked *using* the terms of a linguistic framework, with their governing rules intact. By contrast, those involved in addressing "external" questions, on this model, are engaged in pragmatically advocating for what concepts and terms we *should* use, and/or how we should use them. Along these lines, we can distinguish between internal and external

---

[9] Suppose we reconceive, for example, revisionary metaphysical views about what "objects" there are as proposals that we use the word "object" only to refer to organisms and simples (or people and simples, or only simples)—in order that we can better give a clear and unified response to the special composition question. Such proposals will only be as compelling as the need to meet these supposed theoretical demands.

questions of metaphysical modality. Internal questions are those questions to be addressed *using* the actual term, and aiming to give object-language expression of its semantic rules (or what follows from them)—those can and ought to be addressed by the sorts of methods described in Section 8.3. But other questions remain, which may be deeper and more interesting: external questions about what rules we *should* associate with our terms—what conceptual/linguistic scheme we *should* adopt, and what rules it should be governed by. Such disputes can be perfectly genuine, deep, and significant. But we will engage in them more capably when we are clear about the natures of the disputes in question and the purposes for which the conceptual scheme is recommended.

Seen in this light, the modal normativist approach can provide several interesting methodological benefits. First, as we have seen, if we consider metaphysical modal questions internally, it gives a way of justifying the standard methodology of answering these questions by way of considering intuitions about actual and imagined cases, giving a non-mysterious response to the problems of modal epistemology. Combined with the view that the semantic rules are often open-textured, it also gives us a way of understanding why many debates have seemed so irresolvable, and why in certain situations any answer we give seems arbitrary. At the same time, combined with the view that the semantic rules are open to revision, it provides us a different, more transparent way of addressing fine-grained metaphysical modal questions when we need to do so. It can also account for the felt depth of many debates in modal metaphysics, the difficulties of many of the debates, and the potential significance of the results by noting the potential for *external* metaphysical modal debates as well, understood as involved in a kind of metalinguistic negotiation that may sometimes be very difficult, involve matters of genuine disagreement, and be tied up with norms and values central to our way of life.

Which is the predominant way of understanding metaphysical debates—as internal or as external? What percentage of our debates fall into each category? I won't take a stand on that here. The answers to such questions will depend on one's views about how much conceptual content our shared terms have. But recognizing that such debates may be internal *or* external gives us tools we may use in analyzing, and directing our contributions to, a variety of first-order debates. The modal normativist who is also a meta-ontological deflationist may note and approve of both of these strategies, without giving up the epistemological and ontological benefits that come with a deflationary meta-ontological approach.

Conclusion

My immediate goal in this book has been to develop a clear, plausible, and demystifying approach to understanding talk about what is metaphysically necessary or possible. In developing the modal normativist view, I have aimed to put back on the map a kind of approach to modality that was popular about a hundred years ago, but had been nearly forgotten in recent discussions of metaphysical modality. I have tried to show that the approach, broadly speaking, was not killed off by classic problems such as the embedding problem and the objections notoriously raised against conventionalism. I have also tried to show that a version of modal normativism can accommodate the hard cases of Kripkean *de re* and a posteriori necessities thought to present barriers, as well as a range of other putative counterexamples. All that work aimed to show that the approach is still available.

The more interesting work, in my view, lay in showing that an approach along these lines is not only *available* but *desirable*. For it can enable us to avoid many of the classic ontological problems of modality, resolve the epistemological problems in ways no other defensible view can, and provide a justification and clarification of the methods of metaphysics, wherever it deals with implicitly or overtly metaphysical modal questions. While the details may prove to need adjusting in various ways, if I have at least made the case that a broadly normativist approach to metaphysical modality is more viable and attractive than most of my contemporaries had realized, I will be happy to count that as a success.

But there are also further goals here, beyond theorizing about metaphysical modality. As in most of my recent work, the deeper goals are meta-metaphysical and methodological. The work done here (concerned with debates about metaphysical modality) is part of a larger program aimed at demystifying metaphysics. I have undertaken other

Norms and Necessity. Amie L. Thomasson, Oxford University Press (2020). © Oxford University Press.
DOI: 10.1093/oso/9780190098193.001.0001

parts of that work elsewhere—for example, in *Ontology Made Easy*, where I addressed debates about what exists. There is a common goal of those two books: the epistemological demystification of metaphysics.[1] Otherwise put, in both works I hope to show that those questions of metaphysics that are well-formed and answerable can be answered straightforwardly in ways that require nothing more mysterious than conceptual and empirical work. I made that case for existence questions in *Ontology Made Easy*, and I have made it for metaphysical modal questions here. Any metaphysical questions that remain, beyond those that are implicitly existential or modal, will have to be handled separately. Not everything can be done in a single book—or even two. But I hope that the work done here will at least give those interested in other metaphysical problems some strategies to consider.

The goal in both cases is not the destruction of metaphysics, but its demystification. Or rather, the goal is the demystification and—ultimately—reorientation of metaphysics. For there is a still deeper aim in my recent work: to give an account of what we legitimately can, and should, do in metaphysics, in a way that avoids epistemological mystery, and makes it clear how we can think of the work of metaphysics in a way that doesn't make it look like a second-rate rival to the sciences in purporting to "discover" "deep and hidden" facts.

We can, first, examine how our concepts *do* work—and what follows from that, for other areas of our conceptual scheme, or given empirical facts. This may also involve interesting rectification problems, such as aiming to resolve puzzles or paradoxes our conceptual scheme seems to give rise to, or assessing whether elements of our inherited conceptual scheme may be meshed with the conceptual scheme and empirical results emerging from the natural sciences (in areas ranging from cognitive science to quantum physics).

As I have argued in Chapter 8, however, we can also go beyond asking questions about how our conceptual scheme *does* work, to ask what conceptual or linguistic scheme we *ought to use*. And that task is

---

[1] In fact, the current volume and *Ontology Made Easy* were originally conceived of as a single book directed toward developing a deflationary approach to (much of) metaphysics. As each side got longer, it became too long to contain a single volume, and split into two works.

deep, difficult, and of great worldly importance. This is a theme I have just touched on at the end here, but which I have begun to develop elsewhere (Thomasson 2017a, 2017b, 2018b, 2020) and hope to return to at greater length one day.

Before closing this book, however, it is worth clarifying the three interrelated threads that have been woven throughout this book, and how they interact. Those themes are functional pluralism, meta-ontological deflationism, and the view that meaning is often underdetermined and open for renegotiation. To some extent, these views may be sold separately, but together they form a powerful package. In closing it is worth bringing these themes to the surface and showing what each has contributed to the work undertaken here, as well as making clear how they interact to provide a powerful approach to a range of philosophical problems.

The first thread is the functional pluralist idea that our talk of modal necessities and possibilities fundamentally serves a function other than describing or tracking features of this or other worlds. The functional pluralist idea has roots in the work of such figures as Wittgenstein, Ryle, and Sellars, but has been most recently developed in the neo-pragmatist tradition advanced in work by Price (2011), Williams (2011), and Brandom (1994, 2008).[2] The underlying thought is that we might often make more progress on philosophical problems by stepping back from the canvas. Rather than beginning by asking what modal properties, moral facts, truth, etc. *are*, we should first ask what the *discourse* does for us, what functions it serves. Once we start from this question, we may find that areas of our discourse (like tools) may serve many different functions—and that not all of these functions involve representing, tracking, or describing features of the world around us.[3] The key idea behind the modal normativist view I have defended is an application of this functional pluralist thought: that metaphysical modal discourse does not function to track special modal features of reality, but instead has the function of enabling us to convey, reason

---

[2] That tradition in turn has drawn inspiration from work in the expressivist/quasi-realist tradition in metaethics (especially Blackburn [1984, 1993], and Gibbard [1990, 2003]).

[3] That is, in Price's terms (2011, 20–23), not all have an e-representational function.

with, and renegotiate semantic rules and permissions in advantageous ways, in the object-language. Appealing to the alternative function of metaphysical modal discourse enabled us to avoid the classic epistemological problems of modality, including both the integration challenge and the reliability challenge. For we no longer had to think of modal facts as features of this world or other worlds that we lack the ability to empirically "detect" or come into causal contact with. It also enabled us to see why methods that use thought experiments and intuitions (methods that make use of our semantic competence) are perfectly appropriate in modal metaphysics.

The second main strand of my work here and elsewhere is a form of meta-ontological deflationism, which I have not argued for here but have argued for and defended elsewhere under the label "easy ontology" (Thomasson 2015). Functional pluralist analyses of various areas of discourse can be, and often have been, undertaken without any connection to easy ontology (perhaps in part because these alternative functional stories have often been given by those in the neo-pragmatist tradition who do not want to waste their time on metaphysical questions). But taken apart from an easy approach to ontology, an alternative functional analysis of an area of discourse may look like it is either simply ignoring metaphysical questions (about what modal properties, moral facts, or *really are*), or giving implausible eliminativist answers to them, along the lines of, "There aren't *really* Xs (or at least: we don't have to commit to them), but here's why we talk *as if* there are." And indeed, in some incarnations (Ayer's emotivism, Yablo's early fictionalism), non-representational analyses are put to this sort of work. But there is no need to go that way.

Combining a neo-pragmatist functional analysis with an easy approach to ontology gives us a route, in at least many cases, to simple realist conclusions about the entities in question. In this case, I have argued, we should simply say that there are modal facts, modal properties, and the like. Thus we needn't be either ignoring "metaphysical questions" or defending implausible eliminativist answers to them. Nor need we embrace fictionalism. We can instead get straightforward, simple realist answers that entitle us to say that there are modal facts and properties, in the only sense that has sense.

This is a huge benefit. For it enables us to avoid all the counterintuitive consequences of denying that there are facts, properties, or objects of the relevant kind (modal, moral, mathematical, etc.).[4] In the modal case, we can allow that there are modal truths (and falsehoods), that we can acquire modal knowledge, and that there are objects with modal properties. And this last move is especially important since (as Michael Rea [2002, 94–96] suggested) if we deny that there are modal properties, it seems that we must also deny that there are any ordinary objects at all. But we can accept these realist theses while making it clear that some of the ontological problems thought to face traditional forms of realism are simply out of place here—there are the entities, but there are not the "placement problems" thought to plague such entities, and we don't have to accord them some "secondary" or "reduced" status. Moreover, we can see why it is out of place to press further questions about what non-modal features our modal properties are grounded in, or what the truthmakers are for our modal truths. In short, while one can give an alternative functional story about an area of discourse (including the modal) without marrying it with an easy approach to ontology, in my view one does much better by bringing these two threads—functional pluralism and easy ontology—together. One hope is that this book may bridge the gap between these two areas of literature, giving a kind of example of how the two approaches may be combined, and what benefits it may bring to do so.

Functional pluralism and easy ontology are both general approaches, which may turn out to be applicable in other areas. Can such approaches be combined to also help with other recalcitrant problems—problems about truth, meaning, causation, chance, mathematics, morality, or elsewhere? That is a question I will have to leave for elsewhere, and mostly for others. But I hope I have at least made it clear that such approaches have been wrongly forgotten and ignored. I also hope to have provided a model of how they might work, and a view of what the substantial ontological, methodological, and epistemological advantages will be, where we *can* make them work.

---

[4] It also enables us to do better than fictionalist analyses can, as I argue in Thomasson (2013c).

A third and final thread that has played an important role in this work is the idea that the meanings (thought of here as rules of use) for our terms are often incomplete, open-textured, and open to change and renegotiation. Again, to be clear: the normativist view in itself does not commit one to this view about language—it commits one only to the claim that the metaphysical modal facts and the semantic rules go together, insofar as true claims of metaphysical necessity are object-language reflections of actual semantic rules and their consequences. It does not commit one to particular views about how much conceptual content our terms have, or whether (or how) it is changeable. So one could in principle combine modal normativism with the view that there are no semantic rules (and so no true claims of metaphysical necessity), or with the view that there are detailed and fixed semantic rules that we can tease out to answer any metaphysical modal question.

But thinking of linguistic rules on analogy with other rules makes it natural to think that these (like the rules of games and other social rules) may be open-textured and changeable. And we have independent reason to think that our linguistic rules are often open-ended, and that it is often a matter of decision what to do with them (particularly when new or unforeseen circumstances arise). As I have argued in Chapter 4, by accepting this, we can avoid objections that were thought to undermine the idea that our terms have any conceptual content at all, while also doing better than pure causal theories at making unified sense of "what we would say" in a range of cases.

While modal normativism and meta-ontological deflationism are both, in principle, separable from this view about the openness of linguistic rules, when we bring these threads together, we once again get a stronger view. For by allowing that our terms may have rules that are open-textured and up for renegotiation, we can respond to prominent criticisms of traditional conceptual analysis. We can also come to understand why so many metaphysical modal debates are up for grabs, with no clear answer, and why it sometimes seems that giving any answer would be arbitrary. Still more importantly, we can get a deeper understanding of what we often have been, and can be, up to in metaphysics—as involving not merely analysis of extant concepts (whether of *person, art, freedom*, etc.) as they are, but negotiation of what these concepts *should be*, or what rules *should* govern the corresponding terms. And this, in turn, fits in nicely with a kind of pluralism about *use*. For it makes evident that, in uttering indicative modal statements, one need not be aiming to "report" "detected" modal truths: one may instead aim to communicate, enforce, undermine, *or renegotiate* the rules. This is part of a broader understanding of what work in metaphysics (and elsewhere in philosophy) sometimes has been, and certainly can be, up to: work not just in conceptual analysis but in conceptual engineering (see Thomasson 2017a, 2017b, 2018b). That is to say, we may not only engage in analyzing or communicating what the rules for our terms or concepts *are* (and what follows from this), but also work on determining what terms or concepts we *should* use, and how we should use them (for various purposes). This, as I have argued elsewhere (Thomasson 2020), is work that is as deep, worldly, and important as we could ask for.

The ultimate hope is to gain a conception of metaphysics that removes the epistemological mystery, while retaining the thought that metaphysics may engage in work that is worldly, worthwhile, and important. Reconceiving of the appropriate and manageable work of metaphysics in this way is the deepest goal of my recent work—and a goal I hope to have made a little more progress on with this book.

Bibliography

Adams, Robert Merrihew. "Theories of Actuality." *Noûs* 8 (1974): 211–31.

Armstrong, David M. *Universals: An Opinionated Introduction.* Boulder, CO: Westview Press, 1989.

Armstrong, D. M. *Truth and Truthmakers.* Cambridge: Cambridge University Press, 2004.

Ayer, A. J. *Language, Truth and Logic.* New York: Dover, 1936/1952.

Ayer, A. J. *Wittgenstein.* New York: Random House, 1985.

Baker, Gordon. *Wittgenstein, Frege and the Vienna Circle.* Oxford: Blackwell, 1988.

Barnard, Robert. "A Theory of Logical Normativity." *Southwest Philosophy Review* 29, no. 1 (2013): 49–59.

Beall, J. C., and Greg Restall. "Logical Consequence." In *The Stanford Encyclopedia of Philosophy* (Winter 2016 Edition), edited by Edward N. Zalta. https://plato.stanford.edu/archives/win2016/entries/logical-consequence/

Benacerraf, Paul. "Mathematical Truth." *Journal of Philosophy* 70, no. 19 (1974): 661–79.

Bennett, Karen. "Spatio-Temporal Coincidence and the Grounding Problem." *Philosophical Studies* 118 (2004): 339–71.

Bennett, Karen. "Two Axes of Actualism." *Philosophical Review* 114, no. 3 (2005): 297–326.

Bennett, Karen. *Making Things Up.* Oxford: Oxford University Press, 2017.

Berker, Selim. "Does Evolutionary Psychology Show That Normativity Is Mind-Dependent?" In *Moral Psychology and Human Agency: Philosophical Essays on the Science of Ethics*, edited by Justin D'Arms and Daniel Jacobson, 215–52. Oxford: Oxford University Press, 2014.

Bickerton, Derek. "Language Evolution: A Brief Guide for Linguists." *Lingua* 117 (2007): 510–26.

Blackburn, Simon. *Spreading the Word.* Oxford: Clarendon Press, 1984.

Blackburn, Simon. *Essays in Quasi-Realism.* New York: Oxford University Press, 1993.

Blackburn, Simon. "Attitudes and Contents." *Ethics* 98 (1998): 501–17.

Blackburn, Simon. "The Semantics of Non-factualism." In *The Blackwell Guide to the Philosophy of Language*, edited by M. Devitt and R. Hanley, 244–52. Oxford: Blackwell, 2006.

Blackburn, Simon. "Sharon Street on the Independent Normative Truth as Such." http://www2.phil.cam.ac.uk/~swb24/PAPERS/Meanstreet.htm

Bliss, Ricki, and Kelly Trogdon. "Metaphysical Grounding." In *The Stanford Encyclopedia of Philosophy* (Winter 2016 Edition), edited by Edward N. Zalta. https://plato.stanford.edu/archives/win2016/entries/grounding/

Boghossian, Paul. "Analyticity." In *A Companion to the Philosophy of Language*, edited by Bob Hale and Crispin Wright, 331–68. Oxford: Blackwell, 1997.

Braddon-Mitchell, David. "Qualia and Analytical Conditionals." *Journal of Philosophy* 100, no. 3 (2003): 111–35.

Brandom, Robert B. *Making it Explicit*. Cambridge, MA: Harvard University Press, 1994.

Brandom, Robert B. "Inferentialism and Some of Its Challenges." *Philosophy and Phenomenological Research* 74, no. 3 (2007): 651–76.

Brandom, Robert. *Between Saying and Doing: Towards an Analytic Pragmatism*. Oxford: Oxford University Press, 2008.

Bricker, Phillip. "Concrete Possible Worlds." In *Contemporary Debates in Metaphysics*, edited by Ted Sider, John Hawthorne, and Dean Zimmerman, 111–34. Oxford: Blackwell, 2008.

Bueno, Otávio, and Scott Shalkowski. "Modal Realism and Modal Epistemology: A Huge Gap." In *Modal Epistemology*, edited by Erik Weber and Tim De Mey, 93–106. Brussels: Koninklijke Vlaamse Academie van Belgie (Royal Flemish Academy of Belgium), 2004.

Bueno, Otávio, and Scott Shalkowski. "Modalism and Theoretical Virtues: Toward an Epistemology of Modality." *Philosophical Studies* 172 (2015): 671–89.

Burke, Michael. "Copper Statues and Pieces of Copper: A Challenge to the Standard Account." *Analysis* 52, no. 1 (1992): 12–17.

Cameron, Ross. "The Grounds of Necessity." *Philosophy Compass* 5, no. 4 (2010): 348–58.

Cappelen, Herman. *Fixing Language: An Essay on Conceptual Engineering*. Oxford: Oxford University Press, 2018.

Carey, Susan. *The Origin of Concepts*. Oxford: Oxford University Press, 2009.

Carnap, Rudolf. *Meaning and Necessity: A Study in Semantics and Modal Logic*. Chicago: University of Chicago Press, 1947/1956.

Carnap, Rudolf. "On Explication." In *Logical Foundations of Probability*. Chicago: University of Chicago Press, 1950/1962.

Chalmers, David. *The Conscious Mind: In Search of a Fundamental Theory*. New York: Oxford University Press, 1996.

Chalmers, David. "Two-Dimensional Semantics." In *The Oxford Handbook of Philosophy of Language*, edited by Ernest Lepore and Barry C. Smith, 574–606. Oxford: Oxford University Press, 2006.

Chalmers, David, and Frank Jackson. "Conceptual Analysis and Reductive Explanation." *Philosophical Review* 110, no. 3 (2001): 315–60.

Charlow, Nate. "The Problem with the Frege-Geach Problem." *Philosophical Studies* 167/3 (2013): 1–31.

Clarke-Doane, Justin. "Debunking and Dispensability." In *Explanation in Ethics and Mathematics: Debunking and Dispensability*, edited by Uri D. Leibowitz and Neil Sinclair, 23–36. Oxford: Oxford University Press, 2016.

Creath, Richard. "Quine on the Intelligibility and Relevance of Analyticity." In *The Cambridge Companion to Quine*, edited by Roger R. Gibson, 47–64. Cambridge: Cambridge University Press, 2004.

Cummins, Robert. "Functional Explanation." *Journal of Philosophy* 72, no. 20 (1975): 741–64.

Dasgupta, Shamik. "Realism and the Absence of Value." *Philosophical Review* 127, no. 3 (2018): 279–322.

Davidson, Donald. "Knowing One's Own Mind." *Proceedings and Addresses of the American Philosophical Association* 60 (1987): 441–58.

Devitt, Michael, and Kim Sterelny. *Language and Reality*. Cambridge, MA: MIT Press, 1999.

Dickie, Imogen. *Fixing Reference*. New York: Oxford University Press, 2015.

Divers, John, and Joseph Melia. "The Analytic Limit of Genuine Modal Realism." *Mind* 111, no. 441 (2002): 15–36.

Dreier, Jamie. "Expressivist Embeddings and Minimalist Truth." *Philosophical Studies* 83 (1996): 29–51.

Dreier, Jamie. "Metaethics and the Problem of Creeping Minimalism." *Philosophical Perspectives* 18 (2004): 23–44.

Dreier, Jamie. "Negation for Expressivists: A Collection of Problems with a Suggestion for Their Solution." In *Oxford Studies in Metaethics* (Vol. 1), edited by R. Shafer-Landau, 217–33. Oxford: Oxford University Press, 2006.

Dreier, Jamie. "Quasi-Realism and the Problem of Unexplained Coincidence." *Analytic Philosophy* 53, no. 3 (2012): 269–87.

Dummett, Michael. "Wittgenstein's Philosophy of Mathematics." *Philosophical Review* 68, no. 3 (1959): 324–48.

Dummett, Michael. *The Logical Basis of Metaphysics*. Cambridge, MA: Harvard University Press, 1991.

Duncan, Michael, Kristie Miller, and James Norton. "Is Grounding a Hyperintensional Phenomenon?" *Analytic Philosophy* 58, no. 4 (2017): 297–329.

Elder, Crawford. *Real Natures and Familiar Objects*. Cambridge, MA: MIT Press, 2004.

Evnine, Simon. "Much Ado about Something-from-Nothing." In *Ontology after Carnap*, edited by Sandra LaPointe and Stephan Blatti. Oxford: Oxford University Press, 2016.

Fine, Kit. "Essence and Modality." *Philosophical Perspectives* 8 (1994a): 1–16.

Fine, Kit. "Ontological Dependence." *Proceedings of the Aristotelian Society* 95 (1994b): 269–90.

Fischer, Bob. "Modal Empiricism: Objection, Reply, Proposal." In *Modal Epistemology after Rationalism*, edited by Bob Fischer and Felipe Leon, 263–80. Switzerland: Springer, 2017.

Fischer, Bob, and Felipe Leon. *Modal Epistemology after Rationalism.* Switzerland: Springer, 2017.

Forbes, Graeme. *The Metaphysics of Modality.* Oxford: Clarendon Press, 1985.

Forbes, Graeme. "Critical Study: The Plurality of Worlds." *Philosophical Quarterly* 38, no. 151 (1988): 222–40.

Frege, Gottlob. *The Foundations of Arithmetic: A Logico-Mathematical Enquiry into the Concept of Number* (2nd rev. ed.). Translated by J. L. Austin. Oxford: Blackwell, 1974. Originally published as *Grundlagen der Arithmetik* [1884].

Geach, Peter. "Ascriptivism." *Philosophical Review* 69 (1960): 221–25.

Geach, Peter. "Assertion." *Philosophical Review* 74, no. 4 (1965): 449–65.

Gert, Bernard, Charles M. Culver, and K. Danner Clouser. "Death." In *Bioethics: A Systematic Approach* (2nd ed.), 283–308. Oxford: Oxford University Press, 2006.

Gibbard, Allan. *Wise Choices, Apt Feelings.* Cambridge, MA: Harvard University Press, 1990.

Gibbard, Allan. "Meaning and Normativity." *Philosophical Issues* 5 (1994): 95–115.

Gibbard, Allan. "Projection, Quasi-Realism, and Sophisticated Realism. Review of Simon Blackburn, *Essays in Quasi-Realism.*" *Mind* 105, no. 418 (1998): 331–35.

Gibbard, Allan. *Thinking How to Live.* Cambridge, MA: Harvard University Press, 2003.

Glock, Hans-Johann. "Necessity and Normativity." In *The Cambridge Companion to Wittgenstein,* edited by Hans Sluga and David G. Stern, 180–208. Cambridge: Cambridge University Press, 1996.

Goldman, Alan, and Joel Pust. "Philosophical Theory and Intuitional Evidence." In *Rethinking Intuition,* edited by W. Ramsey and M. DePaul, 179–200. Lanham, MD: Rowman & Littlefield, 1998.

Goldman, Alvin I. "Discrimination and Perceptual Knowledge." *Journal of Philosophy* 73, no. 20 (1976): 771–91.

Grice, Paul. *Studies in the Way of Words.* Cambridge, MA: Harvard University Press, 1989.

Grover, Dorothy, Joseph L. Camp, Jr., and Nuel D. Belnap, Jr. "A Prosentential Theory of Truth." *Philosophical Studies* 27 (1975): 73–124.

Hacker, P. M. S. *Wittgenstein's Place in Twentieth-Century Analytic Philosophy.* Oxford: Blackwell, 1996.

Hale, Bob, and Crispin Wright. *The Reason's Proper Study: Essays towards a Neo-Fregean Philosophy of Mathematics.* Oxford: Clarendon, 2001.

Haslanger, Sally. *Resisting Reality: Social Construction and Social Critique.* Oxford: Oxford University Press, 2012.

Hilbert, David. *Foundations of Geometry.* Translated by Leo Unger. Peru, IL: Open Court, 1899/1999.

Hirsch, Eli. "Against Revisionary Ontology." *Philosophical Topics* 30 (2002): 103–27.

Horwich, Paul. *Meaning*. New York: Oxford University Press, 1999.

Horwich, Paul. *Truth-Meaning-Reality*. Oxford: Clarendon Press, 2010.

Hume, David. *A Treatise on Human Nature*. London: Penguin, 1739/1985.

Hume, David. *An Enquiry Concerning Human Understanding*. Indianapolis: Hackett, 1777/1977.

Husserl, Edmund. *The Crisis of the European Sciences*. Translated by David Carr. Chicago: Northwestern University Press, 1970.

Husserl, Edmund. *Ideas Pertaining to a Pure Phenomenology and to a Phenomenological Philosophy: Second Book*. Translated by R. Rojcewicz and A. Schuwer. Dordrecht, The Netherlands: Kluwer, 1989.

Irmak, Nurbay. "An Ontology of Words." *Erkenntnis* (forthcoming).

Jackman, Henry. "We Live Forward But Understand Backwards: Linguistic Practices and Future Behavior." *Pacific Philosophical Quarterly* 80 (1999): 157–77.

Jackson, Frank. *From Metaphysics to Ethics: A Defence of Conceptual Analysis*. Oxford: Oxford University Press, 1998.

Jenkins, C. S. "Concepts, Experience and Modal Knowledge." *Philosophical Perspectives* 24 (2010): 255–79.

Jubien, Michael. "Analyzing Modality." *Oxford Studies in Metaphysics* 3 (2007): 99–139.

Kaplan, David. "Words." *Aristotelian Society Supplementary Volume* 64, no. 1 (1990): 93–119.

Kment, Boris. *Modality and Explanatory Reasoning*. Oxford: Oxford University Press, 2014.

Kripke, Saul. *Naming and Necessity*. Oxford: Blackwell, 1980.

Lance, Mark Norris, and John O'Leary-Hawthorne. *The Grammar of Meaning: Normativity and Semantic Discourse*. Cambridge: Cambridge University Press, 1997.

Langton, Rae. "How to Get a Norm from a Speech Act." *Amherst Lecture in Philosophy* 10 (2015): 1–33.

Lefftz, Gregoire. *The Identity of Ordinary Objects: An Essay in Deflationary Ontology*. Ph.D. dissertation, Sorbonne University, 2018.

Leon, Felipe. "From Modal Skepticism to Modal Empiricism." In *Modal Epistemology after Rationalism*, edited by Bob Fischer and Felipe Leon, 247–62. Switzerland: Springer, 2017.

Lewis, David K. *Counterfactuals*. Cambridge, MA: Harvard University Press, 1973.

Lewis, David K. "Possible Worlds." In *The Possible and the Actual: Readings in the Metaphysics of Modality*, edited by Michael Loux, 182–89. Ithaca: Cornell University Press, 1979.

Lewis, David K. *On the Plurality of Worlds*. Oxford: Blackwell, 1986.

Lewis, David. "Humean Supervenience Debugged." *Mind* 103 (1994): 473–90.

Locke, Theodore. *Counterpossibles for Modal Normativists.* Ph.D. dissertation, University of Miami, 2018.

Locke, Theodore. "Counterpossibles for Modal Normativists." *Synthese* (2019): 1–23. https://doi-org.dartmouth.idm.oclc.org/10.1007/s11229-019-02103-1

Locke, Theodore. "Metaphysical Explanations for Modal Normativists" (in progress).

Ludlow, Peter. "The Myth of Human Language." *Croatian Journal of Philosophy* 6, no. 3 (2005): 385–400.

Ludwig, Kirk. "De Re Necessities" (in progress; draft as of September 15, 2013).

Lycan, William. "Review of *On the Plurality of Worlds*." *Journal of Philosophy* 85, no. 1 (1988): 42–47.

Mackie, J. L. *Truth, Probability and Paradox.* Oxford: Clarendon Press, 1973.

Mackie, J. L. "De What Re Is de Re Modality?" *Journal of Philosophy* 71, no. 16 (1974): 551–61.

Mackie, J. L. *Ethics: Inventing Right and Wrong.* New York: Penguin Books, 1977.

Mackie, Penelope, and Jago, Mark. "Transworld Identity." In *The Stanford Encyclopedia of Philosophy* (Winter 2017 Edition), edited by Edward N. Zalta. https://plato.stanford.edu/archives/win2017/entries/identity-transworld/

Malgren, Anna-Sara. "Rationalism and the Content of Intuitive Judgements." *Mind* 120, no. 478 (2011): 263–327.

Marcus, Ruth Barcan. "Modalities and Intensional Languages." *Synthese* 13, no. 4 (1961): 303–22.

Marion, Matthieu. "Wittgenstein, Ramsey and British Pragmatism." *European Journal of Pragmatism and American Philosophy* 4, no. 2 (2012). https://doi.org/10.4000/ejpap.720

McCracken, Michael. *Prospects for a Deflationary Account of Propositions.* Ph.D. dissertation, University of Miami, 2009.

McSweeney, Michaela. "Logical Realism and the Metaphysics of Logic." *Philosophy Compass* 14.1 (2018). DOI: 10.1111/phc3.12563

Menzel, Christopher. "Actualism." In *The Stanford Encyclopedia of Philosophy* (Summer 2018 Edition), edited by Edward N. Zalta. https://plato.stanford.edu/archives/sum2018/entries/actualism/

Mill, John Stuart. *A System of Logic, Ratiocinative and Inductive: Being a Connected View of the Principles of Evidence and the Methods of Scientific Investigation* (Vol. 1, 9th ed.). London, 1843/1875.

Millikan, Ruth. *Language, Thought and Other Biological Categories: New Foundations for Realism.* Cambridge, MA: MIT Press, 1984.

Moore, G. E. *Lectures on Philosophy.* London: George Allen and Unwin, 1966.

Mulligan, Kevin, Peter Simons, and Barry Smith. "Truth-Makers." *Philosophy and Phenomenological Research* 44, no. 3 (1984): 287–321.

Nolan, Daniel. "Hyperintensional Metaphysics." *Philosophical Studies* 171 (2014): 149–60.

Nozick, Robert. *Invariances: The Structure of the Objective World*. Cambridge, MA: Harvard University Press, 2001.

Palmer, Frank R. *Modality and the English Modals* (2nd ed.). New York: Longman, 1990.

Papafragou, Anna. "The Acquisition of Modality: Implications for Theories of Semantic Representation." *Mind and Language* 13, no. 3 (1998): 370–99.

Parfit, Derek. *Reasons and Persons*. Oxford: Oxford University Press, 1984.

Peacocke, Christopher. *Being Known*. Oxford: Oxford University Press, 1998.

Perez Carballo, Alejandro. "Structuring Logical Space." *Philosophy and Phenomenological Research* 92, no. 2 (2016): 460–91.

Pettit, Philip. *Rules, Reasons and Norms*. Oxford: Clarendon, 2002.

Plantinga, A. *The Nature of Necessity*. Oxford: Clarendon Press, 1974.

Plantinga, Alvin. "Two Concepts of Modality: Modal Realism and Modal Reductionism." *Philosophical Perspectives* 1 (1987): 189–231.

Plunkett, David. "Which Concepts Should We Use? Metalinguistic Negotiations and the Methodology of Philosophy." *Inquiry* 58, nos. 7–8 (2015): 828–74.

Plunkett, David, and Tim Sundell. "Disagreement and the Semantics of Normative and Evaluative Terms." *Philosopher's Imprint* 13, no. 23 (2013): 1–37.

Preston, Beth. "Why Is a Wing like a Spoon? A Pluralist Theory of Function." *Journal of Philosophy* 95, no. 5 (1998): 215–54.

Price, Huw. *Time's Arrow and Archimedes' Point*. New York: Oxford University Press, 1996.

Price, Huw. "Metaphysics after Carnap: The Ghost Who Walks?" In *Metametaphysics*, edited by David Chalmers, David Manley, and Ryan Wasserman, 320–46. Oxford: Oxford University Press, 2009.

Price, Huw. *Naturalism without Mirrors*. Oxford: Oxford University Press, 2011.

Price, Huw. "Ubiquitous Pragmatism." In *The Practical Turn: Pragmatism in Britain in the Long Twentieth Century*, edited by C. J. Misak and Huw Price, 149–62. Oxford: Oxford University Press, 2017.

Price, Huw, with Simon Blackburn, Robert Brandom, Paul Horwich, and Michael Williams. *Expressivism, Pragmatism and Representationalism*. Burlington, VT: Ashgate Publishing, 2013.

Prior, Arthur N. "Worlds, Times and Selves." In *Papers on Time and Tense*, edited by Per Hasle, Peter Ohrstrom, Torben Brauner, and Jack Copeland, 241–56. Oxford: Oxford University Press, 2003.

Putnam, Hilary. "The Meaning of 'Meaning.'" *Minnesota Studies in the Philosophy of Science* 7 (1975): 131–93.

Quine, W. V. O. "Truth by Convention." In *The Ways of Paradox and Other Essays* (rev. and enlarged ed.). Cambridge, MA: Harvard University Press, 1935/1976.

Quine, W. V. O. "On Carnap's Views on Ontology." Originally published 1951; reprinted in his *The Ways of Paradox and Other Essays*, 203–11. Cambridge, MA: Harvard University Press, 1966/1976.

Quine, W. V. O. "Two Dogmas of Empiricism." In *From a Logical Point of View*. Cambridge, MA: Harvard University Press, 1953/2001.

Quine, W. V. O. "Two Dogmas in Retrospect." *Canadian Journal of Philosophy* 21 (1991): 265–74.

Ramsey, Frank. "General Propositions and Causation." In *Foundations: Essays in Philosophy, Logic, Mathematics and Economics*, 133–51. Atlantic Highlands, NJ: Humanities Press, 1978. Originally published in 1929.

Rea, Michael C. *World without Design: The Ontological Consequences of Naturalism*. Oxford: Clarendon Press, 2002.

Restall, Greg. "Multiple Conclusions." In *Logic, Methodology and Philosophy of Science: Proceedings of the Twelfth International Congress*, edited by P. Hájek, L. Valdés-Villanueva, and D. Westerståhl, 189–205. London: KCL Publications, 2005.

Restall, Greg. "A Cut-Free Sequent System for Two-Dimensional Modal Logic, and Why it Matters." *Annals of Pure and Applied Logic* 163, no. 11 (2012): 1611–23. consequently.org

Ripley, David. "Paradox and Failures of Cut." *Australasian Journal of Philosophy* 91, no. 1 (2013): 139–64.

Roca-Royes, Sonia. "Similarity and Possibility: An Epistemology of *De Re* Possibility for Concrete Entities." In *Modal Epistemology after Rationalism*, edited by Bob Fischer and Felipe Leon, 221–46. Switzerland: Springer, 2017.

Rosa, Emily. "A Close Look at Therapeutic Touch." *Journal of the American Medical Association* 279, no. 13 (1998): 1005–10.

Rouse, Joseph. "Temporal Externalism and the Normativity of Linguistic Practice." *Journal of the Philosophy of History* 8 (2014): 20–38.

Roy, Tony. "Things and *De Re* Modality." *Noûs* 34 (2000): 56–84.

Russell, Gillian. *Truth in Virtue of Meaning: A Defence of the Analytic/Synthetic Distinction*. Oxford: Oxford University Press, 2008.

Ryle, Gilbert. *The Concept of Mind*. London: Hutchinson, 1949.

Ryle, Gilbert. "'If,' 'So,' and 'Because.'" In *Collected Papers*, Volume 2, 234–49. London: Hutchison, 1950/1971.

Sagoff, Mark. "On Restoring and Reproducing Art." *Journal of Philosophy* 75, no. 9 (1978): 453–70.

Salmon, Nathan. "Review of 'On the Plurality of Worlds.'" *Philosophical Review* 92, no. 2 (1988): 237–44.

Schechter, Joshua. "Explanatory Challenges in Metaethics." In *Routledge Handbook of Metaethics*, edited by Tristram McPherson and David Plunkett, 443–59. London: Routledge, 2018.

Schieder, Jakob. *Between Meaning and Essence: Explaining Necessary Truth*. Doctoral dissertation, Humboldt University of Berlin/Kings College London, 2016.

Schiffer, Stephen. *The Things We Mean*. Oxford: Oxford University Press, 2003.

Schlick, Moritz. Allgemeine Erkenntnislehre. Berlin: Springer, 1918.

Searle, John. *Speech Acts.* Cambridge: Cambridge University Press, 1969.

Searle, John. *The Construction of Social Reality.* New York: Free Press, 1995.

Sellars, Wilfrid. "Counterfactuals, Dispositions and the Causal Modalities." In *Minnesota Studies in Philosophy of Science, Volume 2: Concepts, Theories and the Mind-Body Problem*, edited by Herbert Feigl, Michael Scriven, and Grover Maxwell, 225–308. Minneapolis: University of Minnesota Press, 1958.

Shalkowski, Scott. "The Ontological Ground of the Alethic Modality." *Philosophical Review* 103, no. 4 (1994): 669–88.

Sidelle, Alan. *Necessity, Essence and Individuation: A Defense of Conventionalism.* Ithaca: Cornell University Press, 1989.

Sider, Theodore. *Four-Dimensionalism.* Oxford: Oxford University Press, 2001.

Sider, Theodore. "Reductive Theories of Modality." In *The Oxford Handbook of Metaphysics*, edited by Michael J. Loux and Dean W. Zimmerman, 180–208. Oxford: Oxford University Press, 2003.

Sider, Theodore. *Writing the Book of the World.* Oxford: Oxford University Press, 2011.

Sinott-Armstrong, Walter. "Expressivism and Embedding." *Philosophy and Phenomenological Research* 61, no. 3 (2000): 677–93.

Skorupsi, John. "Mill on Language and Logic." In *The Cambridge Companion to Mill*, edited by John Skorupsi, 35–56. Cambridge: Cambridge University Press, 1998.

Skyrms, Brian. "Possible Worlds, Physics and Metaphysics." *Philosophical Studies* 30 (1976): 323–32.

Sosa, Ernest. "Experimental Philosophy and Philosophical Intuition." In *Experimental Philosophy*, edited by Joshua Knobe and Shaun Nichols, 231–40. Oxford: Oxford University Press, 2008.

Spelke, Elizabeth. "Principles of Object Perception." *Cognitive Science* 14 (1990): 29–36.

Stairs, Allen. "Review Essay: On the Plurality of Worlds." *Philosophy and Phenomenological Research* 49, no. 2 (1988): 333–52.

Stalnaker, Robert C. "Possible Worlds." *Noûs* 10, no. 1 (1976): 65–75.

Steinberg, Alexander. "Pleonastic Possible Worlds." *Philosophical Studies* 164 (2013): 767–89.

Strawson, P. F. "Truth." *Analysis* 9 (1949): 83–97.

Strawson, P. F. *Analysis and Metaphysics: An Introduction to Philosophy.* Oxford: Oxford University Press, 1992.

Strawson, P. F., and H. P. Grice. "In Defense of a Dogma." *Philosophical Review* 65, no. 2 (1956): 141–58.

Street, Sharon. "A Darwinian Dilemma for Realist Theories of Value." *Philosophical Studies* 127 (2006): 109–66.

Street, Sharon. "Mind-Independence without the Mystery: Why Quasi-Realists Can't Have It Both Ways." *Oxford Studies in Metaethics* 6 (2011): 1–32.

Tanesini, Alessandra. "Temporal Externalism: A Taxonomy, an Articulation, and a Defense." *Journal for the Philosophy of History* 8 (2014): 1–19.

Thomasson, Amie L. *Fiction and Metaphysics.* Cambridge: Cambridge University Press, 1999.

Thomasson, Amie L. "Foundations for a Social Ontology." *Protosociology* Vol. 18–19: Understanding The Social II: Philosophy of Sociality (2003): 269–90.

Thomasson, Amie L. *Ordinary Objects.* New York: Oxford University Press, 2007a.

Thomasson, Amie L. "Modal Normativism and the Methods of Metaphysics." *Philosophical Topics* 35, nos. 1 & 2 (2007b): 135–60.

Thomasson, Amie L. "Answerable and Unanswerable Questions." In *Metametaphysics*, edited by David Chalmers, David Manley, and Ryan Wasserman, 444–71. Oxford: Oxford University Press, 2009.

Thomasson, Amie L. "Fiction, Existence, and Indeterminacy." In *Fictions and Models: New Essays*, edited by John Woods, 109–48. Munich: Philosophia Verlag, 2010.

Thomasson, Amie L. "Experimental Philosophy and the Methods of Ontology." *Monist* 95, no. 2 (2012): 175–99.

Thomasson, Amie L. "2012 Nancy D. Simco Lecture: Norms and Necessity." *Southern Journal of Philosophy* (2013a): 143–60.

Thomasson, Amie L. "The Ontological Significance of Constitution." *Monist* (2013b): 54–72.

Thomasson, Amie L. "Fictionalism vs. Deflationism." *Mind* 122, no. 488 (2013c): 1023–51.

Thomasson, Amie L. "Quizzical Ontology and Easy Ontology." *Journal of Philosophy* 111, nos. 9–10 (2014a): 502–28.

Thomasson, Amie L. "It's a Jumble out There: How Talk of Levels Leads Us Astray." *American Philosophical Quarterly* 51, no. 4 (2014b): 285–96.

Thomasson, Amie L. *Ontology Made Easy.* Oxford: Oxford University Press, 2015.

Thomasson, Amie L. "Metaphysical Disputes and Metalinguistic Negotiation." *Analytic Philosophy* 58, no. 1 (2017a): 1–28.

Thomasson, Amie L. "What Can We Do, When We Do Metaphysics?" In *Cambridge Companion to Philosophical Methodology*, edited by Giuseppina d'Oro and Soren Overgaard, 101–21. Cambridge: Cambridge University Press, 2017b.

Thomasson, Amie L. "How Can We Come to Know Metaphysical Modal Truths?" *Synthese* (special issue: *New Directions in the Epistemology of Modality*) (2018a): 1–30. https://doi.org/10.1007/s11229-018-1841-5

Thomasson, Amie L. "Metaphysics and Conceptual Negotiation." *Philosophical Issues* 27 (2018b): 364–82.

Thomasson, Amie L. "What Can Global Pragmatists Say about Ordinary Objects?" In *The Nature of Ordinary Objects*, edited by Javier Cumpa and Bill Brewer. Cambridge: Cambridge University Press, 2019: 235–59.

Thomasson, Amie L. "A Pragmatic Method for Conceptual Ethics." In *Conceptual Engineering and Conceptual Ethics*, edited by Alexis Burgess, Herman Cappelen, and David Plunkett, 435–58. Oxford: Oxford University Press, 2020: 435–58.

Toulmin, S. E. "Probability." *Proceedings of the Aristotelian Society* Supplementary 24 (1950): 27–74.

Vaidya, Anand. "The Epistemology of Modality." In *Stanford Encyclopedia of Philosophy* (Winter 2017 Edition), edited by Edward N. Zalta. https://plato.stanford.edu/archives/win2017/entries/modality-epistemology/

Van Inwagen, Peter. "Metaontology." *Erkenntnis* 48 (1998): 233–50.

Vavova, Katia. "Evolutionary Debunking of Moral Realism." *Philosophy Compass* 10, no. 2 (2015): 104–16.

Vetter, Barbara. *Potentiality: From Dispositions to Modality*. Oxford: Oxford University Press, 2015.

Warren, Mark. *Lightweight Moral Realism: Objectivity and Reasoning without Heavyweight Facts*. Ph.D. dissertation, University of Miami. Ann Arbor, MI: UMI/Proquest, 2014.

Warren, Mark. "Moral Inferentialism and the Frege-Geach Problem." *Philosophical Studies* 172, no. 11 (2015): 2859–85.

Wells, Gordon. *Language Development in the Preschool Years*. Cambridge: Cambridge University Press, 1985.

Williams, Michael. "Pragmatism, Minimalism, Expressivism." *International Journal of Philosophical Studies* 18, no. 3 (2011): 317–30.

Williams, Michael. "Knowledge in Practice." In *Epistemic Evaluation*, edited by John Greco and David Henderson, 161–85. Oxford: Oxford University Press, 2015.

Williamson, Timothy. *The Philosophy of Philosophy*. Oxford: Blackwell, 2007.

Wittgenstein, Ludwig. *Tractatus Logico-Philosophicus*. Translated by C. K. Ogden. London: Routledge, 1922/1933.

Wittgenstein, Ludwig. *Wittgenstein's Lectures: Cambridge, 1932–35*, edited by Alice Ambrose. Totowa, NJ: Rowman and Littlefield, 1932–35/1979.

Wittgenstein, Ludwig. *Wittgenstein's Lectures on the Foundations of Mathematics: Cambridge, 1939*, edited by Cora Diamond. Ithaca: Cornell University Press, 1939/1976.

Wittgenstein, Ludwig. *Remarks on the Foundations of Mathematics*, edited by G. H. von Wright, R. Rhees, and G. E. M. Anscombe. Translated by G. E. M. Anscombe. Cambridge, MA: MIT Press, 1956/1978.

Wittgenstein, Ludwig. *The Blue and Brown Books*. Oxford: Blackwell, 1958.

Wright, Crispin. *Wittgenstein on the Foundations of Mathematics*. London: Duckworth, 1980.

Yablo, Stephen. "How in the World?" *Philosophical Topics* 24, no. 1 (1996): 255–86.

Yablo, Stephen. "A Paradox of Existence." In *Empty Names, Fiction, and the Puzzles of Non-Existence*, edited by Anthony Everett and Thomas Hofweber, 275–312. Palo Alto: CSLI Publications, 2000.

Yablo, Stephen. "The Myth of the Seven." In *Fictionalism in Metaphysics*, edited by Mark Eli Kalderon, 88–115. Oxford: Oxford University Press, 2005.

Zimmerman, Dean. "Theories of Masses and Problems of Constitution." *Philosophical Review* 104 (1995): 53–110.

Index

For the benefit of digital users, indexed terms that span two pages (e.g., 52-53) may, on occasion, appear on only one of those pages.